Angels

DON'T WARN
FOR
NOTHIN'

THE SPIRITUAL WARFARE MEMOIR
OF
Rozaletta A. Tru

Dedication

I would like to dedicate this book to several people: first, to my son, DeLon; and then, my siblings; my devoted readers; and lastly, but not least, to the love of this life.

DeLon, there was no mediator between us, no person to bridge that gap of understanding for you, reinforcing the respect of the role of a guiding parent. I hope this book serves as that conjoining piece that enables you to better comprehend the mother whom God chose for you and our purposeful paths on this earth.

To all of my siblings, in which; one is no longer with us on this earthly journey, being the eldest of the combined thirteen of us, maternally and paternally—the age gaps between us, in addition to having different mothers and fathers, have led us all to share different experiences in our lives. Therefore, comprehending the other's perspective and outlook about life has been challenging. My hope is that one day, we all can celebrate together.

To my maternal siblings whom I am naturally closer to, simply because I helped look after you four when we were younger—I hope this book gives you some clarification as to who your big sis is; how I've developed such a hardened exterior in a way and made some decisions that you might have perceived as callous.

To the multiple readers and listeners of this memoir, know that this book offers an exclusive view of how the

ANGELS DON'T WARN FOR NOTHIN'

spiritual realm affects the physical world and the nature of man, with my life as the prime example. On this journey, you too will know the intimate parts of me, share in my fears, misfortunes and hopefully my awesome victories as this life continues and the story develops. I hope this book will touch you enough to encourage and not discourage you, but also to uplift whatever good God has invested within you.

Finally, to the one I felt an innate connection with—a once dear and precious soul to me in the beginning, who has since found mental easement in being the opposite of his objective in my life. My hopes are that one day your eyes, too, will be uncovered and the awakened man within you shall arise; able to discern fully your purpose on this earth and to uphold your intended role in my life, if God be willing.

CONTENTS

ACKNOWLEDGMENTS

Firstly, I want to acknowledge the Holy Father. Our Lord God who is arched in Heaven and whose name is highly praised. His Kingdom shall come and His will be done on Earth as it is in Heaven. Amen.

Secondly, I would like to acknowledge my son. De-Lon, you are not to blame for the division in our family. You were and have been a victim of your circumstances for a long time. Now an adult, you were manipulated since a young boy by those you believed had your best interest at heart. And sadly, you are still blinded to that fact. As a result, you were thrown back to the streets. That first started right before you were born; but then again and again, from a small baby to a toddler. And yet once more in your adolescent years, when you were blessed with a steady home, thrown into those streets, only this time by your own doing, but with their "helping" hand.

Misled to go against your own mother, the only being alive whose blood prominently runs through your veins; the given one God chose for you to come into existence in. And for you to revolt against that Godly, reverent connection is you being a menace to yourself. My role as a parent is to steer you in the direction of righteousness; to encourage you to optimize your God-given abilities and be a success in life as the head and not the tail.

However, those closely around us, unbeknownst to me

11

during that time, influenced you to think the opposite. Instead, you felt lowly and untrusting of your mother. The words of that fruitless person caused you to believe that you were deprived as a kid, instead of loved; and made you think that all I wanted was to "control" you rather than want the best for you. That sort of division and resentment placed in one's heart about their own mother or father is dangerous for all parties involved. And as a defiant child, it causes one's true blessings and growth to be hindered; the Holy Bible speaks of these things.

Even more upsettingly, no one cared enough to correct your diverted ways. Now exposed to the world with an immature mind and unanchored spirit, you were beguiled by worldly temptations, surrounded by nonbelievers and people who selfishly used you. Son, the mind can be our worst enemy; however, there comes a time when you have to start feeding that righteous spirit within you, which is in your control.

DeLon, this life was not given to you for you to do whatever you want with and be unproductive. Despite the forewarnings I spoke to you about, and you finding out things the hard way, by now it should be very apparent that what I speak to you is truth, and for your benefit. My hopes are that you will soon understand that the destructive behavior you have been conditioned to have toward your mother is called being brainwashed, and that so-called "bond" you supposedly have or had with that person is, or was, really a curse.

Also, I'd like to acknowledge the men in this world and send a message to all of my male readers. We women are not here to bow before you, so that you can rest your foot

upon our backs and treat us as property. We stand as en
tional creatures for a purpose. We are the adjoining pa
the oracles, the portals of life that metamorphize God's
breath of soul into bone and flesh. Women are biologically
created to receive and yield in whatever way it is manifested. We are the yoke of life, the mothers of this earth. Our direct ecosystem, when carrying child(ren), should be stress-
and worry-free, because whatever we feel or go through, so
does that umbilically attached child(ren) growing within us.

Therefore, if you are fortunate enough to become a father, be highly mindful of the delicate process of creation.
For women are true spiritual vines, physical conductors of
God; so as highly valued as we are to the Lord, we then, too,
should be to man. For when we are cherished and honored
by our intended counterpart, engaged righteously, that enables doorways of energies unknown to us to be discovered
and unleashed through your honored affection. That type of
connection allows a man to feel that transference of power,
one being of great joy, love and all the pleasures God intended for a woman to yield unto her man. Therefore, wom-
en should not be abused or misused, but adored, fulfilled
and uplifted for we are the glory of man! Hallelujah.

Finally, I would like to acknowledge myself, because I
have endured such deep betrayal and hurt in this life. However, through it all, I have sustained a positive outlook, been
productive steadily within my career and been self-reliant
with only the grace of God as my aid. Therefore, a high-five
and kudos to me. This sister-girl is a conquering warrior-
ess! I have kept the Faith, knowing that *all* things work for
the good of those who love the Lord—and everyone knows

that I love the Lord. The pain and tears that I have felt and cried throughout the years are ones of a Tru testimony, for the Lord did not allow me to go through these things to be silent.

When I think back on all the suffering that could have been avoided, the tears still well up in my eyes. However, if I had not gone through those things, I would not have this story to tell. Therefore, when I say, Angel's Don't Warn for Nothin', it goes deeper than what anyone could possibly imagine and beyond what I could ever foresee.

Introduction

This memoir exclusively tells of the journey of a true one—Olivia Rao. It contains detailed consequences from the good as well as the seldom, but catastrophic, bad choices that Olivia has made. There is some sexual content involved, as well as raw theory processes intertwined throughout her story, alongside a series of controllable and uncontrollable circumstances.

Olivia is a rebel at heart, but good in nature. She overcomes some hardships as a youth, but still makes life harder for herself by leaning to her own understanding instead of completely trusting in God—a level of trust that is yet progressing. Steadily fighting the good fight, Olivia realizes that the choices she makes, be they good or bad, are really those of a spiritual warfare- evil versus the goodness within her preternatural surroundings. Choosing the high road, Olivia finds herself alone on a path of righteousness unknowingly; the once loyal become disloyal and the snakes close to her eventually reveal themselves. As to what extent of the lowly cowardice and evildoing nature of those in Olivia's circle, will be revealed in greater depth in ADW4N Vol. 2.

As for this volume of Olivia's journey, it is her introduction to the world and to herself. Olivia, being a teenage mom, is discovering who she is as a woman, as she sets on a path toward stability. Along the way, she connects to a person who stimulates her to the core. However, the negative forces around them cause things to go astray. Oblivious of the stronghold from the soul tie created unbeknownst with this one, Olivia tries to move on, but finds herself entangled in a thick web of lust and love. Haunted by her past poor decisions, she breaks free from it all and tries her darndest to not look back, but after so many years, her heart still yearned for that one.

As you read her story, my hope is that the reader will understand the depth of Olivia Rao's testimonies. As she grows, Olivia learns that the best choice in life is to stay within God's peace and uphold His laws, because His laws are intended for our benefit and favor. Olivia believes wholeheartedly that God lives in us all, as He does in every living thing. However, with that said, Olivia also has a reckoning about the sinful nature of men and the evil forces behind it. Within these shared tours of her life, Olivia's aspirations are to enlighten her readers about the power of choice, with the understanding, there are good and evil spiritual kingdoms at bay; and how both majorly influence the physical life of (wo)man. Olivia's aim is for her readers to grasp these notions and in turn harness that Godliness—that good nature—within themselves.

Job 12:10—In whose hand is the soul of every living thing, and breath of all of mankind.

A Peculiar Child

CHAPTER ONE

When I was a small child, I recall my mother saying how she saw spirits and believed that meant she was born with a black veil on her face. One of her ghostly encounters, she shared with me, occurred when a classmate of hers passed away; he was a close acquaintance to my mother. She said that his spirit visited her on the day of his burial; he appeared to her and she became so frightened that she started screaming and ran right through him.

I remember hearing that story at the age of five and being so creeped out that I prayed I would never see anything like it. Thankfully, I have not seen any haunting ghosts or human-shaped spirits in a frightening manner. However, I have had my share of bizarre encounters of the unknown throughout my life. I have felt, seen and heard the presence of various entities of the spiritual realm and perhaps even physical life too, beyond this world.

Growing up, I have always had some sort of insight and an in-depth remembrance of things significant to me. I recall thoughts and memories beginning as early as the age of two; like the time when my mother and I lived with my Aunt Rena for a spell. We were in the dining room and I was sitting in the highchair as she spoon-fed me smashed peas that I utterly disliked and resisted eating when she tried to feed me. Moments like that along with being potty trained are memories that I can still recollect vividly to this day.

Becoming older, I would observe things that would normally be overlooked by most. Discovering the gift of insight, I recall being over to my maternal grandmother Big Mama's house; who you will learn in detail about within the story. On this particular day, she asked me an unusual question. I was sitting on the sofa in her living room as she was sitting across from me on her loveseat in a peaceful stillness. I was quietly sitting there too, highly content. I had been noticing Big Mama's skin, hair and how her whole appearance underwent a change within a short time span.

Big Mama broke the silence in the room and asked me, "Do you know what my fountain of youth is?"

I answered, "Yes."

Surprised, her eyes opened a little wider. She leaned forward to further ask, "What it is then?"

I replied, "Your garden."

Not expecting my response, she said, "Yes—yes, it is. How did you know?"

Just to give her a quick answer, I said, "Because I just know." I didn't want to go into any further details, but before she had even asked that question, I had already observed the answer.

Big Mama loved gardening and was very dedicated to it. She had a vegetable garden in her back yard, a rose garden in the front yard and various flowers planted around her home. Before sun-up, she would be outside tilling to the ground and sometimes even until sundown. Big Mama devoted many hours and days into growing her gardens. And my grandmother benefited from her gardening in more ways than what she knew.

One day, Big Mama decided to let the vegetable garden go, and I happened to be there to witness the post, physical effects of that decision. During that moment, I saw Big Mama's skin wrinkle and become sort of pale. Her hair turned all the way gray, as if she had no strength to keep herself up. She appeared somewhat fragile at that period. Big Mama was already up in age; however, she never looked old to me until after she gave up her gardening.

Months later, Big Mama returned to gardening full-fledged and I was there again to see her physical features improve. Her skin firmed up again; her rich melatonin showed beautifully in her complexion once more. My grandmother literally reversed the hands of time right before my eyes. After that experience, Big Mama was well aware of the blessings yielded to her from cultivating the ground. She started dying her roots black again and within no time, the Big Mama we all were familiar with was back. The strong and youthful appearance of our grandmother had resurfaced right along with all those nutritious vegetables she tended to. Gardening was Big Mama's fountain of youth, and now we both knew it.

As a youngster, I was also aware of the various feelings that temptations brought. I understood the difference between good and evil. I could feel it. When I acted up or lashed out, I was cognizant of the energies that excited those outward behaviors. Sometimes I would give into those sinful feelings, but oftentimes I would resist them. I understood, even then, the spiritual gratification of doing the right thing over choosing wrongfully. Those times when I withstood from giving into temptations, I could feel the warmth of my spirit radiate within me; like the Godliness invested would flex internally every time I resisted the enemy. I comprehended, too, the eternal treasures and peace merited in Heaven for the good done on earth that surpassed evil. Yet, like many of us, I also became momentarily distracted by the desires of my flesh.

Growing up in church as a child meant being in a strict and unyielding environment. In church I was restricted of this and that. I could not play. I could not laugh or talk with my churchgoing friends. While inside the church house, we kids had to be still in our seats and remain quiet. As time went on, I began to think that church and going to Heaven would be extremely boring and dull. I had interpreted within my five-year-old mind that to do evil or sinful things were fun and exciting. To do or be good meant being muted and living an uneventful life. I thought in hell, one could have sex, smoke cigarettes, and have all the amusement that he or she desired. Therefore, I wanted to feel that excitement; I wanted to have the fun that I thought Heaven could not deliver. Therefore, I began to pray to go to hell.

For weeks I prayed effectually to be sent to hell. However, God cut that perverse behavior short very quickly. On a night like any night, I got into bed to go to sleep for school the next morning. Staying with Big Mama at that time, I had my own room and a cozy bed. I fell right to sleep and had a dream unlike any other dream.

In this dream, I was in the spiritual realm outside of Heaven, standing in a line of about five to six people. We were waiting before some golden gates; everything else was white, and under our feet, were fluffy white clouds. At the two golden gates, I noticed that there were two beings, one on each side of the gates. I do not recall exactly what they looked like, other than both were pale looking and identical to each other with dark, beady eyes. They had a scroll in their hands and when the next person in line was up, they both would look at the scroll, simultaneously nod their heads yes and the golden gates would open, allowing that person to walk into Heaven. One by one, a soul went in as the golden gate opened before us and closed behind each one that entered.

Finally, it became my turn to be up next to go through the golden gates. However, the two beings looked down at their scroll, then looked up at me with a blank stare and continued to look at me without any expression. I was not paying full attention to them at first, because I was distracted from the excitement of being right there before the gates of Heaven. I was standing in place but focused on looking in-between the golden bars in an attempt to see what parts of Heaven I could. My attention was off the two beings that guarded the gates until I felt their gazes upon me. Now standing side by side, they redirected my attention toward them. They looked at me with those dark, beady eyes and both shook their head, No.

In an instant, the white cloud which had firmly supported my steps now parted under my feet, and I plummeted. The fall was so steep, it took my breath away as I dropped below and screamed endlessly in fear. It was a long fall with darkness all around me. As my body swayed from side to side while nose-diving at a rapid speed downward, I could see a small, reddish sphere. The further down I dropped, the more that fiery atmospheric domain got bigger.

Then I woke up hyperventilating from the dream.

I immediately sat up, in an attempt to pull myself together. My stomach and heart felt like they were in my throat. Still short of breath and shivering in fear, it took me all of five minutes of sitting up to somewhat gather myself. Once I was able to steady my breathing, heart still beating rapidly, I hopped off that bed and dropped to my knees to plead for forgiveness, because I now did not want to go to hell.

The Lord corrected me of that spiritual corruption in a heartbeat. Although I did not reach hell, the fall alone was devastating enough to get me back on the right spiritual track and have me in fear of the Holy Father. I was on that floor sincerely begging for forgiveness from God. I was crying and pleading so hard that snot ran down my nose uncontrollably and the tears pouring down my face obscured my vision. Drastically, I petitioned for God to not send me to hell as before requested.

After that mind-altering dream, my eyes were open to a vital lesson pertaining to Heaven and hell. If you don't make it into Heaven, the descent into hell is not like a walk in the park or a slide down a pole. You plummet with all force and gravity leading you there, and it's a long, gut-wrenching fall.

After that, I never again prayed for such an immoral thing. God quickly showed me, that wasn't really what I wanted—ever.

In Close Sight

CHAPTER TWO

I've always felt that God had a close eye on me. Somehow, He would manifestly correct me and I explicitly got the point. I was always somewhat of an outsider, one who never really fit in with the "in" crowd. If I started to, something would occur that would cause the dynamics to change. Therefore, much of my life I was often viewed as being strange or mysterious.

As a youngster, the first thing my eyes were open to about my uniqueness happened when I first noticed this rugged heart-shaped mark—a birthmark. That's located on the top part of my right arm, along my radius bone, inches from my wrist. Shortly after discovering this, I was over at my Grandmother Letta's house. Amazed at my finding, I ran to the kitchen where everybody was bunched up at.

Gathered around the stove and oven, my dad, grandmother and some his siblings were either cooking, eating or both, because it was Thanksgiving Day. My dad was standing in the doorway of the kitchen when I saw him. Excited and holding my right wrist in my left hand, I went to him.

"Daddy, daddy, look!"

However, he was too distracted with everything that was going on. He barely looked at what I was showing him, and nonchalantly said, "Uh-huh, yeah." Then shooed me away.

Obviously, he did not share in my excitement of my new discovery of the birthmark. Therefore, like a deflated balloon, my shoulders dropped, and I slowly walked off in complete disappointment. That was my last time to make an attempt to show anyone else of kin my special heart-shaped mark.

I do not believe I was born with a black veil over my face as does my mother. However, I do believe there is something uniquely different about me, which the entirety of, is still unknown to me currently. Although, even with my insight, I have had my fair share of shortcomings. I have made poor decisions out of anger or despair, despite my beliefs. That disorderly conduct exposed me to great ordeals in life; even when I thought I was through the rough patches. Those deeply regrettable choices would haunt me for years and continue to do so presently, in more ways than one, which you will soon learn about.

All it takes is one wrong decision and your whole natural course of life can be thrown off with a major detour. Life-altering decisions that can easily be referred to as the 80/20 rule; when 20 percent of your choices affects 80 percent of your life. All it takes is one careless judgement to dramatically affect your purpose in life, and the lives of those around you. To be, or not to be, depends on the choices you make, choosing right over wrong.

Thankfully though, along with His infinite and unmatched power, our God miraculously redeems. He is greater than all the humanly mistakes we can ever make in this lifetime and the next. God knew our path and all the intimate choices we'd make, even before we entered into this physical world. And the Lord has the power to turn all those wrongs into a great right and make our paths straight. However, in God we must believe and unceasingly trust that He is able.

Time of Innocence

CHAPTER THREE

There was a moment in my life when I had no cares in the world. During those times, I was an athletically built, slim, fit six-year-old child. My mom would always tell me that I was as healthy as an ox. The only child in her house at that time, I had nobody to look after but myself and my baby dolls.

Back then, my mother was the favorite aunt to all my big cousins. She was the baby of five girls, with there being a one- to three-year difference between her siblings There was a nine-year age gap between my mom and the eldest of the sisters. Therefore, by the time my mom hit her adolescent years, the two eldest sisters were well into having children of their own. So, I can only imagine that when it came to babysitting their kids, mother was the Queen Bee. My mother herself was practically raised up with the first niece and nephew of the family, and because of that, she developed a closely knit relationship with my older cousins. She was known as the fun-loving auntie to them.

At this period in life, my mother was a saint somewhat to my dad's mom and me. On the days I visited my paternal grandmother, Letta Vaye, she would always tell me the story about the day she got saved. My mother, who was heavily into church then, invited my grandmother to accompany her and on that very day, my grandmother Letta was introduced to Christ and dedicated her life to Him. Grandmother Letta continued to have a trusting and unyielding relationship with God. For in her own words, Grandmother would say, "I've been saved ever since."

As for me, still in my early childhood at that time, my mom was a great mother too. She always kept a clean house and cooked dinner every night. I loved her boiled cabbage. She made sure I attended school every day, bathed, neatly dressed and hair primly combed with either a press or French-braided style. But most importantly, she cared about my education. For two years of my preschool life, I attended a private school, Northside Christian Academy. Therefore, I thought very highly of my mother then, and my Grandmother Letta did too, for reasons of her own.

Mother and I attended church services on a regular basis, some weekdays included. I recall being a small child sitting with my back resting against the church pew, my legs not even long enough to dangle over my seat. I observed the church members and how some of them reacted during the Pastor's sermon or when the church organs got to playing music. Various church members cried or spoke in this funny language. In some cases, their bodies would jolt and move around aimlessly in the room until they became limp. Then they would collapse on the floor and lay there motionless.

I grew up in a Baptist church, where they called that speaking in tongues and getting the Holy Ghost. I recall seeing my mother do that very same thing and I cried out in fear, because I thought she might have been hurt. One of the church members would pick me up and console me as I would see another member lay a large white cloth over my mother's body. That happened often, and at that time, the rationale of it all was beyond my understanding. However, somehow, with the lessons in church, I did comprehend the concept of having morals and values. I understood what was right and wrong in the eyes of God. And although it frightened me, I knew that those people were being moved by the Holy Spirit.

Down the course of life, my mother changed and not for the better. A series of events took place that caused her to be withdrawn from family members and the church. I was probably about eight or nine years old when I last attended church with her; and didn't attend myself for many years after that. But somehow, those morals, values and that internal energy that I felt in my spirit, especially when I did good; would carry and keep me throughout my life.

At some point, my mother began having a contentious, strained relationship with her mother, Big Mama. For whatever reason unknown to me and perhaps Big Mama too, mother started to distance herself from Big Mama. Despite, Big Mama giving my mother almost anything she wanted and considerably helped her out. I recall months going by where I would go without seeing Big Mama until that one rainy day, I spotted her outside where mother and I lived.

I was outside playing by myself and by happenstance, I ran into my cousins Kimberly, Cynthia and Anthony who were with Big Mama. Next to the green painted, four-unit, bilateral apartment complex, my mom and I lived in was a medical office. That was literally like thirty steps away, east of our home. My grandmother, who made it crystal clear for all of her grandchildren to call her Big Mama, had my cousins with her as she went to her doctor's visit. My cousins saw me outside playing and once Big Mama parked her car to go inside the building, they came running toward me. Big Mama saw me too, paused, then went on to her appointment. My cousins, however, kept running and when within arm's reach, cheerfully embraced me.

It was already cloudy that day and after a few minutes, it began to rain. So excited to see each other, instead of retreating for cover, we pulled off our shoes and started playing in the rain. We ran around and around that small, two-tiered green duplex until we were exhausted. Barefooted, hair wet and clothes so drenched, it stuck to our skin like a wet napkin. We weren't even concerned with getting sick or in trouble that day. All you heard was boisterous laughter all through the air. We had no worries, no cares, and no fears of any sort.

It was truly a time of innocence.

The Woman with the Iron Fist

CHAPTER FOUR

Big Mama, my mother's mother, was a two-time divorcee. By the time I was born, I only knew her as a single mother and grandmother. She worked two and three jobs not only to support her household but as her daughters became mothers themselves, she also helped take care of her grandchildren. Big Mama was a country girl born in Parkin, Arkansas. She came from a family of thirteen; ten girls and three boys.

Big Mama would always tell me many stories about how they grew up. I remember her telling me that her mom was a full-blood Cherokee Indian and her father, a Geechee African. She went on to say how her mother had such beautiful, long, black, straight hair, but her father's hair was just the opposite; reddish brown, dry and nappy. Big Mama said she hated combing his hair, because afterwards it would always look the same; balled up and parted as if a comb had never been taken to it. However, he would always ask one of his girls to comb his hair. As it would turn out, all the boys' hair took after their mother's low-maintenance mane. And as for the girls, well, their hair wasn't as tightly-curled and unmanageable as their father's hair; however, it still required some tending to—well, perhaps a lot of tending to.

She also would tell me how their father and his friends used to make moonshine, and could barbeque and smoke meats exceptionally well. So good, in fact, that after hours, some of the local Sheriff's men would set up a picnic area behind their home some ways off, camouflaged behind a few trees and bushes; and Big Mama's father would be out all-night smoking meats for those police officers. She said they would have a heyday drinking moonshine and eating BBQ all throughout the night. Big Mama said she never saw the officers, but boy, could she hear them carrying on clear past one or two in the morning, just laughing and talking.

As Big Mama and all her siblings got older, it wouldn't be too long before they started to have families of their own. Big Mama moved to a few different towns in Arkansas, but by the time she had her last daughter—my mother, Grace—Big Mama decided to relocate to Tulsa, Oklahoma. My mother was about two years of age at the time. Tulsa would be where Big Mama would get settled and raise her five girls. Eventually, six out of Big Mama's thirteen siblings (five sisters and one brother) would also migrate here and raise their families as well. Ironically, all the sisters who settled in Tulsa bought homes and lived in close proximity to one other.

Although Big Mama didn't have much of an education, she knew how to survive and was a very sharp and wise woman. My grandmother told me that when she was in the third grade, she was pulled out of school to go work in the fields and pick cotton. As a child noticing how my grandmother conducted herself; her having only a third-grade education never stood out to me as being a hindrance to Big

Mama. She worked multiple jobs and had good credit to purchase what she wanted.

She could richly live off the land. She had a huge vegetable garden filled with okra, tomatoes, greens (turnip and mustard), and cabbage. Big Mama was the best from-scratch home cook I ever came across; she seasoned her food to perfection with just the right balance of salt. She could make some of the best homemade, yeast cinnamon rolls that you ever wanted to eat; fresh out the oven, they would melt right in your mouth. Also, Big Mama was an exceptional storyteller. The stories she told were filled with such detail and intensity. When hearing them, you could actually visualize and feel every word she spoke. Indeed, Big Mama was brilliant within her own right.

And oh, how this woman was strong in every way— mentally, physically and spiritually. She weighed about a buck-sixty (160 lbs.), 5'2" in height; so short she had to make a homemade pillow to sit on, just to see above the steering wheel as she drove. In addition to that, she had these big hands and feet for her body size; wearing a size 10 in shoes. However, what she lacked in height, she made up with tenacity and vigor, because Big Mama was one tough cookie and a very smart little lady who made the best out of what she had.

Although Big Mama was a small woman, she ruled with an iron fist. She had the respect of all her grandkids, her five daughters and their men too. She would not hesitate to pull a baseball bat, a gun, a knife or a machete out on anyone, if they threatened the safety of her or any of her children. Just ask my dad. He and Big Mama would have their run-ins on several occasions. My father told me himself that twice he had to run down the street dodging bullets because he and my mom got into a scuffle and Big Mama stepped in. He learned very quickly to not doubt the strength of a little old black lady named Big Mama.

Needless to say, nobody—whether friends, family or people in the neighborhood—in their right mind challenged Big Mama. In her home, she had three guns that she hid exceptionally well. All my years as a kid growing up in that house, when given any opportunity, I would search high and low for hours trying to lay eyes on these legendary guns that I've heard so much about. But I could never find them. She owned a machete too; I saw plenty of that. That's what Big Mama used to chop down old bushes or tree limbs. Big Mama loved flowers along with her huge, better than supermarket vegetable garden. She loved working outside in her yard. She taught me how to fish, mow the lawn and cook a few dishes. I felt blessed and protected just to have Big Mama as my grandmother.

Through my lenses, I never saw any weakness from her, not even on her dying bed. She was a true matriarch. However, she did have one soft spot—my mother, the baby of all her babies.

Grace

CHAPTER FIVE

Coming of age, my mother blossomed into a beautiful, brown-complected, stylish young lady who became popular amongst her peers. Her given name was Grace, but all her family and friends called her Gracie. Gracie, like the majority of the black kids who lived in North Tulsa, attended Booker T. Washington (BTW), now a historical black high school. Grace always looked the part. She was nicely dressed; her hair full and luxurious, worn in either a blown-out Angela Davis Afro or in a pressed, straightened-out bouffant style, favoring Diana Ross in the Supremes.

Grace had older sisters who had jobs in addition to her mother, Big Mama, and they all steadily provided for her as well. There was no tangible item that she lacked in her high school years. Grace was one of the few kids in high school who had her own vehicle. And since this was back in the early '70s, everyone at BTW knew of Grace.

Big Mama would tell me stories of how she had a hard time getting Grace across that graduating stage. My mother was constantly skipping school to hang out with friends. However, she would get caught because one of the neighbors or an associate of her mother would spot her and call Big Mama to let her know of Grace's whereabouts. Big Mama would have to leave work to go find her daughter and take her back to school.

One of my aunts said that my mom experimented with drugs back then. Considering it was the early '70s, that was of no surprise to me, even though I can say as a kid and even as an adult, I never witnessed my mother drink alcohol, smoke a cigarette or partake in any type of illegal drugs. Although I do recall being about ten years of age, living with Big Mama—mother came home late in the wee hours wearing this black satin two-piece pants suit, and she was sloppy drunk. The blazer was only fastened by two buttons, and it had a deep V-opening. I could clearly see that she had no blouse or bra on underneath it.

I was in the hallway when she brushed by me, reaching for the bathroom knob, rushing inside as she kneeled over the bathtub throwing up. I turned away and went back into my bedroom and went to sleep. But that was the only time where it was evident that she had been drinking alcohol.

Ralph

CHAPTER SIX

When I was a kid, my mother spoke very little about my dad. The things she did share at that time, though, were enough to satisfy my growing and easily distracted mind. Grace said that she and my father were high school sweethearts. Familiar with one another already from the neighborhoods, dad enrolled in BTW after being kicked out of Central High School, then located in downtown Tulsa. And in the hallways of BTW in 1972, Ralph made his move.

When Ralph and Grace began dating, mother said that he used to be insecure and ashamed of his eyes and how they changed colors. That was shocking to hear because my daddy was fine—like, Billy D. Williams fine. He was tall and brawnily built with a natural, sun-kissed, golden-brown glow; his eyes were green that turned to grey, and sometimes blue in color too. So, to hear that he was self-conscious of the color of his eyes blew my mind. Especially when all his siblings, with the exception of one, had those "funny" colored eyes. And they got it from their father, my grandfather TR, who was a dark brown man in complexion with deep, sea blue eyes.

Mother also mentioned how smart my dad was too. She said that he could have been a doctor. Ralph was good in math and he loved crossword puzzles. However, the challenges in life took their toll. Along with hanging out with the wrong crowd, not having that proper mentorship, plus the pressures of life that came with being the eldest of six siblings; and having a father who ran out frequently on the family and a mother with a disabling disease such as polio—my father took to the streets in pursuit of that fast money.

Grace and Ralph's relationship lasted well beyond high school years, but it was a rocky one until it was no more. Grace had me at the age of 22 in 1977. And since I was a kid, I can count on one hand the number of times I saw them together. Although I never witnessed any violent temperament between them, I did hear stories about their volatile confrontations. Big Mama would have to intervene and break up a few fights, because some of the situations went down in her home. My dad became very unfavorable in Big Mama's eyes. And as dominating as Big Mama was, I have no doubt that she had a role in making sure my mom and dad stayed apart.

I recall the story my paternal Grandmother Letta told me about. It happened on the day my mom brought me home from the hospital after giving birth. My dad went over to Big Mama's house to see me, but Big Mama would not let him in. In his face, Big Mama told him that I was not his baby and that he should leave. My father, having a quick temper apparently, got mad. In a rage, he picked up a big rock and smashed Big Mama's car windshield to pieces. Big Mama reacted by going for her pistol. She shot at my dad as he ran off down the street trying not to be caught by one of those flying bullets. I am sure nobody was laughing when it happened, but the way my Grandmother Letta had told that story, I was in tears from laughter and she was too.

Although my father was embarrassed about his unique features at first, I assume the continuous attention he got from the ladies helped him get over his insecurities. Further putting a dent in his relationship with my mom. Dad became very popular, and with the steady attention he was getting from other females, he figured out fairly quickly that having "funny colored eyes" wasn't so bad; and absolutely nothing to be ashamed of. I gathered that my mom and dad had an intermittent relationship throughout the years, but the final straw was when my mother got word that my dad had gone to Dallas with two other women and had a threesome. I suppose you can say Ralph was a rolling stone.

My dad did some time in the pen too, on numerous occasions. I can recall one time taking this long drive in the back seat of a car in the heat of summer with no AC. We were all packed tight with just the window air to give us a breeze; we were sweaty the whole way there. I remember my aunt Sheila and Janet being in the car. I don't know who drove. But when we got there, they unbuckled me out the back seat and grabbed me out the car. I may have been about three or four years of age.

My dad, laying eyes on his daughter, picked me up and bear-hugged me. His arms totally wrapped around my little body. Kissing me, he pressed his face up against mine, and I remember feeling his sharp, prickly beard hairs jabbing their way into the side of my face. It shocked me, because it was so unexpected and uncomfortable. It felt like a hundred little prickly pins instantly jabbing my skin, but I didn't flinch a bit. Instead, I let him snatch all the kisses and hugs he could. Then after a short time, we all gathered back into that hot, humid car; sandwiched in, and sweaty, and drove back to Tulsa.

My dad ended up having eight more children after me. No other ones from my mother, but allegedly between those two women he went to Dallas with. Three by one and five by the other, who he would eventually be common-law married to. I got to know my younger siblings by the brief interactions I had when I went over to their places as a kid. Although we did not visit on birthdays or share holidays together, still yet- we all knew one another.

False Hope

CHAPTER SEVEN

The only other person I saw my mom, Grace, date when I was a kid, was this man named Gabrielle. When Gabrielle came into the picture, my mom and I were staying at the Washington Heights apartments located in North Tulsa. I loved our apartment. It had this huge living room, so spacious that I used to run and do cartwheels up, down and all around it. Our apartment had this cute little kitchen nook, with a dining space just big enough for our small two-seated dinette table. It had an L-shaped hallway that led from the kitchen to the bedrooms, which were a nice size too. My mom's room was large enough to fit her king-sized bed, and my room was large enough for my full-sized bed, dresser and toy chest.

When mother introduced me to Gabrielle, I was in kindergarten. By his appearance, he looked decent. Gabrielle was dark-complected, with a low to near-bald haircut. He wasn't unattractive, but he wasn't really cute either. His medium-built body stood taller than my mom's 5'5" feminine frame by an inch or two. He wore a fresh, fragrant cologne that made him pleasant to be around and had a nice smile. I am unsure if Gabrielle was muscular or not, because the times I saw him, he wore a suit and tie.

While my mother and Gabrielle were together, I don't recall having much interaction with him, with the exception of one time. I distinctively remember one morning when he woke me up for school. Gabrielle teased me about having a hole in my cheek, because when I sat up from my pillow, I had a long streak of slobber going down the side of my cheek. He wiped my face dry, then gave me a soft pinch on the cheek before leaving my room. And that was as much as I could recollect of him from a six-year-old's perspective.

I don't know what kind of charm Gabrielle had, but he had my mother's nose wide open. Mother really liked him. I overheard her evening talks with Big Mama, saying how Gabrielle was a successful businessman. That he had all this money and he wanted to marry her. Mother seemed very delighted with Gabrielle and obviously envisioned a future with him.

One day, my mother gathered me in the car and drove to pick up Big Mama and my Aunt Armostean too. We drove somewhere a-ways from North Tulsa. It was an area of town I'd never been before, the far west of Tulsa. I recall looking out the backseat window as our car passed some huge two-story homes. There was a lot of land between the homes, so it appeared that it was a newly developed neighborhood. She finally slowed down and parked alongside this gorgeous two-story home with big sash windows.

We all got out of the car to go inside the house. I remember walking in and seeing just three feet from the entry, there was some broken tile in the flooring. Seeing it too, my mom hurried where the defect was and said they were going to get that fixed. But other than that, the house was remarkable. It had a big, open floor plan with a nice big kitchen. She said that Gabrielle was buying the house for her. Hearing that made me excited, because I could just imagine myself running all around in that big house; for it was five times bigger than our quaint apartment out North. My mom appeared thrilled too; it showed all over her face and throughout her body language. Big Mama looked over everything and had a smile on her face, but for whatever reason, did not seem too convinced of our possible new reality.

Shortly after visiting the potential new home, I am uncertain which event took place first, but some major things went down. I recall hearing my mom wailing through the walls of my bedroom. I went out in the hallway toward her room to see what was wrong; but her bedroom door was closed. I could hear her letting out this lamenting cry. I may have overheard a man's voice in there too; that part of it was also unclear.

Later in the week, while I was over at Big Mama's house, some pieces of the puzzle had come together for me. My Aunt Armostean had arrived over there. When she came, I was playing with my toys in the den, which was adjacent to the living room, where the adults were talking as I listened in. Armostean talked about Gabrielle being a crook, showing Big Mama this article in the newspaper titling him a con artist. That sudden news certainly came with a lot of gossip and shock.

Needless to say, the move into that big, nice house out West was now just a fantasy. Along with my mother's blissful marital future with Gabrielle, because I don't recall seeing him much at all after that.

My mom would eventually recoup and bounce back from the devastation of that relationship. The terrible blow of finding out that her fiancé, her "successful" businessman beau, was a well-known con artist. Every word he spoke that my mother held onto so dearly, was an outright lie. It didn't seem to have broken her spirit, or perhaps it did—she just had a good way of concealing those emotions. Either way, on the outside, my mother appeared to be managing it well. She was still that crazy, fun-loving auntie that all my big cousins adored.

Growing Up Martin-Style

CHAPTER EIGHT

Growing up, everyone called me Red because I had reddish sandy-brown hair that was curly from wearing a Jerri curl. My hair was thick, and I had lots of it too. I assume it was easier to just slap some hair chemicals on it, to break it down enough to where all you needed was some curl activator and a hair pick or comb to manage it. Back then in the early '80s, Jerri curls were a black man and woman's hair savior. Everywhere you went, it seemed like the majority of black people were donning the curl, with me included.

As youngsters, all of Big Mama's grandkids played hard. Even us girl cousins, and we could hang with the boys, like some true tomboys. I remember one time we were playing in the front yard of my Aunt Rena's house with the other neighborhood kids. We decided to play football. We all got into formation, five kids on one side and the other five on the opposing side, facing each other. None of us wore any head gear. The only type of armor we had was on the shoulders, where we cut up shipping boxes that posed as shoulder pads.

Someone did the countdown... One! Two! Three, hike! We all went charging into our opponent. Colliding, our heads bumped one another, our boxed-shoulder pads were knocked off; for sure I knew somebody got hurt. I know I was, but I didn't let that interrupt my game time—not one bit. We got up from the unexpected soreness of that crash and continued playing the game. We were a tough bunch.

In the summer days, Big Mama would watch us all when our moms were at work and needed a sitter. I remember one day my mom, being off from work, drove up to the house. Seeing her in the driveway, my older cousins came running out the house to greet her as she stepped out of her powder blue, 1982 sedan Malibu. She reached in her purse and pulled out a hundred-dollar bill and gave it to one of the eldest cousins, Nalla, to split amongst the crew. There were about four of them, and needless to say they all jumped in the air with sheer joy and excitement. I was around six, and my older cousins' ages ranged from twelve to sixteen. Back in that day, being a kid and getting a hundred-dollar bill to be split four ways was a lot of money. They thought they were rich. Especially after walking out of Gibb's candy store, where everything—soda-pop, chips and candy—cost a quarter.

At that time, my mom worked at the Convention Center in downtown Tulsa. She seemed to always have money, and that made her happy, which in turn made me happy. We dressed good, ate well and overall lived well. But like all good things that come to an end, so did our comfortable lifestyle.

Things Change

CHAPTER NINE

It's amazing how much change time brings or how drastic life can be from one moment to the next. Within the following two years, I was no longer the only child. My mother had another child, a boy named Israel. So, at the age of eight, I was now a big sister.

We had moved back in with Big Mama. My mom was now unemployed and in-between jobs. She had gotten into some trouble with the law. Apparently, all that good eating and extra cash flow we had going on came with more than what we bargained for.

On some evenings back then, my aunts used to all go over to Big Mama's house, sit around the living room and gossip. They would discuss the situations of whichever sister had the most drama going on at the time. And around that time, my mother was commonly the topic of discussion. Through those living room conversations were how I heard about what was going on with my mother.

I overheard from the relatives that when my mother was working at the Convention Center, she was also collecting a welfare check and food stamps. It was reported, charges were filed and she had been found guilty of welfare fraud. Rumors had spread about the neighborhood, and so it was told, the informant was one of my father's jealous girlfriends whom he had kids with. She had turned my mother in out of spite, even though my mother and father weren't together.

I had heard many stories concerning my father. I knew that Ralph was a diehard ladies' man. All the ladies wanted them some Ralph. However, it was no secret that there was only one lady who forever captured his heart; and that was my mother. Grace was envied for being the love of my dad's life, and because he made it no secret, my mother was disliked for that reason alone.

Going back and forth to court, my mother ended up losing her job downtown, which definitely caused hardship in our household. With the new addition to the family and mother's present legal troubles, by the time I hit the third grade, it seemed life got extremely difficult from there on out.

My mom had been found guilty and penalized for committing fraud. She was ordered to repay the money in a timely fashion or else face prison time. Because I was so young, I didn't understand what was going on regarding her legal matters. However, it was apparent that whatever she was doing or the lack thereof was unsatisfactory to the judges, because for the next five to six years she would intermittently spend the majority of that time in prison and absent from the lives of her children.

Doing prison time somehow changed my mother. She was no longer the fun-loving mommy I looked up to and adored. She didn't attend church anymore, and barely cleaned up the house. She would sleep all day and cook dinner at night when it was time for us to be in the bed. Mother wasn't concerned with our schooling or anything else, for that matter. Big Mama had to step in and take us to and from school at times or my aunt would give me a lift while picking up her daughter, because we attended the same school. It was like life had defeated my mother and she didn't even bother to try anymore.

That period was also when her hateful ways toward me began. The motherly spirit she possessed, which used to give me inspiration and happiness, had gone away to prison with my mother and did not return when she did.

It seemed like for every spell mother was free, she would get pregnant, have another child, be there with us for a short span, then get locked up again. The authorities would usually arrest her when she went for her quarterly visits to the parole officer or had to appear in court. That ongoing process began to be such a burden on me, because it was I, who would be the one taking care of her kids in her absence.

I recall one time—I was twelve years old, and my mother went to visit her parole officer. I was left to babysit my two little brothers, Israel and Isaiah, which was nothing out of the norm. She was gone all day. All day turned into all night, which led into the next morning. There we were, home alone with nothing in the fridge but a gallon of milk. My brothers, two and four years old at the time, got hungry and so was I. To ease the edge of our hunger, I may have popped some popcorn, made a peanut butter sandwich or something simple to get us through the night. We managed, still yet, as the hours went by, so did our growing concern.

I was worried out of my mind about the whereabouts of

our mother. Did she get into a wreck? Was she kidnapped? My mind was wearied with all sorts of dreadful thoughts as to why she had abandoned us. Our telephone was turned off, so there was no way to reach out to anyone. Israel, who was the second oldest, would cry all through the night, asking for his mama. He would get severely asthmatic at times, so along with being concerned with the whereabouts of our mother, I also was fearful of Israel getting overly upset and having an asthma attack with no adult present.

Going into the second day, late in that afternoon, we got a knock at the door. Happy and excited, I rushed to the door to open it, only to find that it was our grandmother, Big Mama. She said our mother had gotten arrested, and instructed me to gather our things and go with her. My heart sank, and in a low, broken up voice I muttered, "What?" That was the only word I could say out loud before the tears started to stream down my face uncontrollably. And I thought to myself, *not again.*

I never liked for anyone to see me cry, but this time was more challenging than others in fighting back the tears. Our mother was sent away again, and I was very hurt by it. Gathering our things, I was constantly using my arm sleeve to wipe my eyes dry. However, the tears were falling faster than what I could wipe away. Going to each one of our bedrooms, I packed as much as our belongings as I could and loaded them in the car.

My little brothers were in the back seat buckled down, and me in the front. My grandmother put her car in reverse and began to drive away from our home. On the way to Big Mama's house, the tears steadily fell. I had my face turned toward the passenger window, away from Big Mama, so she could not see my eyes as the tears freely flowed. The feeling of shame and extreme sorrow overwhelmed my soul, because our mother was locked up again, away from her children.

When we reached Big Mama's house, my little brothers, clueless to the extent of things, got out of the car and ran inside. I, however, was feeling the weight of the world on my shoulders and it was heavily tugging on those heartstrings, because I could not stop weeping. I grabbed our things and took them in the house. Then I settled myself in one of the two spare bedrooms where I closed the door behind me. I lay on the single bed to bury my face in the pillow as I cried some more. Uncontrollably weeping, it felt as though the tears were endless.

After a short while, my cousin Markie came in the room where I was, and lay down in the other single bed adjacent to me. He appeared to be asleep, but I knew that he wasn't. I lay there, still overwhelmed with the burdensome thoughts of my mother being incarcerated again and me having to look after my brothers once more, in addition to attending school.

Then, all of a sudden out of nowhere, although I could not physically see it, I sensed or envisioned it. There was an angel in that room with us. It was in the corner of the room next to the bedroom closet. Hovering with its his legs folded and one elbow resting upon his knee as his face sunk in the palm of his hand looking down at me. Then he raised the other hand, snapped his fingers, and voila! Just like that and in an instant, the glooming sadness that weighed on my twelve-year-old heart was no more. My eyes, that just a second ago, could not stop the tears from flowing now, were suddenly dry. I couldn't force another tear out even if I wanted to. The weariness that heavily oppressed my young mind was immediately lifted—poof, gone, in a snap!

I got up from the bed and shoved Markie, because I knew he was pretending to be asleep and perhaps there to be nosey. He got up from the bed and shoved me back. Then simply as that, we ran out of the room laughing and playing as if I didn't just experience such emotional hardship. I felt a peace within me that everything was all right. Oddly enough, I found myself cheerful and smiling that entire day. And as a matter of fact, never again did I feel such depths of sorrow regarding my mother's imprisonment departures.

Sadly, my mother would be locked away for months and in some cases years. It would be Big Mama and later, my Aunt Armostean who would step in and share the responsibilities of caring for my brothers and me. That process of my mother going in and out jail continued on up until baby number four, Christian. With Christian, my mother was actually pregnant with her while incarcerated. I remember being on the phone and asking her, "Are you pregnant?"

My mother sat on the other end of that receiver while she was behind those bars and told me a flat-out lie. "No, I am not pregnant." I was relieved but not totally convinced. It would be me who had to look after my siblings, and Big Mama, who kept us all. Big Mama worked at night, so that left me to take care of my two little brothers when she would leave for her second-shift job, which was not easy for an elementary school aged child.

After a while, my Aunt Armostean began to help out and took in my little brothers, Israel and Isaiah, to go stay with her and her family. That was a huge relief for me, because at the age of twelve, going to school and dealing with those types of responsibilities was a huge load to carry. Therefore, with the boys staying with her, now I could just look after myself. Now, since my aunt took on the role of caring for my little brothers, who at the time were ages three and five, I could just be a kid and play with my toys. That lasted for a short while until baby number four came along. I appreciated my aunt and Big Mama for looking after us. However, the recurrent separations between my brothers and me, during our mother's incarcerations, in time I would later see, caused our family unit to be weakened.

After months of living burdensome-free under Big Mama's roof, mother gave birth to Christian, then got locked right back up again. She missed out on Christian saying her first words, taking her first baby steps, but I was there to witness it. I coaxed my little sister as she took one step after the other. A little over a year passed before mother was released from prison this go-round. And like before, mother would stay at Big Mama's house until she got on her feet or obtained some housing assistance. That entailed applying for Section 8; a government assisted program that paid a portion or 100 percent of the rent for qualifying families. Mother got approved and knew some people who rented homes that would accept the voucher.

The house was very nice, with three bedrooms, one and a half baths, two living areas and a full dining area. My mother got a job as a private-duty worker for an elderly woman named Ms. Wakefield. From what I understand, she and her family were financially well off. She also had rental properties and allowed my mom to rent this house from her.

Moving into the house wasn't an easy process. I recall being at Big Mama's place, in bed sleeping. The bed seemed extra warm and cozy that night. It was so quiet and peaceful. It felt so good that I may have been sleeping with a smile on my face. Then, all of a sudden, my sleep was disrupted by mother. She was shaking my shoulder at four in the morning, telling me to get dressed. I was going with her over to the rental house to wait with her for the electricity to get turned on. Sorely annoyed, I did as mother said.

We went to that house with no electricity or heat to benefit us. It was dark and grossly cold in there. To keep warm, we lay on this mattress and buried ourselves under the covers. I was too through, so to speak; I went from a peaceful environment and sleeping in a cozy, warm bed, to this freezing, teeth-chattering, dark house. Exhausted, I attempted to go back to sleep, but that was almost impossible to do in those conditions. I laid in this extra firm bed, with nothing but the body heat of my mom and a few light blankets to keep her and I from freezing until sunrise. Later in the day, the PSO man eventually came to turn the electricity on and I was glad for that.

It was very challenging for me to adjust to our growing family. Living with my mother, it was as if I was the more responsible one. It seemed like my time was more devoted to looking after the kids than her. She would often say she was going to work, then be gone for days. It was seldom that she would have a real job, like a regular 8 to 5. Instead, she would do odd jobs like picking up sticks from off the side of the road or private duty work.

Mother would be gone with her guy pal Gaeta Wayne, "working" as she would say. He'd drop by to pick her up, and she'd be gone for days, leaving me to take care of the home and look after my little brothers and now sister. The majority of the time when my mom left us, we would either be low on food or the baby was out of pampers.

Although I've never witnessed my mother smoke a cigarette or drink any sort of alcoholic beverage, her actions often made me wonder if she did drugs. All those long escapades she'd be gone on, for days "working," and when she did come home, she had not one pamper, no food or any money to show for her time being gone.

Now, I love my mother and there was a point in my life when I tried to please her consistently, but never could. She was too greedy and ornery; the more I gave, the more she wanted. Living with my mom, I would always try to keep the house clean. And instead of her appreciating it and wanting to keep a clean house herself, she would do something like pop some popcorn for my little brothers. And what would they do? Within minutes, they would have popcorn literally covering the entire living room floor and just moments after I had cleaned it. Honestly, I couldn't even tell if they ate any of it. I never saw them in action, but they might as well have just thrown the whole bowl of popcorn in the air, because that's what the floor looked like after they were done with it.

It bothered me when mother did things like that. Usually when she carelessly would dirty up things, I would just bite my lip, containing my frustration and clean it up again, then retreat into my bedroom. The four surrounding walls of my bedroom were my place of refuge away from the disorder that lurked throughout the rest of the home. My bedroom was my calm place to escape; that's where I spent the majority of my time when my mother was home. By keeping myself out of sight, I was able to avoid some of the havoc stirred up amongst the walls of our home, mainly caused by her lack of goodness.

Behind Our Four Walls

CHAPTER TEN

Like every coin has two sides, according to the basic introduction of Psychology, so do people. There is a good and an evil side in every person. To everyone on the outside, my mother was the sweetest person. However, behind the four walls of our home, I regularly saw that other side, her evilness. The outside world viewed my mother as a Christian woman—a happy, sweet lady. But behind closed doors, mother's conduct was the opposite of that and she gave me sheer hell.

Typically, a mother would be encouraging and supportive to her children. My mother was not. For the life of me, I could never rationalize her changed behavior toward me. Some mothers deal with addictions which deprive their children of a healthy maternal relationship. My mother, on the other hand, didn't drink or do any drugs as far as I knew. No, she was just downright spiteful for no reason at all.

I caught her one time, talking on the phone to Big Mama, telling her how lazy and no-good I was. I had come out of my room to look in the refrigerator, and there she was on the living room couch, sprawled out with the phone receiver to her ear, saying, "Yeah, she don't do nothing." When mother saw me look over at her, she smirked and continued to talk down on me, as if telling blatant lies was the thing to do.

I couldn't believe it. After all, I was the main one, if not the only one in the house, who cared enough to keep it clean and do minor upkeep when things got broken due to their carelessness. Therefore, to hear her say those awful things about me was mind-boggling and painful. I tried to figure it out. I wondered if she just didn't have anything else to talk about or wanted to create some drama. But nonetheless, she most certainly told some tall tales that day to Big Mama and whoever else that might have been willing to listen on the other end of that receiver.

This woman I called mother unjustly told false rumors about me and painted a negative image about me to the outside family. It was a consistent, evil habit of hers to bad-mouth me behind my back. And she often said cruel, hurtful things to my face.

I could be just walking down the hallway of our home, headed to the kitchen or something. We'd pass by one another and out the blue, she would stop me with her lips all turned up into a sneer and tell me I looked just liked my daddy. Then she'd go on to say that I wouldn't be shit, just like he wasn't shit. I would stand there, and have this blank expression on my face as I looked at her without saying a word. Mother would just stare at me with a bitter look on her face as she watched me retreat back to my room.

At times, she would call me a "bitch" and "streetwalker" for reasons unknown to me. In fact, I didn't even know what a streetwalker was until I finally asked her one day. I knew it meant something negative though, because when she said it, I could hear the venom and resentment in her voice. In my head, I did walk the streets, as did all the rest of the kids in the neighborhood, but I usually made it in the house before the streetlights came on. So, I didn't understand the reasoning for her strife.

Her favorite thing to call me, which was also unwarranted, was "demon" or "devil." No matter how I attempted to avoid her, she always managed to slip that in somewhere as she was speaking to me. During that time, at the age of 14, I was still very innocent-minded. Besides the occasional harassment that the eldest sibling might show toward the younger ones, there was no justifiable cause for my mother to consistently call me a devil or any other demeaning name for that matter.

For the life of me, I could not understand why she acted so angrily toward me. I mean, it's not like she got pregnant with me by accident. Nope, her best friend in high school told me later on that she got pregnant on purpose and even went to the extent of taking fertility pills. Her pregnancy with me was intentional; she wanted to have me. Despite how unfavorably mother viewed me as I grew up, throughout her hostility, I still found myself trying to please her constantly beyond my hurt.

As children growing up into the adolescent years, we naturally have insecurities and/or lack confidence. Self-assurance is a mental strength that is developed with time and is built by steady encouragement. In most cases, we ourselves don't even realize our own gifts or the greatness of who we are and what we can accomplish until somehow, we are made aware of it. So, imagine the bigger disadvantage we face when our surroundings are a negative space. We grow up doubting and undervaluing ourselves. And dealing with this woman that I called mother, behind those four walls, was a daily mental war zone. The way she consistently put me down, it was like she wanted me to be nothing and wanted me to believe that I would be nothing.

However, I was unwilling to give into the bullshit. I would not allow her to get into my head. I countered her jealousy and strife by telling myself, "I *will* be somebody; I will be a success in this life and the next."

There were days when she attempted to keep me from getting my education. During my freshman year in high school on multiple occasions, I had to aggressively protect myself from her physical attacks because she wanted me to miss school, and I wasn't having that. She would initiate a fight or urge me to stay home to watch her kids. However, I refused to give in to her nonsense on every level- mentally, physically and verbally.

Despite her being my mother and the head of our household, I could not make sense of her rationale for being so abusive. How could a person bring children into this world just to watch them fail? It made no sense. And besides school became an escape from the constant negative bashing I dealt with at home, I also valued my education, and I wasn't going to let her or anyone deter me from getting my high school diploma.

Although I remained adamant about going to school, mother's verbal assaults did hinder me some. I was severely discouraged from verbalizing my thoughts and displaying any sort of talent publicly. Hardly anyone knew that I had a strong voice to sing with. I was terrified to open up that part of myself to others out of fear that it would be rejected, as it was by my mother behind our four walls.

Back then in my bedroom, I used to put on full concerts, with my face made up, wardrobe changes and all. I imagined myself performing in front of thousands of people. I sang to the songs of En Vogue, Whitney Houston and Mariah Carey. I couldn't quite hit all the high notes of Mariah, but I dang sure came close and ran neck-and-neck with En Vogue and Whitney. I practiced their songs for hours in my bedroom. Sometimes my mother would leave me alone, but other times she would yell for me to shut up or say that I couldn't sing. She was so discouraging.

As far as communication, I was always a quiet soul. I seldom volunteered information and never got into gossiping. A lot of times, I would keep my opinions to myself unless asked, and it was very difficult for me to verbalize my inner thoughts, especially in relationships. Behind our four walls, mother was successful in discouraging that part of me too. She always told me, "Don't talk when grown folks are talking." And usually, that meant to not converse with her either. Therefore, coming of age and to this day, I still find it challenging to gather enough nerve to express vocally my thoughts and musical gifts.

As far as a mother-daughter relationship, I had missed out on that for some time now. That motherly love that I remember so vividly at age seven began diminishing around the age of nine and was nonexistent when I reached my teens. I don't recall ever sitting down with my mother at any time in my adolescent years and having one conversation with her. We hardly ever talked. She would bark orders at me about the chores she wanted me to do. I would tell her when I needed some pads for my menstrual cycle or other personal hygiene products, and that would be the gist of our communication. I remember when I first got my menstrual, I didn't even tell her until a year later, because I feared she would think I was having sex or something. My flow was super light anyway and didn't come every month, so I was able to manage it myself. But when I did gather the nerve to finally tell her, all she said was, "It's about time!" Go figure! All that worrying for nothing.

All in all, it was tough growing up as a kid. As children, we deal with our own awkwardness, in addition to our uncontrollable home situations; then we have to turn around and go to school, and deal with kids who like to pick on other kids. But you know what? That does build character; I can say it did for me.

At Gilcrease Middle School, I was one of the heaviest kids in the entire school and I was only in the sixth grade. So, I got talked about and ragged on regularly, and the source of all that trouble came mainly from a kid named Alvin. I was always his target for jokes, and boy, did he bring some attention to my worn-down shoes, my high-water pants or my overweight body. But I have to be fair—when I scored something new, he brought attention to that too.

However, his days of making me the butt of jokes came to an end after we had a scuffle in the library and ended up almost breaking the library projector. Alvin was so busy dodging blows from me that he didn't realize the projector cord was behind his leg and slowly heading for the floor with every step back he took. The teacher had to make a rapid decision between saving the projector from hitting the floor, or rescuing Alvin from me. She chose the projector. After catching the large piece of equipment and making sure it was stable, our sixth-grade teacher then put a halt to our physical confrontation. After the fight was over, I earned the nickname Thunder Fists, and after we both returned to school from a three-day suspension, all Alvin talked about then, was how I kicked his butt. We became good buddies after that.

Going into high school, I did not want to be fat. I constantly imagined myself stepping out of my 180-pound fat suit. And by the time I graduated middle school, that's exactly what happened. I began making the effort to lose weight. I significantly reduced my calorie intake by limiting myself to one big chocolate milk shake a day, and I burned off the calories by exercising vigorously. When I say exercise, I mean dance. I love to dance, and back then I would be in my bedroom for hours dancing and working up major sweats.

And it worked. By the time I hit ninth grade, that fat suit was no more. I had lost forty pounds and grew a few inches taller. I slimmed all the way down and had solid muscle mass. I stood 5'8", weighed 140 pounds with a four-pack, and did not do one sit-up to get it. I was lean and trim. I looked good and felt great.

Coming of age, we don't realize things about ourselves, like natural talents, until they are somehow brought to our attention. Our eyes have to be open to them. In high school, although I was now slim and trim, I was not aware of my athletic abilities. At least not until I happened to be running down the school hallways with one of the fastest girls at McLain High. Her name was Kay; she was one of the top high school athletes in track and field. When it happened, we were not competing against each other at all, but for whatever reason we were running top-speed down the hallway. I put a little spunk to my speed and breezed right by Kay.

At that moment, I realized, "Hey, I'm pretty fast and long-winded too," because I wasn't at all out of breath. I began to see myself as an exceptional competitive long-distance runner. So, the next day after school, I sought to try out for track and field, but just my luck, I couldn't find where the team met.

Later when I got home, I mentioned to my mom that I wanted to run track. But she said no. She wanted me at home after school to look after my brothers and sister. And I did just that, so my aspirations of running track my freshman year were put to a halt.

That wasn't the only time I found a sport I was good at, only to lack mom's support. When I was in the fifth grade attending Roosevelt Elementary, I wanted to play softball. And I was very good at it. Attending practice regularly, every time I stepped up to the plate, I would hit a home run. I was a heavy kid for my age, still a shorty too, but I had some muscle mass underneath that flab, because one by one—bop! None of those kids could catch my hits; it was homeruns all day. So, not only would I have been a great asset to the team, but playing a sport would have aided me in being more active and social.

Mother knew I really wanted to play softball, as did the coach. He went out of his way to talk to my mom about me playing. All she had to do was sign the consent form; the coach would have taken care of everything else. But, did mom sign the papers? Nope.

It seemed like my mother was continuously trying to hinder my inner shine. Naturally, I am a homebody; I absolutely enjoy being in the comforts of my own home. And peace is what I got when mother left to run errands or what have you. I love the outdoors too. In our backyard, we had a huge pecan tree. It yielded fruit, but for whatever reason the whole time we stayed in that house, I never ate a pecan from it. Either the squirrels would eat the pecans, or they just wilted.

One day I was in the backyard, enjoying the weather outside; spring was the season. The flowers had bloomed and looked so beautiful that it prompted me to write a poem. I created one page, poetically describing the beauty that surrounded that tall, full-bodied pecan tree. All the words just seemingly flowed together so well; you could visualize exactly what I was describing. I read it over and over again, proud of what I had done. Later that day, I placed the poem on the table in the kitchen, then got distracted with doing something and forgot to pick it up.

The next day, I remembered that I had left my poem lying around and went to find it. I wanted to put it with my other keepsakes. But the poem wasn't on the table or anywhere in the kitchen. I steadily searched for it. However, my poem was nowhere to be found.

Frustrated and disappointed, I stepped outside the house in the backyard and slumped myself on the first step. As I sat there, I just so happened to look down—and saw scattered on the ground all these small fragments of paper with the colored ink that I had used for writing. It was my poem! Someone had ripped it into tiny pieces. There in the frame of the backdoor were the remnants of about five or six pieces of what was left of my beautiful creation. The culprit was either my mother or brothers, but more than likely- it was my mother.

My heart was broken. But like so many of the other things that bothered me throughout the years, I got over it. This person I called mother and lived with certainly appeared to be the same one I adored when I was age six. However, spiritually something about her had changed. This woman here that I continued to call mother had grown a black heart toward me, or so it felt.

Freshman Fun

My freshmen year was the most fun I had all throughout high school. During that year, I had my best friend/cousin to run and chat with during school hours. My grades were decent. I had plenty of friends and I always got along with everybody. I never really had any enemies or fall-outs with anyone, but I was severely shy. I never wanted to stand out in the crowd. Later in life though, I would find out that it's not good to just blend in, especially if your natural course is to be that star and shine brightly. A lesson I am still working on for myself. However, aside from the shyness, my freshman year was filled with new and cool experiences.

My first kiss was during my ninth-grade year. I remember it all too well. It was a high school field trip to the Oklahoma City Science Museum that ranged from freshmen to seniors. During our tour of the place, a senior basketball player, who was very popular and very handsome by the way, grabbed me by the hand and pulled me into an exhibit room covered with mirrored walls all around. Mirrors reflected multiple images of us; it was so cool. I stood admiring Shea's statuesque 6'5" athletic build, displayed in a 360-degree view along with myself.

Cheesing hard and uncontrollably, my cheekbones began to hurt as my heart pitter-pattered with excitement. Before that day, I had no idea Shea even liked me. He may have spoken to me in the school hallways, but that was about it. He was super cute and being a good basketball player, Shea was well known throughout the entire school. Therefore, we were familiar with each other, but never did I have such an attraction for him until we both stood face-to-face in that mirror maze.

I tried to conceal it some, but with the mirrors all around us, it was hard not to notice my beaming Kool-Aid smile. Occasionally, I would cover my mouth with my left hand, hiding the slight overjet of my front two teeth, but none of that made a difference to Shea. He looked down at me with his big, brown, pretty eyes; he had a big smile on his face too, showing off his pink, luscious, full lips. Shea embraced me and leaned down to my 5'8" build and gave me a kiss. At first, it was a nice and subtle peck; he was warming me up. Then he leaned in more for a full-throttle kiss, using his tongue to enhance the experience.

"Yes!" I thought to myself as I finally got to feel those beautiful, plush, silky-soft lips up against mine, and he did not disappoint. I wanted more, but we had to go.

We stayed in the exhibit for no more than five minutes, because we had to catch up with the rest of the class. However, that was an experience I wouldn't forget. Shea picked the perfect spot to unknowingly give me my first kiss. The place had dimmed lighting, it was private and with the cool imagery of our reflections multiplied a thousand times with a 360-degree view, I can honestly say I looked good kissing that fine, tall specimen of a man. Whew!

Getting back in line with the class, my senses were on

high alert. It was funny too, because I noticed my kissing buddy was also making eye contact with a fellow classmate of mine, Jennette. After further observation, I put two and two together and realized that two-bit two-timer was flirting with her too. I was sorely disappointed, and without hesitation, I didn't give Shea anymore of my attention that day or during that high school year. However, I did continue to cherish my first kiss.

Later in my freshman year, I would have two boyfriends during the school year. Therefore, I had ample opportunity to practice my kissing skills, not that I needed it; but that's the most action both of the boyfriends got from me. I never really wanted to go all the way, so to speak, with any of them. I got just as much pleasure from the anticipation of it all, and that was good enough for me. However, because of me not going all the way, I was labeled a true tease. And I couldn't argue with that even a little bit, because I truly was naturally and loved it.

Meeting Eric

CHAPTER TWELVE

After school, I always walked over to Big Mama's house, because she lived just six blocks away. Occasionally, my best friend, Wanda, would walk with me because she lived nearby. Sometimes, I would stop at Wanda's house and hang out a bit before walking up the street to Big Mama's.

One day after school, I was doing my regular routine, stopping at Wanda's for a short period. Only this day, I was getting a lot of attention, certainly more than usual sitting on Wanda's porch. I may have gotten a little bold too, because I would wave at random guys driving by in their cars, and for one reason or another, they felt the urge to turn around and pull up to where I was—for a closer look at the scenery, I suppose. However, I quickly turned down their advances and continued hanging out with my friend.

On that very same day, a guy was riding his bike down the street. I didn't know him personally, but I recognized his face and was aware of his bad reputation. His name was Eric. He'd attended the same middle school as I did for a while, but his presence there was a brief one. Eric either transferred out, or more than likely got kicked out. That day, for whatever reason and despite his bad rep, as I saw him ride past me on that bike, I wanted his attention. So, I called out his name boldly: "Eric!" He kept on riding down the street as if I never had said a word.

Not thinking anymore of it, I went back inside Wanda's house and turned my attention to something else, totally forgetting that Eric had completely ignored me. Although I really wasn't interested in getting to know him, I called for his attention because it was something to do, and I didn't have anything else to distract me. I simply saw a familiar face, someone I happened to know, and called his name. I didn't expect anything to come of it.

However, something did happen. Eric turned around. The next thing I knew, there was a knock on the screen door and a person yelled through it, "Did somebody call Eric?"

I was totally caught off guard and scared. Thank goodness Wanda's mother hadn't arrived home yet. I would not have known how to explain that a random boy was at her house on my account. I rushed to the front door, a little stunned by his boldness, and responded, "Yes, I did." Then I opened the screen door, hurried out, and walked him to the curb. While I did, he asked me how I knew him. So, I went on to say that I remembered him from Gilcrease Middle School, intentionally neglecting to mention his bad rep. Then at the end of our light and very brief conversation, Eric asked for my number and I gave it to him.

There wasn't an instant attraction, but Eric was cute. He was light-complected, as if either his mother or father was white. He had dark brown, wavy, thick hair that was low-cut and faded in the back. He was slimly built with nice muscular tones. Eric stood at a height of about 5'11", a few inches taller than me. He had dark, deep brown eyes that were slanted and almond-shaped. He had a nice smile too with nice teeth; and he most certainly was a talker.

He Got Me

CHAPTER THIRTEEN

After a few weeks of getting acquainted with him, I developed a liking to Eric. Honestly, it may have been more that I felt sorry for him. During our long, conversational hours on the phone, I had learned that Eric was really a good kid who got up caught up in bad things by hanging with the wrong crowd. He seemed to be the target of a lot of negative attention because growing up in the heart of the hood, in the North Tulsa streets, if a person had something that others wanted, it would get stolen.

As the youngest of two children growing up in a two-parent home, Eric had most of the latest dress apparel, and plenty of it. Back then, gangster Nikes were very popular, and Eric had them in every color. There were kids in North Tulsa who didn't know where they would get their next meal, much less have more than one pair of decent-looking shoes. And here Eric was, this high-yellow complected kid with new gear on every day, it seemed. It made him a target for unwanted attention. The kids who lacked guidance and a stable home, who didn't care much about anything, would make many attempts to start a fight with him and take what he had. Sometimes they would be successful in their thievery attempts, but other times they wouldn't.

From all the conversations we had, I gathered Eric was a young misfit who only wanted the acceptance of his peers. But either way, he snagged my attention. And with our daily phone conversations, Eric snatched my heart too.

My routine walks from school over to Wanda's house soon became a detour to Eric's place, where we got real cozy, real fast. We did a lot of kissing and grinding, which blew my mind. And soon after, my sexual imaginations got the best of me, and I decided to take the plunge and let him have my virginity. Wanda and I had been planning on losing our virginity on the same day anyway, so who else better to give it up to?

The attraction for Eric was there, and I sincerely developed feelings for him. The thought of him consumed my guarded rational thinking, and soon I became weak for him. Eric was just a year older than me, but he seemed a lot older. And with his maturity, good looks and tender touch, Eric had managed to ravish my heart and do what no other could before him.

He got all of me. And as a naive, young lady, I can tell you from experience—falling in love in your youth can be set up for a lot of future heartache.

Young Love

CHAPTER FOURTEEN

Still in my freshmen year and dealing with all the demands of my mother, it was challenging for me to be a part of any school activities. However, the activities that Eric and I were involved in did not require a permission slip; and whatever free time I had available before seven p.m., I used it hanging out with him. Even if it was just for thirty minutes, I somehow made a way to lay eyes on my babe. Usually when we saw each other, it was during the day. Due to my curfew, I seldom saw him at night. However, in the daytime, I took full advantage in receiving all those kisses and heartfelt embraces before I was expected home to look after my siblings.

We didn't see each other every day. However, we talked on the phone every single night. Even on those nights that he would go out with his rowdy friends, no matter what time he got home, Eric would always—every single night—call me to say goodnight and tell me he loved me. That alone was enough to allow my heart to fall deeper for him.

It's funny about that young love. In its early stages, everything seems perfect. Of course, in the beginning of our relationship, I saw no faults in him. However, as the relationship progressed, my eyes were open to some things that stood out as odd to me.

For instance, Eric smoked cigarettes. He was sixteen

and smoked cigarettes, but even more bizarre, he smoked those cancer sticks with his mother. They often shared a pack between each other. I couldn't believe it. They would sit at the dining table, having a casual conversation with one another, and Eric would say, "Mama, give me a cigarette." And she would reach in her purse and pull out a smoke. Never have I seen anything like it that before.

Eric smoked weed too. I did not witness that until later in the relationship. However, when we started to get serious, which was rather quickly, he did tell me that due to his excessive weed smoking, he couldn't have any kids. At that time, I wasn't an advocate for weed smoking. As a matter of fact, I was downright against it. But I did find it to be a relief in a twisted, upside-down smiley-face type of way that he had fertility issues, because I, by no means, wanted to have a kid anytime soon. Especially not while in high school. Although he could've been pulling my leg, I thought there was some truth to it. After a while, we stopped using condoms and every month like clockwork, the red tide came through, which thoroughly made me happy.

As time went on, things remained good between Eric and me. At least as good it could be, considering the relationship was kept tightly under wraps from my family, which is how I liked it. Only a few people knew I was seeing him. I kept my grades up, still enjoyed all my friends at school, and saw my young love when I could. He would walk over to see me too. We would meet either down the street from my house or somewhere close by. However, in the early phase knowing each other, Eric never came over to my house. We kept my mother completely oblivious to our relationship.

I was happy to have someone to confide in. And to make things better, it wasn't with anyone from school. Therefore, no one knew about my personal dealings, and I didn't have to worry about anyone spreading my business amongst my peers.

Looking back, I see now that I desired his attention and love, because that's what I lacked at home. Growing up, I never missed not having a father around. Having a mother's love is what I missed in my life. Having Eric as a confidant to open up to and talk about my dreams and admirations with, was refreshing to me and the best part about our relationship.

Revealed

CHAPTER FIFTEEN

During Christmas break, Eric and I got to see a lot of each other. By that time, I had fallen head over heels in love with him. One evening he asked me to meet him at the corner down the street from my house. Considering we had just seen each other earlier that day, I wondered if things were ok with him. So, I agreed, hung up the phone, grabbed my shoes and headed out the door. He was waiting at the street corner for me and greeted me with a hug and a kiss.

Jokingly, I said, "What, miss me already?"

But Eric was not laughing. He had a serious demeanor about him, one I didn't see too often. He released his embrace, rested his hands on my shoulders, looked me in the eyes and said, "I think I got you pregnant, Olivia."

"Huh, what?! How do you know?" I asked.

He replied, "Because I busted a big nut in you this time."

I looked at him, blinking my eyes as I shook my head from side to side. "But you told me that you couldn't have kids," I said.

"I know," he responded. "But today was something different. I think I got you pregnant with a boy."

"Ok, what?" *Now, that's totally absurd,* I thought to myself. *How is he just going to know that I'm pregnant and that it's a boy at that?* If he was pulling my leg, I did not find it amusing. As a matter of fact, I began to get perturbed. By that time, I had already been out too long and needed to get back to the house, so I quickly made my exit.

But before I left him, he pecked me on the cheeks. Then, off I went down the street and back home. I didn't know if there was any truth to what he told me, but as a fifteen-year-old, I found the sudden claim highly disturbing.

Days went by, until it neared the time for my monthly period. When that time came, my period was nowhere to be found. I thought to myself, *Maybe I'm stressed and it's delayed a bit.* I wasn't having any morning sickness or anything, and that was a definite sign of being pregnant, right?

Weeks later, I still hadn't gotten my period. And I suddenly found myself hungrier than I've ever been in my entire life. That day, when lunch period hit, I met up with the usual friends to grab something to eat. I stopped at three different places. I went to Arby's and ate a twelve-inch sub. Still hungry, I then went to Fastop gas station for nacho chips with chili, cheese and jalapenos. After all of that—I was still feeling like I could eat more, and shortly after, ate two glazed donuts. Finally, my hunger was quenched. I couldn't believe how hungry I was. Yet, I still did not think that I with child.

A few months went by, and still no period. Finally, I admitted to Eric that I could be pregnant, but still wasn't certain. I didn't dare tell my mother anything. I didn't know how I was going to reveal that information to her if I was.

She and I barely talked.

I steadily and patiently waited for my period to come. It got to the point where it consumed me. My mind started playing tricks on me. I would feel some moisture in my panties and rush to the bathroom, happy and excited that I would be greeted by Aunt Flo, but nothing. Frustrated to the utmost, I shook it off and looked forward to the following month.

At school, there were sign-ups for baseball, and I thought, *maybe I'll try out for that.* I filled out the consent form, but had to have a physical before everything was final. I went up to Westview Clinic, a local medical facility located on the hill of 36th Street and North Cincinnati. I filled out all the paperwork and waited in the lobby for the nurse to call me back.

The nurse came from the back and called my name. "Olivia Rao!" She stood there with part of herself hidden behind the waiting door. I followed her to a clinical room, where she took my weight. "143," she said as she jotted it down on the clipboard. The nurse checked my temperature and all that, writing down my vitals on a stack of papers held by her clipboard. She said, "Ok, the doctor will be in to do the physical shortly."

I said, "Ok," and sat up on the clinical table, mind totally clear. I wasn't expecting anything out of the ordinary.

After a short wait, the doctor came in and repeated the same questions as the nurse. He took his stethoscope and started listening to my heart. He said, "Did you know you an irregular heartbeat?"

I said, "Yes."

He took the stethoscope and rested it on my back, then asked for me to lie down on the table. I leaned back, and he listened to my heart again. Then, he took the stethoscope and moved it down toward my stomach. He lifted it and rested it back down on my stomach, listening intently. Then, he raised his head and looked at me.

"You're pregnant."

I quickly rebutted, "No, I'm not!'

"Yes, you are!" he said.

Then the tears started to pour. I begged the doctor, "Please don't tell my mother. Please don't tell!"

The doctor was a black man, maybe an African black man because when he responded, his voice had a deep, robust sound to it. "It is the law," he told me. "I must tell your mother."

I sat up on that exam table boo-hooing. I couldn't believe this was happening to me. What was I going to do with a baby at sixteen? My mind was heavy, and I couldn't see past being sixteen and pregnant. My life was over—or so I thought.

After I was all cried out, I lay on that exam table just staring up at the ceiling tiles in disbelief about my new reality. I thought about how irate my mother's reaction would be after hearing the news. But the main thought that weighed heavily on me was that I was going to be a teenage mom. Something I'd never wanted.

After a while, my mother walked through the door, looked at me and said in a surprisingly calm voice, "I knew you were pregnant."

At that moment, I was overcome with so much shame, I could do nothing but be in silence. I felt so exposed too, because my secret was out. Now that I was pregnant, it was evident that I was having sex. After leaving the doctor's office, I would be no longer in denial about my pregnancy. I had been forced to face my reality, forced to see the truth from where I really stood.

Weeks later, I got set up to receive prenatal care and my first ultrasound. It showed that I was six months along and having a son—just as Eric said.

The Biggest Reveal

Chapter Sixteen

Going into my sophomore year carrying a child was not what I intended for myself. I had aspirations of going to college and being successful in every way. I wanted to be married first, before pushing that baby carriage, but life doesn't always pan out how you expect it to. I was living the consequence of my actions, so I had to deal with it and make the best decisions for my circumstances and future.

I immediately unenrolled myself out of McLain and enrolled into Margaret Hudson, a school for pregnant teens. I attended there for half a semester. Eric was going to P-12, an alternative school for kids in the adjoining building to Margaret Hudson. So, Eric would pick me up for school and take me home.

Now a soon-to-be mother, dealing with home life didn't seem as burdensome. Somehow, I felt strangely liberated from the constant pressures of looking after my siblings. With my very own little one to look after, my perspective changed. However, that liberated feeling came short-lived, because although there was relief from consistently babysitting my siblings, what followed was a whole new level of stress that I have never fathomed until it happened to me. It made the last three months of my pregnancy extremely stressful.

It's funny about people, so much that I wonder at times, is it human nature to take advantage of another when he or she is vulnerable? When I became pregnant, within my circle I saw a different side of people that I never imagined I would. Some of those people became controlling and disorderly. Some showed their darker sides, disrupting the peace and stability of me and my unborn child. The top three creators of the chaos in my life were my own son's father, Eric; my mother, Grace; and my Big Mama, Addie Mae.

With Eric, prior to my pregnancy we never had any issues. However, that all changed when I got pregnant. That extended time around each other permitted Eric opportunities to act a plum fool around me. For example, one day when I was over his house, Eric had just finished off an eight-point beer and began to be disgruntled toward me. He threatened to hit me with his fist if I did not get up and wash the dishes. Apparently, the alcohol made Eric want to exert some authority over me.

However, my pride and prowess would not let me give in to Eric's menacing behavior. In the middle of the threat, his mom came home. Shockingly, she too had no control over her son's actions and was helpless in the matter. Despite, the anger and aggression Eric displayed, he did not hit me. Still, I got very upset—to the point where I became physically ill the next day.

That was the type of thing that began to transpire during my pregnancy. Spending more time with him allowed me to recognize those very serious underlying issues.

To the outward eye, Eric was an attractive guy, but like

most men, he had many flaws. He had a nice body to caress, soft hair that I loved running my fingers through, but on the flip side, Eric was terribly weak-minded and a habitual liar. He could easily get persuaded into doing the wrong things with just the minimal amount of pressure from his peers.

Furthermore, he'd fabricate a lie in a heartbeat for no reason at all. Even though Eric knew that he was my first and only lover, he had the nerve to tell his momma that he didn't think the baby was his. He told his momma the baby could belong to Shea, the guy I went to high school with and had kissed literally once. I couldn't believe he said that, and I think his momma half way believed it too. That taught me, though—you have to be careful about what information you disclose to people, because Eric made that story up solely due to me sharing with him about my first kiss. He used what I disclosed to him in confidence and fabricated a whole story that was totally false. My relationship with him taught me that looks aren't everything; you need to have a strong mind to come with it too.

The more time I got to spend with Eric, the more I realized this dude was a little too crazy for my comfort. On our very first official "date" together, I was about eight months along. I wanted to go to the movies, so that is where we headed on a beautiful sunny day. On the drive there, I imagined cozying up with my babe while watching our movie of choice, and I was excited. When we arrived to theatre, we were thirty minutes early before the show started.

Next door to the theatre was an arcade, so Eric and I decided to play some games to pass the time. In the midst of us doing so, this guy walks in the arcade that Eric recognizes from years back. The guy was with his girl too. Eric, being the super chatty person he is, stopped his game to talk to the guy, then invites him to come along with us to the movies.

I was semi-distracted playing Ms. Pacman, but shortly after, I did notice the guy tap Eric on the shoulder and whisper something in his ear. Not thinking anything of it, I turned all my attention back to my game, because those little ghosts were getting hard to dodge. The next thing I knew, Eric came to me and said, "We about to rob the place. Go out to the car."

I shook my head in disbelief. He then leaned in closer to uncover a pistol he had in his pants, concealed by the bottom of his shirt. Now I was afraid and shocked; this fool was really about to rob this arcade with me being enormously pregnant.

My mind was in a whirlwind at what was about to take place. Not to mention how terribly disappointed I was about how our very first date took such a crazy, dangerous turn. But I wanted to protect myself and my baby, so I got the hell up out of there. My pregnant self, wobbled fast out of that arcade. I got a good distance away too before I saw Eric dash out of there like a madman. Seconds later, his homeboy scurried out behind him, heading in the opposite direction. I was so frightened and now uncomfortably hot from the speed-walking I had done in the hot sun while carrying an extra fifty pounds of baby weight. I could not believe what I was experiencing at that moment. I kept thinking to myself, *what insanity have I gotten myself caught up in dealing with this boy?*

Predominantly, I had made good choices in life. I never skipped school or broke many rules, and I absolutely did not come remotely close in my actions to the foolery that I was witnessing with Eric. The father of my child. My belly stuck out so far; it overshadowed my feet, it was huge. Just putting on shoes posed a strenuous task. And here I was, out in the hot sun and close to being an accessory to strong arm robbery. Eric turned a seemingly great day and one of the few highlights of our relationship into a twilight zone experience.

All in all, Eric had robbed the store for about three hundred bucks. He pulled out this scrunched up cash from his pants pockets to show it to me. I saw that his knuckles were scuffed-up from climbing fences or what not in efforts to flee the crime scene. Looking at the money- *So what?* I thought. I felt so let down by his decisions. Soon, his homeboy found us and they split the money. I was not moved at all by it. It certainly was not worth the risk of losing his freedom or mine either, for that matter. If Eric had pulled a stunt like that before I got pregnant, I would have run out that arcade and kept running right past his crazy ass without looking back.

However, here we were—bonded by our unborn child.

A few days after that absurdity, I was able to shake off the weariness and get back to a sense of normalcy. Nevertheless, dealing with Eric on a daily basis made it challenging for me to maintain a peaceful mental state. Usually, the drama would start with Eric being unable to hold his liquor. The other disorder stemmed from his mother spoiling him beyond belief. The biggest drama to unfold and cause me anguish for years to come was under her consent.

At that time, keep in mind, Eric was just a year older than me, seventeen. One day after school, he called me to say: "I met this girl working at Church's Chicken. She's pregnant and homeless, so momma said she could stay with us."

Listening to those words made me furious inside. I could not believe his mother consented to that while I was across the way, big and pregnant with her son's child. I thought, *where will she sleep*? I was young and naive, but dang it, I was not stupid.

Eric said there was nothing going on between them, which was hard for me to believe when most likely she would be sleeping in his bed. I knew this because Eric's mom had that thick, hard plastic on her couches in the living room. No one could sleep comfortably on that. His mom slept in the second bedroom with the TV on, while the third bedroom was taken up by Eric's dad. So, where else would this girl be sleeping?

I was fuming. But what could I do? Absolutely nothing; I could not control someone else's household. He was allowed to do that under his mother's consent. It didn't make a difference that I was pregnant with her grandchild and it didn't matter how it made me feel.

To add insult to injury, Eric would talk to me about this girl's situation. He told me how she didn't want to be pregnant. She would cinch her belt extra tight around her waist in hopes of miscarrying. Eric said he even dropped weights on her stomach in an attempt to help her get rid of the baby.

Now, my pregnancy was unexpected too, but I never even considered doing anything extreme as that. From the stories I heard, this chick had some underlying issues of her own. Clearly, she was mentally disturbed. Furthermore, come to find out, she attended McLain High during the years that I did, but she was a grade or two above me. When Eric told me her name, I knew exactly who she was.

That chick wasn't around for too long, but she did leave an impression in more than one way. Weeks after Eric broke the news about his new guest, he called me, just as he regularly did. We talked for about an hour. Right before we hung up, he said that he loved me.

Upon ending our conversation and out of nowhere, I heard a shattering noise in the background. Then I hear Eric yelling, "This bitch done hit me in the head with a plate!" His "live-in" friend overheard our conversation, got jealous, and reacted. Eric, still with the phone in hand, started tussling with the girl. I could hear them scuffling around in the kitchen. After so long of hearing the mess, that was taken place, I finally hung up. If I had any suspicions about Eric and that girl having sex, after that day, I was certain they were. Shortly after that, she moved out, but she and Eric still remained friends.

The dynamics of my own relationship with Eric changed significantly after that. I remained very much in love with him, but his immaturity, egoistic and negative behavior hindered the love from freely flowing. I cried a lot of tears and endured all sorts of hurt. Eric knew he had me in a vulnerable situation because I was carrying his child, and with that came his dark side. He never became physically abusive toward me. However, he was mentally abusive and attacked me until my self-esteem became very low.

I've heard people say that when you're young, like I was, you don't know what love is. That is untrue. Eric was my first love. And when you've never felt the feeling of heartache or fear, you love without caution. You love wholeheartedly. Unfortunately for me, by loving him in that way, I suffered dearly.

When Eric said something demeaning or hurtful, I couldn't even get angry about it. I was so weak in love; all I could do was look at him as he carried on with his insults. I couldn't walk away or raise my voice in defense. I was too sapped in love to even defend myself, and Eric knew it.

Right then is when I became aware of the type of love I carry. It is a pure and selfless love that is often too raw and genuine for most people. Therefore, it is a must that I am careful and be very selective to whom I give my heart to, because it can be debilitating. Consequently, the one I choose to open my heart to, could act as a real kryptonite for me.

Dear Mother

CHAPTER SEVENTEEN

Being eight months pregnant, I knew it was time to buckle down. I was about to have a real, live human being come from my body, and I needed to prepare for his arrival. Therefore, all frivolous spending came to a halt. I started to save all my checks from my summer job, not spending a dime. I would cash my check and put my money up in my bedroom.

My dear mother, however, did not give a damn about me preparing for my unborn child. She would find my money wherever I stashed it and simply take it.

Of course, I would confront her about it. There would be some type of argument, but really, what could I do about it? Nothing. The times when I was away from home for the day, I would return to find my room completely demolished—mix tapes ruined, wall posters destroyed, clothes thrown all over the floor. Sometimes, I would go in my room, close the door and just cry. I had no privacy at home, and whatever sense of peace I had, my mother wouldn't let that last too long.

My mother caused unnecessary and unjust stress in my life repeatedly. She would call up Big Mama to gossip. She'd get Big Mama all stirred up over lies. I don't know what was said, but Big Mama got to saying I shouldn't have anything to do with Eric and his family, and that she would take care of me and the baby. Apparently, Big Mama thought she could come in-between my son and father as she had once done between me and my father.

But I wasn't having it. My son was not going to be deprived of his family on either side. When I spoke up and said that, Big Mama got to talking about disowning me. Of course, I didn't want that to happen either; however, I had to stand my ground for my child's sake.

Another one of my mother's motherly moments occurred on a night I was at home alone. I was in my little brothers' bedroom watching TV, when she and my little brothers came home. She came barging into the room unexpectedly, storming in and hollering at me for no reason. I spoke up for myself. We went back and forth arguing; I remained sitting as she stormed out the room.

The next thing I knew, she came back in carrying a plunger and attacked me with eyes full of rage. It was a natural instinct to raise my arm for protection, blocking the plunger from hitting any other parts of my body. She repeatedly struck me, as if trying to either break my arm or that wooden handle. I felt the intensity of each blow, but my arm was not going down. Finally, she got fed up and threw the plunger down and said that I had to get out her house. Dear mother continued to holler and curse at me. She wished harmful things upon my unborn child; she even threatened to call the police, as if I had initiated the attack and not her.

I sat there, still on the bed, witnessing her evil nature through my dry eyes, because not one tear was shed. However, I was very hurt by her actions. I looked down and noticed multiple knots on my right arm from defending against those blows as I continued to sit in silence.

Dear mother returned to the room to let me know that my aunt was coming to get me. "Get your shit and go," she ordered.

Quietly, I went to my room to gather my things. I grabbed two large, black trash bags and put all my clothes in them. I stuffed whatever else I could in the bags too, trying to get all my belongings in there. Both bags were filled to maximum capacity. When my aunt came, I dragged each heavy load to her car with my very pregnant belly, got in, and we drove off.

Arriving at my aunt's house, I got out the car and grabbed my bags to go in. Armostean lived in a three-bedroom, one-bath home with her husband and children. She had a total of three kids, but only two lived at home. The middle child, Teko, had cerebral palsy and stayed at a facility for the mentally handicapped. Since the bedrooms were all being occupied, I took my things to the den. Armostean gave me some sheets, a blanket and pillow to make myself a bed on the sofa. I put my things away in the den storage closet. By that time, a few tears managed to trickle from my eyes and down my face.

Feeling emotionally hurt and frightened for my future, I lay myself down on the sofa bed and rested my weary mind.

The next day, I awakened early. My body was still tired, my right arm sore, bruised and still knotted from defending myself. I remained quiet, withdrawn in deep thought. Although living at home wasn't an ideal situation for me, it was still home. It was what I was used to. But now, that had been taken away from me. The question rang in my head, "What am I going to do, being sixteen, with child and nowhere to call home?" The thought troubled me, but I was grateful to my Aunt Armostean for taking me in, even if it was momentarily.

I got up from the sofa, put away the blanket and pillows, and made up the couch as it was before. I wanted it to feel like I wasn't even there. With this sudden change of events, I felt like I was a burden. Therefore, I stayed in the den for most of the day, secluding myself from everyone in the house as much I could. Initially, I even tried to refrain from eating, because I didn't want anyone to feel they didn't get enough food due to there being an extra mouth to feed. Being eight months pregnant, I couldn't starve myself for too long, but I did wait until everyone else had eaten; then I ate what was left.

After a little while, I began to feel somewhat comfortable. However, Armostean always had a way of reminding me that this was not my home. If I left out an article of clothing accidentally or the couch pillows were left on the floor or not set properly, she'd let me know. When something went missing or got broken, of course I would be the first person everyone would blame—even though I never touched a thing that didn't belong to me, unless told to do so. From time to time, I felt like Cinderella under their roof, but that didn't make any difference to me. Out of the four maternal aunts I had, Armostean was the only one who ever opened her door to me.

Although my circumstances were tough, I went on

about my day-to-day activities. I went regularly to my doctor visits, and attended school. I began spending more time with Eric and his family since I didn't have to be in by nine p.m. anymore. I would often attend church and go to the mall with them.

Eric's mom loved to shop. She'd be at the mall every weekend. During the times I was with them, we'd all go to the mall. Eric's mom would buy herself and Eric some things; then she'd ask me if I wanted anything. Despite her friendliness, I would always decline, because again, I didn't want to be a burden to anyone. Eric's mom had already gotten our child so much already and that was good enough for me.

Still, being a minor myself, I was often concerned with how I was going to support my child. Eric's mom stepped in and took a lot of that burden away from me, and I was appreciative for that as well. Being at the mall with them, though, she asked me so many times if I wanted anything and one day I finally said, "Chocolates." That was the least inexpensive thing I could think of at the time that I liked.

So, she grabbed me a large bag of M&Ms, plain. And that would become her gift to me every year, for years to come.

The Arrival

CHAPTER EIGHTEEN

Weeks had passed, and surprisingly, I was doing ok so far. It was a Wednesday evening and Armostean had made juicy steaks for dinner. Everything my aunt cooked was delicious. Armostean was known for being the next best cook in the family after Big Mama, and I can vouch that rank was well deserved. And it turned out food was not scarce under their roof.

I sat in the den that night and scarfed down a big meal. I ate a giant bowl of vanilla ice cream, drenched with chocolate syrup, then turned around and ate a whole six-ounce steak, baked potato and salad. It was so good; I was licking my fingers. Sometimes, with a few of her dishes, I would even lick the plate or take my index finger and swipe clean the inside of the bowl, to take in all that yummy goodness. Yes, it was that delicious.

Later that night, we were all in the dining area playing card games. Armostean and her hubby may have been either in their rooms or away. However, my cousins and I were home, sitting around the table, flipping cards. We stayed up playing for hours, and it was so much fun. I was winning most of the card games, so I was having a blast. It felt good to laugh and enjoy my surroundings for a change.

When it was time for bed, I got up from the chair and noticed a small puddle on the cushioned, cloth seat where I sat. Thinking that I must've laughed too hard with a loose bladder, which was common during the pregnancy, I cleaned the chair, went to bed, and didn't think anymore of it.

The next day at school, coincidently, the teacher began talking about what happens when a pregnant woman's water breaks. As I listened to her explain the phenomenon, I became curious, so I raised my hand to ask, "How do you know when your water breaks?"

She answered, "If you get up and there's a puddle, that's a clear sign that it has happened."

I recalled getting up the night before and seeing that wet spot. However, I wasn't experiencing any pain, or labor pangs, or anything that I was aware of that would indicate I was in labor. After class was dismissed, I went up to the teacher and calmly said, "I think my water broke. I got up from the chair and saw a puddle."

She tilted her head, squinted at me and replied, "Are you sure? Here, take this pH paper and place it on the inner lining of your underwear." I went to the bathroom and did exactly what she instructed me to do, then returned and showed her the pH paper. She looked at the coloring of it and said, "Yep, your water has broken."

The teacher called my cousin Nella, who came right over and took me to the hospital. I still wasn't having any contractions and surprisingly, I wasn't afraid. Because my water broke the night before, the medical staff were concerned that I would have a dry birth. The nursing staff hooked me up to monitors, tracking my contractions. Looking at the line go up and then down, the nurse asked me,

"You don't feel that?"

Oblivious to what I should be feeling, I shook my head no in response, because I felt no pain. Not at that time, at least.

Hours later, Eric got word that I was in labor and came up to see the birth of his child. It was just him and me. I had requested for no one to be in the delivery room but the father, and the staff honored that. With no epidural, hours later, I finally started to feel the contractions. Following them was a huge sensation to push. I didn't go to Lamaze classes, but I'd seen enough on TV to know how to breathe.

I kept telling the staff, "I have to go the bathroom, I have to use the bathroom!"

The nurse said, "No! If you do, your baby will be in the toilet!"

I kept doing that fast breathing I'd seen on TV. After each contraction, the pushing sensation increased, making it more challenging to resist the strong force of thrusting. The breathing technique made it manageable to refrain from pushing as instructed. The goal was to hold off on any type of pressing, because I was not yet dilated to that magic number, ten.

Finally, the doctor said to me "Ok, *push!*"

With every ounce of strength in my body, I screamed and pushed as hard as I could. The nurse shouted, "Stop screaming!"

Huh? Isn't that what they do in the movies? I thought.

Screaming wasn't helping the baby come out any faster, though, so I followed her order. I pushed again with all my might, this time only letting out a huge grunt.

"Almost! Keep pushing!" the doctor told me.

I gritted my teeth, with sweat beads on my forehead, and again, I gave another robust thrust, using all my energy. Then I heard a cry.

"It's out; it's a boy!" the doctor shouted.

I rested my head back on the pillow, so immensely drained that I could barely keep my eyes open. The nurse laid the baby on my chest, but I could only see his skin tone. I did not have enough energy to focus on anything more.

"What is his name?" the nurse asked. I chose the baby's first name, and Eric chose the middle name. I said, *DeLon*.

In the recovery room, I slept as my family members gathered to see my newly born child. Although I was asleep, I could hear their voices. Eric's mom was there as well. With the bit of stamina I had, I did manage to open my eyes briefly for a glimpse of everyone around my baby. Before falling back to sleep, I saw Eric's mom cradling my child with the other relatives in the room watching. I overheard my Aunt Armostean say, "Well, he'll most likely grow up to be ugly, because he's cute now." Someone giggled. Hearing them, I wanted to get up and join them in checking out my child, but my body lacked the energy and strength.

I was so drained by pushing out an eight-pound, two-ounce, 22-inches long human being, I didn't even wake to eat. The nurse kept asking if I wanted any food and without opening my eyes, I shook my head, no. The nurse came up to my bed again to ask if I wanted the baby to stay overnight with me. Yet again, I shook my head, no. There would be no other person in the room besides me, and I would be in deep hibernation mode. Although, in hindsight, I should have kept my baby right by my side.

The next morning, I was refreshed, dressed and ready to receive my child when the nurse brought him in the room. I held him in my arms and looked over every inch of him. He was perfect, with adorable big hands and big feet. DeLon was fair-skinned and had dark features like his father. He had dark brown eyes that were slanted and almond-shaped, like Eric's. His hair was dark brown too, almost black, straight and laid flat on his head. I gazed at him as he looked back at me. This beautiful specimen was my child, and I, his mother.

Later that day, Eric came to pick us up and take us over my Aunt's house. Armostean had a room ready for us. The baby bed was set up, and I had the room all to myself. It was nice. I don't recall which one of her kids gave up their space, but I appreciated it.

My son, DeLon, was a good baby. Yes, he cried, but not excessively. He slept when I slept. He was rarely sick and smiled all the time. My son was a happy and healthy baby, and I adored every bit of him. The feeling of actually being a mother was surreal still, but DeLon made me a proud mama. He gave me purpose.

Months went by. My son was growing like a weed, and all so precious. I moved forward with my education, unenrolling myself out of Margaret Hudson School and back into McLain High. After living with Armostean and her family for those few months, she sat me down to finally have that talk. She said she had spoken with my mother—dear mother—who said that it was ok for us to move back home. Surprisingly, my mother had also had a baby, a little girl, named Hannah. She was born just three months after my son. Apparently, dear mother was carrying too on the night she attacked me and threw me out of the house. I was the eldest of now four maternal siblings, and my son had an auntie who he was three months older than.

Not knowing what to expect with the move back home, I grabbed those two, legendary, black, giant trash bags of ours and hesitantly began to place our clothes in them. Even though DeLon had accumulated a lot of stuff since his arrival, along with my items, surprisingly all of his things fit magically in those bags too. DeLon's swing and other baby toys, I hand-toted to the car. It took about three trips back and forth before we were all packed up. Then I took my son and went to the car to wait for our aunt to take us to dear mother's house.

I dreaded being back under my mother's roof. The thought of all her negative behavior made me feel dispirited. I had not really talked to her since the night she forced me out. Whatever arrangement she and Armostean had concerning me, I knew mother would not keep it. Before too long, she'd be back to her old ways again. Moreover, now there would be two infants living under one roof. Which, to me, was just as humiliating as being a teenage mom. However, I knew I didn't have much choice in the matter. When

Armostean pulled up to the house, I took a deep breath, gathered my wits and opened the car door to get out.

Dear mother stood in the opening of the entryway, holding her baby Hannah, and watched as one bag after the other was taken out of the car. Armostean went inside to talk to mother. After unpacking all our things from the car, I went inside as well. They were talking as I went to my bedroom. Mother had leased me a brand-new bedroom suite. The waterbed that was there previously, a hand-me-down from another Aunt, had been destroyed by my brothers. Like the little hellions they were, they threw darts at it, and amongst destroying my bed caused the room to flood. However, everything had been all cleaned up and the new bedroom suite was nice, with a regular mattress. Very much my style. I liked it way better than the waterbed.

Looking at our new bedroom gave me a slight feeling of relief. I exhaled and thought, *Living here might not be so bad after all.*

Getting settled in was overall a smooth transition. Armostean had given me her bed set covers, which were plush and super cozy; so sleeping in our new bed was like napping on a cloud. I really liked my room. DeLon got comfortable quickly too, in addition to mother getting really close with him as well. Plus, my brothers weren't being so roguish either. I had my privacy, my things remained intact, and being there felt like home once again—at least for the moment.

Moving back home had some perks too. While I attended school, childcare was not an issue. Grace did not work, so she would watch DeLon during the day. At night, she would come in my room and ask to hold DeLon. One time, Eric had snuck through the window to see us. He ran to hide in the closet when my mom came in and asked to hold DeLon. We both were scratching our heads about that situation, but I let her hold him. After a while, she would return DeLon to his room and place in the bed.

When DeLon was nine months old, I got word that Eric had caught a case. He had been in trouble before with misdemeanors in years prior, and now he would do time at L.E. Rader, a correctional center for minors. Although Eric was only seventeen at that time, he was charged and sentenced as an adult due to his previous offenses in conjunction with the case. And from what his mother told me, the fact that Eric refused to snitch on whoever his distributor was. His only drug case with a street value under $500 had sent Eric up the creek for drug trafficking.

Eric's mom was embarrassed about her son going to prison. She made everyone close within the circle say that he was away at college. I kept in touch with Eric through letters and phone calls. He kept trying to set up rides for DeLon and me to go down and see him, but I was afraid to go somewhere out of town riding with a total stranger.

One time, his sister Tammy, who was significantly older than him, made arrangements with me to pick us up and take us to see him, but she never arrived. DeLon and I was up early and ready; however, Tammy was a no-show. I got the feeling Eric's mom might have told her not to pick us up that day, because she didn't want the lie to be disturbed.

Eric was away at college.

True Colors

CHAPTER NINETEEN

Mother would always be cool for a little while, but eventually, she'd show her true colors. I don't recall specifically the reason for her kicking us out this time. However, with dear mother, it always had to do with money. I never minded giving; however, she wanted to keep taking until there was nothing left, and I could not allow that, especially with a little one to look after. Nevertheless, when I did stand my ground, that's when her unpleasant side would come out and her attack would always be, "Get out!"

As a result, DeLon and I were displaced quite a bit during my teen years. We moved a total of ten times from when I was sixteen to nineteen years of age; six of those ten times were in my high school years. During those times, I learned a lot about how family can really be. Some felt like it was too much of burden to help me, and others just didn't want to be bothered. However, with each closing door that was shut behind me with baby in hand, I learned that I could not lean on my family. Therefore, I got closer and closer to God with steady prayer.

On our last go-round with staying with mother, of course things went the way they usually did, with no surprises. However, instead of migrating between members of our maternal family for a temporary place to stay, my then best friend Keneitha offered a room in her two-bedroom apartment that DeLon and I could stay in. And I was so grateful.

I met Keneitha at Margaret Hudson. We found out that our fathers used to run the streets together back in their heyday. Also, the father of Keneitha's son, Mauri, was my sixth-grade classmate at Gilcrease Middle School; his name was Mason. With our kids being just a month apart, we had a lot in common and became really good friends.

DeLon and I stayed with Keneitha and her family, for about a year until our friendship was tested. Keneitha wanted me to do this check fraud scheme that some people around us were doing. Apparently, that was an easy come-up back at that time. However, I refused. And that hurt our friendship, so then we parted ways unexpectedly.

Year of '96

CHAPTER TWENTY

The year of 1996 was a very pivotal one for me. I was a year out from graduating high school, at the tender age of nineteen, blossoming into a lovely young lady and gratefully overcoming the uncontrollable situations of homeless dependency. As I matured into my responsibilities, I was gaining stability with every steady paycheck I had coming in, and it came with a pension.

I had been working as a dental assistant for over a year at what used to be the first black hospital in Oklahoma, which was monumental. It was established after the 1921 Tulsa Race Massacre, when over 800 people had to be admitted into a hospital. In 1932, the Red Cross finally stepped up and opened the Maurice Willows Hospital, located in the heart of North Tulsa, on the corner of East Pine Street and North Greenwood Avenue. The facility has since been re-named twice, and the latest name is Morton Comprehensive Health. Prior to that, though, countless of black people, old and young, died because the white-only hospitals, which were all of the hospitals in Oklahoma, refused to give any medical treatment to the non-white population. This renowned black hospital is now a federal medical facility that offers treatment for medical and dental services. And as a young, black mother, for this historic and sentimental place to be my very first job out of high school, I felt fortunate and proud.

I took advantage of the opportunity given to me through a health program offered by my high school. Mr. Batson, the school's physiology teacher, directed and oversaw the program. That opportunity opened the door for me to observe and have hands-on training in the medical field of my choice, which was dental. My volunteered twenty hours a week shadowing the dental staff turned into a full-time paid position. Dr. L. Christopher, the director of Morton's dental department at that time, said that I had caught on so well, she felt it was fit to offer me a permanent position. And of course, I gladly accepted. For I really enjoyed being there and providing exceptional service to the patients.

Months later, I was introduced to a guy named Byron through my cousin, Marjorie. Now, Marjorie was a free-spirited, cute, upbeat, brown-skinned girl with beautiful, brown, long, thick hair. Marjorie was always laughing and cracking jokes and had a sparkling personality. She had this bright smile that showcased her cheeky dimples every time she grinned.

Marjorie and I went to middle school together. Back then we knew we were cousins, but we didn't get to really know each other until after we both graduated high school and started hanging out. I loved Marjorie. She was one of the few female friends I had who I could go out with and never feel any sort of negativity or jealousy from her. She had so much confidence within her, and I adored that about her. She had no issues when it came to going after what she wanted, and I totally respected her for that.

As I mentioned, through Marjorie, I was introduced to Byron, who was a nice, decent-looking guy. When we met,

I was enjoying my freedom. After I had gotten over the break-up hurt of an ex, it was a relief to not be in a consuming and unfulfilling relationship. When I met Byron, he had recently broken off an engagement with his live-in fiancée. She moved out, and apparently Byron was single and ready to mingle.

Byron and I talked and developed a mutual understanding as to what we were comfortable with in this new friendship. We both agreed that we didn't want the restraints of being in a committed relationship. However, we liked the comfort of having only one sexual partner. Therefore, we thought it would be more suiting for us to be monogamous sexually, yet still carry the title of being friends.

Now when I met Byron, I had experienced two lovers by then. With those past lovers, sex benefited them more so than me. I mean, I did get aroused, but mostly sex for me was an expression of my deep care to that person. And because I had love for each of them at a period in time, sex for me wasn't all about them pleasing me. I got more satisfaction knowing that they enjoyed me. However, with Byron, he gave me a whole new perception on how sex should be.

After hanging out with Byron, we periodically talked on the phone and shared some good conversations. He invited me over again, but this time without Marjorie and Rick present. He asked me to come over to his place around nine p.m., and I agreed. I ran late, which was not unusual for me, and when I got there an hour after my expected arrival, all of the parking spots were filled at his complex. I went around the apartment parking lot, searching for a place to park. Finally, I found one spot that was quite a-ways away from his complex. I was late enough, I thought, so that parking spot would have to do.

About the time I got to his apartment, it was a quarter past ten. Upon walking to his door, I noticed a note taped to the door. It read, "Olivia, I have a warm bath waiting for you. Come in and have your clothes off by the time you reach the bathroom door." As I refolded the note, my heart began racing. A feeling of excitement, nervousness and shock rushed over me all at once. After finally gathering the nerve, I turned the door handle and entered into his home.

Although I was over an hour late, Byron was still in the tub waiting for me. I heard him splashing the water. By this time, my heart rate had increased to 180 beats per minute seemingly. This was so unfamiliar to me; never have I felt so many emotions simultaneously. I closed the front door behind me and proceeded to take off my clothes as the note instructed.

The living room was dark, with only the light from the slightly cracked bathroom door illuminating the hallway and parts of the living room. I tiptoed my way down the hall and slowly pushed the bathroom door open. This once shy, self-conscious girl stood there in his bathroom doorway completely nude. I had gathered some wits about myself and did exactly what Byron had instructed.

I could tell Byron had been in the bath water for some time. The suds in the tub had dissipated, with only a few, small mini-ones floating around. His fingers were all welted from being submerged in water. But, as his eyes looked upon me, he gleamed and greeted me with a huge smile as he remained in the bathtub waiting on me to join him.

Byron had rose petals floating in the bath water that scurried around as I placed one leg at a time in the water to sit in the tub, facing him. He had two glasses of champagne waiting on the side of the tub, tucked back in the corner where I didn't see them at first. My heart skipped another beat. He leaned toward me to make a toast, and as our glasses were in the air to meet, he leaned in deeper to kiss my lips. I was so nervous, I could feel my heartbeat throb through the tips of my toes, but I kept my cool and returned the kiss as the rose petals floated around us.

We got out the tub. Byron grabbed a towel to dry me off, and I felt so pampered and relaxed from the glasses of champagne we had consumed. I stood at his bedroom door gazing onto the bed and before I knew it, Byron had picked me up from behind and placed me on his bed with the instruction to lie back. Byron slowly spread my legs apart, then nose-dived smack into my honeypot.

Oh, the joy!

If there was any doubt that he would be getting a piece of me that night, it went away, along with the juices that flowed from my body with every caress and lick given. He raised his head to move upward and kissed me on the neck, then planted subtle kisses on my lips as he eased his manhood inside of me. What pleasure was this? I had never felt such sensations, never knew that sexual intercourse could be this blissfully explosive.

I used to hear the saying, "being on cloud nine." Well, I never knew what it meant until that evening with Byron.

With all the multiple orgasms I experienced that night, I literally had an out-of-body experience that floated me to cloud nine, and perhaps even to ten. All those harmonious pleasures that I experienced simultaneously overwhelmed my sensory input, and I was quivering in delight.

Let me tell you, I have always had high endurance and stamina, one of my many blessings. However, that night my body was exhausted from the steady, up-and-down culminations from having numerous orgasms. Amongst the loud, uncontrollable moans that escaped from my lungs with every breath, I began to beg him to stop. My body could not endure anymore. And finally, after so long, he did. I lay limp in his bed, with barely enough strength to lift my head. When I did manage to gather the energy to focus my eyes, I looked for the time—it was three a.m. From the moment I stepped into the tub until being thrown on the bed and worked over nonstop, Byron had me for four hours. After that, I dropped my head back into the bed and passed smooth out.

Later that morning, I had heard someone in the living room. I turned to see if Byron was lying beside me still— and he was. *Who could that be?* I thought. Still drained from earlier, my body remained rested and motionless. I opened my eyes slightly, so I could see through my eyelashes. Someone was walking toward the bedroom door, and I needed to see who that was. I couldn't completely focus or see the face clearly, but it was a full-figured, fair-skinned woman, roughly at a height of 5'5" who stood there.

Lying there playing possum, I watched the woman stand in the doorway, watching us. My first thought was that this must be his ex-fiancée. The second thought was figuring out how I was going to muster up enough energy to defend myself, if his ex decided to run up and charge at me in a jealous rage. Thank God, she did not make a move. Instead, she gazed at us for a few minutes, then silently walked away, not making her presence known.

Still physically weak, but mentally alert, I listened carefully as she left the apartment and closed the front door behind her. Relieved that there was no drama taking place, my mind began to settle down, and I sank deeper into the mattress as I closed my eyes and drifted into another four to six hours of sleep.

When I woke up, I checked my pager to find that I had eight messages. It was about one in the afternoon, and Byron had already left to go to work. As I was getting dressed, his home phone rang; the answering machine picked up after the fourth ring. I overheard a female's voice leaving a message and it sounded familiar; strangely, it was my cousin Mara. She said, "I know you did it. I know you killed my cousin."

Puzzled by what I was hearing, I thought, *What, killed*?! I rushed to the phone to catch it before she hung up. "Mara! What is going on?"

"Olivia?" she responded. "We thought you were dead. Your car was found in a field way out in the country set on fire. The firefighters thought your body may have been in the trunk."

"What?!" I responded. My body began to shake uncontrollably, but this time out of fear. *Is this really happening*? I thought to myself.

117

Mara continued to say, "Everybody thinks you're dead."

Shocked by what I was hearing, I told her I would call her back. Immediately, I ran out of the apartment and rushed over to where I had parked my car. The space where I had left it was empty. My car had been stolen. All I could do was stand and stare at the empty parking space. Apparently, not only was the car stolen; it was set on fire—and my family thought that I was burned alive inside the trunk. What were the chances that something so bizarre as this could happen on the most exhilarating night of my life?

The eerie feeling that came over me at first seeing the car gone eventually passed. Still standing there, my head fell back, facing up to the clear blue sky. The subtle winds grazed my skin sparingly as I let out a huge sigh and reflected on the positive. For one, two and three: I was still alive, healthy and well. Furthermore, I only paid six hundred dollars for the car; and no matter how much I racked my brain around it, there was nothing I could do to control the circumstances.

The only regret I had was losing my son's professionally done photos, which were stored in the back seat of my car. His photos were the most darling images too, capturing all of his witty two-year-old expressions. They were so precious and dear to me; my heart still breaks just thinking about it.

Still, I was thankful to God that I followed my first thought upon parking there, which was to take my income tax check with me. I had it stored in the glove compartment of my car. That night, right before I locked my car doors to walk over to Byron's apartment, I placed it in my purse. Oddly enough though, I wasn't even upset about the car. After what I had experienced earlier that day, how could I be upset at anything? Other than my baby's pictures being gone, a night like that made the loss of my 1980 blue Cutlass Coupe that I paid $600 for, totally worth it.

I called my cousin Mara to pick me up. She came shortly after and took me home. Naturally, she had so many questions for me. And on the fifteen-minute drive to my house, I gave her all the juicy details of that night. We talked the whole way there.

When I got home later that day, my mom was surprised to see me. It wasn't a surprised look of relief though; like, *oh my God, I'm glad you're ok.* It was more of a surprising look of disappointment. As I walked through the front door, she saw me and said, "What? We thought you was dead." Hearing her voice, my younger brothers and sisters came running in the living room where we were.

Now, my mother had plenty of hateful ways that I've dealt with throughout the years. And she had a way with spreading that hateful venom to my younger siblings as well. As soon as one of my little brothers saw me, he started singing, "Ding-dong, the witch is dead; the wicked witch is dead!" Instead of my mother and siblings greeting me with gratefulness that I was alive, she had them all singing to the tune of *The Wizard of Oz*. My little chubby brother continued to sing it, and then they all chimed in and started singing along, with smiles on their faces, "Ding-dong, the witch is dead; the wicked witch is dead."

Forcing myself to remain unaffected by their antics, I walked past them and headed to the den where my son and I slept. While they continued to taunt me by repeating that song, I remained silent and unbothered by their actions. I went to lay down on the couch to rest my mind and ponder how I was going to get another car.

I'm sure if the average person were experiencing this, they would be distraught. However, because I'd spent so many years dealing with my mother and going through my life's hardships, I had developed an extremely hard shell. Therefore, to hear them chanting that song as if it was in celebration of my life being taken, if indeed what the firefighters assumed was true—well, yes, it did slightly bother me. But I quickly dismissed the feeling. By that time, I had gotten accustomed to my mother's evil ways sadly which is why I often referred to her as dear mother stemmed from the 1981 classic movie, Mommie Dearest.

Soon after that, another situation would take place in which my mother's most treacherous moment would transpire. We had one of our many arguments concerning money, which occurred more often than not. I had just walked through the front door when my mom approached me, fussing about giving her some money to pay the water bill.

Now, I would give my mother money just because, but our problems occurred due to the fact, she wanted all my money. On top of that, dear mother was horrible with managing money and at that time, I wasn't earning much. Therefore, I told her I would pay the bill myself instead of giving the money directly to her. But that wasn't what she wanted to hear. So, the argument progressed. In an attempt to prevent the situation from getting more heated, I walked away, went to the den and sat on the couch.

Unfortunately for me, the den didn't have a door to shut her out, and it was next to the kitchen. Just before I had arrived home, mother was in the kitchen cooking rice. Still angry and cursing at me, she went to the kitchen, grabbed that pot of boiling rice, and stood over me with it in her hand. As I sat calmly on the couch, trying not to provoke her, she threatened to throw the boiling rice in my face. I could feel the steam from the pot on my skin and see the bubbles foaming in my peripheral view. Yet, I did not move or flinch. Instead, I sat there, thinking of a way to not have that rice scald my face. In the middle of her ranting threats, I suddenly knocked the pot of rice out of her hand.

Mother was stunned by my actions. She immediately screamed, "Girl, is you crazy?!" Hot rice and water went flying everywhere.

I quickly got up, relieved the boiling rice did not land anywhere near my face. However, I did not go unscathed. Some of the boiling water had singed my right hand; the water was so hot; it caused my hand to bleed. But I didn't say a word. I just got up and walked over to my friend's house who lived a few blocks away to tend to my wound and take a breather. When I returned home, I packed our things, and my son and I moved out.

Dealing with situations like that stemmed from my mother's love of money, and that changed my outlook on a lot of things concerning life and money.

Gone but Not Forgotten

CHAPTER TWENTY-ONE

After many occasional fun times, my monogamous lover-friend, Byron, informed me that he and his fiancée were getting back together. We took a walk around the apartment complex to a swing set located in a children's playground for the residents. And there he broke the news.

I sat on the swing and swung back and forth as I listened to his explanation as to why he decided to go back to his cheating fiancée. Although I felt a certain way about it, I made no attempts to persuade him otherwise. I had my own reserves about Byron and was unsure if I wanted to deal with, if we became in a serious relationship. And everything has its way of working out.

Therefore, the breakup was perhaps right on time. After all, we did have that understanding in the beginning before we became intimate that we were just friends, so although I did care for him, I was not too emotionally invested. After the end of his explanation, I told him that I understood, got up from the swing and walked off. Byron remained sitting as he watched every step that I made away from him.

My heart wasn't broken by Byron's sudden decision, but I must admit I did feel somewhat disjointed leaving him for the last time. Ironically, I had no interest in looking back. Granted, he was the best lover I had ever experienced by far, yet after that day on the swing, I was no longer sexually attracted to him. He made his choice, and so did I.

But oh, do I cherish the memories.

Summer Love

CHAPTER TWENTY-TWO

Months later, I was back to my old routine—hanging out with my road-dog Marjorie. We were hitting the streets of Tulsa, meeting new people and creating fun times for ourselves. One night, we just happened to pull up at the Hood Store, a little convenience store located in my old neighborhood at 46th Street off of North Cincinnati Avenue. We were already parked, and just sitting in the car talking before we went in.

Two guys got out of their car and passed in front of us to go into the store. They noticed us; we noticed them. They both were tall, good-looking and strongly built. One was mocha-brown-skinned; the other one was a darker brown with a smooth, creamy complexion. The darker one looked over to the passenger seat at Margie, then quickly switched his eyes over to the driver side at me.

As I saw him switch his body position to walk over to my side of the car, I adjusted myself in the seat anticipating his arrival. While the darker complected one, was checking us out, I had already peeped him. He was the one who had piqued my interest too. His friend walked over to Marjorie's window and initiated a conversation with her. The dark, creamy brown one introduced himself to me as Rendell and the other guy across the way was his best friend, Sean. I introduced myself to him, and Marjorie to Sean.

I felt an instant attraction. Rendell was all man. And I knew it. He and his friend didn't even make it into the store. Rendell cut the conversation short by telling us to follow them to their neighborhood park, Cheyenne. And that's what we did. We met up there and talked as if we'd known each other for years. He told me he was mixed with black and aborigine, which explained his dark, full, straight hair and dark, milky skin. During our acquainting, I peeped over at Marjorie and Sean; and it appeared that they were hitting it off pretty good too.

After a while, it got really late and we had to part ways. We exchanged numbers, and Marjorie and I went on about our business. Our encounter was nice, but I really didn't think much about it; after all, it was the summertime. That wasn't anything different than what Marjorie and I had been doing all summer long. We'd have a few drinks or a puff or two, share some good laughter and fun with the fellas, then go about our merry way. And that night with Rendell and Sean was nothing out of the ordinary for us.

The next day, after my usual routine of getting the day started, I hopped in my ride, and just as I put the key in the ignition, I get a call. *What do you know? It's Rendell Schwann*, I thought to myself. He had called me to find out what I had up. After some small talk, he invited me to hang out with him. And that was quite all right with me because I thoroughly enjoyed his company. Rendell was a good person, and I felt that spiritually, so I made myself available for him when he called.

The more time I spent with Rendell, the more I got to know him. I found out he was twenty-four years old, worked as a barber, and lived at home with his mother. However, he was in the process of getting his own apartment. He was also working on getting his own barber shop. I liked Rendell a lot; he was a confident, genuine, intelligent, self-sufficient, young man. Most importantly though, he was unselfish and had a huge heart, and that's what I genuinely liked most about him.

When Rendell and I first met, I was still working as a dental assistant, but got laid off shortly afterwards. All the Morton employees, along with myself, had gotten word that there would be layoffs in the near future to aid with budget cuts. Since the clinic was government funded, a government official was sent to analyze the situation and make the necessary cuts, so that the clinic would no longer in the red. No one knew when or who would be laid off, not even the CEO. All the employees were nervous, of course, because at any time someone's livelihood could be negatively impacted by that decision. In the dental department, a few doctors were trying to decide for themselves which ones were expendable within the department and who were not. One even suggested to get rid of all the assistants. However, it wasn't their decision to make.

When we finally got word of how the government official decided to downsize the health services to get Morton functioning back in the black, it was a big surprise to us all. The unsettling news was that the entire dental department would be eliminated from the services of Morton. Therefore, everyone got laid off in the dental department, with a severance package of course. I was nineteen at that time, debt free, and had a son to spend time with. For me, the transition from working every day to not, and still receiving income with the weekly unemployment checks; went smoother than expected compared to some. It felt more like a breather than a doomsday. When I went down to the unemployment office to file my papers, the unemployment officer said that I was the youngest person he ever saw collect benefits.

Thankfully, though before all the Morton layoff drama took place, I had just gotten rid of some excessive debt. A month or two before the talk of job losses swarmed the place, I had returned a brand-new Chevy Corsica to the dealership. Due to seeing through televised commercials that it was a bad deal, a week after purchasing it. When the dealership finally returned my down payment, I took the money and paid cash for a white 1982 Grand Prix that had a maroon, cloth top and plush, maroon fabric seats. The car had a powerful engine in it too, a 301 motor. Which usually is the deciding factor for me regarding car purchases; they have to have some get-up-and-go to 'em because apparently, I have a thing for speed. And I would not waste my time on a car if it did not have some go to it. The initial start could be slow, but once that motor warmed up, I liked to step on the gas and fly down those highways. The Grand Prix was a later model than the Corsica; however, that baby rolled, and comfortably too, minus the car payment.

As a young mother, I had breaks from mommy duties from time to time that benefited everyone, or so I thought. My son's paternal grandmother would keep DeLon every other weekend to spend time with since his dad was locked away. Eric had been incarcerated since DeLon was nine months old; so DeLon only knew of his father's name, but not the actual person.

My son, three years old at this time, was zealously curious as to where his father was. He constantly would ask me, "Where is my daddy? Where is my daddy?"

And I would just say, "He's away at college," the lie his grandmother wanted to sustain, to prevent others from knowing the truth.

I allowed my son's paternal grandmother to keep him, because I believed it was vital for DeLon to have a relationship with his family on both sides. That also enabled me to have some free time. Plus, DeLon was crazy about his Grandmother E. They went shopping every weekend that she had him, so he got spoiled too, like his father. Eric's big sister was married with a family of her own, so DeLon got to build a relationship with them too, as well as their other family members in California and Florida, along with their Tulsa kin.

After my layoff, Eric's mother kept with her usual routine of keeping DeLon. And on those weekends that my son was with his grandmother, I was over to Rendell's place. Our weekends together progressed into spending every day together, and it all felt very natural, as if everything was intended. In my eyes, Rendell was perfect. He fit in with my family. Plus, I could be myself around him, dress up or down; either way, he liked it. He was never insecure about anything concerning me, and I found comfort in knowing that. Even though at times, Rendell could be a bit of a turd.

It was a strange thing too about Rendell concerning me.

When I was with him, he would trigger something internally that prevented me from overeating. As much as I love to eat, for I am a true foodie at heart, when I was around him, once my hunger was satisfied, no matter how much I enjoyed my food, I would just stop eating. When I was with him, I had no desire to overindulge in food, as I commonly did, and that is the peculiar truth.

However, what really captivated me about Rendell and truly touched my soul was how refreshingly encouraging he was toward me. In all my teenage life, I had never known anyone to encourage me in the various ways that he did. No family member, friend, and much less a boyfriend had ever uplifted me in the ways that Rendell so effortlessly did. It was another bizarre feeling, because I did not recognize what my life and spirit lacked until I started receiving it from him. It was like an awakening in my soul. I was being verbally inspired by Ren on a daily basis, and he was oblivious to the empowerment that I was gaining from his positive mindset.

Rendell opened my eyes as to what I needed in a relationship, which was to have my spirit positively fed. He added to my natural inspiration of being a mom and the drive to be more than my yesterday and shine in all my greatness. He motivated me in that way, so I knew wholeheartedly that he was my missing link. I felt a sense of protection with Ren, unlike what I had felt with anyone else. Before we had graced each other's presence, I had no idea where my life was headed or which direction I would go, but somehow once he and I connected, I felt like my feet were placed on solid ground and our paths that led us to meeting that night were predestined by God. I recall sharing that with Ren one night, but I don't think he truly fathomed what I was saying.

One night Rendell came home after a long day's work, and I was there as usual. He was tired and didn't want to go out anywhere to eat, so we ordered in. We were in the living room eating dinner. I sat in the recliner chair, my favorite seat in the apartment. As we ate, we talked about our siblings, what it would be like with our own kids, and so on. And at that moment, I had this strong urge to open up more to him. To tell him about my hardships in life growing up, dealing with an envious, hateful mother, battling homelessness, on top of trying to finish high school and provide for my little one.

However, that second thought popped up in my head and worked its way to the forefront. I thought, I will have plenty of other opportunities to open up to Rendell. It doesn't have to be tonight. That part of my life was a highly sensitive topic and made me slightly uncomfortable to even discuss. Therefore, I listened to that second thought and refrained from divulging that personal and sentimental part of my life to Rendell at that moment.

In hindsight though, I wish I would have trusted my first mind and went forward with being transparent with Rendell. Perhaps it would have touched his heart and made him more attentive to the delicate parts of me and at the same time make him conscious of the strong and good-natured woman he had before him.

Rendell was highly knowledgeable of many things,

which made me even fonder of him. I was a book-smart person. I knew about what I learned in school and things that I leisurely read about, like makeup applications, skin care—you know, girl stuff. However, I was not informed of the everyday quirks of simple living. I knew how to fix something if it got broken or construct objects using written directions, because I am good with my hands.

However, Rendell knew how to restore things. He saw the worth in unsightly objects. For example, when he first moved into his apartment, he had this old, round wooden table. It was very sturdy and had some potential, but it looked rundown. I recall looking at it and turned my lip up at it. Rendell had me put this polish on it and buff it in good, and by golly, that table looked brand-new and gorgeous, to my surprise. It was instances like that where Ren shined.

Being with Rendell every day abetted my confidence. I appear tall and attractive with long thick legs; my walk and stance has always been strong. However, mentally I was this super-shy young lady who was completely apprehensive in speaking her mind. So, it was good to have that positive reinforcement, Ren provided me. He had this natural ability to inspire people, and with him by my side I was constantly being motivated. Slowly but surely, I was easing my way out of that insecure shell of mine and stepping into the shoes of a confident woman who spoke her mind. I knew I had someone special by my side. With time, I would be that bold and gorgeous woman on his arm that Ren would be proud of and exceptionally close to, because he would be there to witness the growth. Or so I thought.

As a youth, my shyness caused me to feel more comfortable blending in with the crowds rather than standing out. I found myself holding back on my God-given talents, just to accommodate those around me. It was like I was putting other people before myself. If I saw that someone was jealous of my natural beauty, I would dull my looks somehow, just so they wouldn't feel that way. I have always had a high energy level too. When I worked at Morton, I would work a full eight-hour day, seeing an average of fifty patients a day. Afterwards, I would hit the gym and work out for a good two hours. So, it was easy for me to leave someone in the dust figuratively speaking. When someone did accompany me to the gym, I would not overly exert myself, just so the other person wouldn't feel inadequate.

Holding myself back though, time and time again, eventually led to me feeling as if I was trapped in a box. Therefore, I knew that it was imperative for me to be more confident with who I am naturally, despite what anyone thought. But I needed a little boost.

When it came to having a potential life mate, there was no compromising. No matter what kind of education or money they had, it was vital that their energy level be equivalent to mine. The love in my life had to be by my side in whatever I was doing. He could not lag behind or be ahead, and he most certainly could not just watch from the sidelines. My life mate had to be parallel to me. And when it came to Rendell, that's what I felt he was—my equal.

Rendell wasn't intimidated the least bit by my natural beauty or sex appeal. He encouraged the sexiness to be revealed and he adored it when it was. Not once did I see any type of competitiveness in his eyes or witness any hostile conduct concerning me, which drew me closer to him. Therefore, the shyness and deep insecurities were beginning to dissolve. The admiration I had for this man ignited an internal flame that was being fueled by his affection and encouraging words. This reluctant, sometimes stuttering young lady, who had endured so much as a youth, was like a hummingbird in extreme climates. She got through, but now was on the brink of emerging as a raving phoenix.

Having that strong, spirited force within me and now physically beside me with Rendell was amazing. I felt I had everything I needed to stand confidently and bold in this world. A world that I didn't have a clue about, but soon, would understand the nature of it and how traitorous it could be.

Open for Love

CHAPTER TWENTY-THREE

With the struggles behind me and high hopes ahead, I could foresee a fulfilling future. My mind was at ease, my soul was at peace, and my heart was once again open for love. To my right, I had a strongly built, intelligent, handsome man to hold and uplift me; and to my left, I had my good-natured, brilliant and adorable son to love and keep me focused. And with those two most valuable people in my life, I could not and would not go wrong. Once my mind was set on something, nothing could stand in my way or prevent me from achieving it.

I honestly enjoyed every bit of the time we spent together, which was every day. Rendell had given me the key to his apartment, which made me feel even more secure in the direction we were headed. We were both on the same page about God (believers), and we both were benevolent spirited people. Rendell worked Tuesday through Saturday and was often tired when he got home from work, so if all we did for the night was lay-up and watch TV, that was still all right with me. Although, we did manage to go out on occasions.

I recall the time we went to the flea market. It was me, Rendell and his best friend Sean. We were walking through the market, looking at different items until we came across a man selling jewelry. He was selling a herringbone necklace with a matching bracelet for $160. Seeing that, Rendell reached in his pocket and pulled out all the cash he had to buy the gold jewelry as a gift for me. It took me by surprise, because it was totally unexpected. However, Rendell was short $60. He looked over to Sean to ask him if he had any cash to add to it. Sean looked stunned too and shook his head, no.

Witnessing this, I bit my lip in frustration, because we had just left the ATM right before heading to the flea market, and I didn't pull out any cash. I was so upset with myself. I wanted that herringbone jewelry set so badly, but the seller wouldn't budge on the price, so we walked away without it. I had secretly hoped that Rendell would return to the flea market to get it for me, but it never happened.

Looking back, I wish I had bargained with that jewelry guy or told him that I would bring him back the difference later. For me, it wasn't just about having some gold jewelry around my neck and wrist. That bracelet and necklace would have served as a reminder of what Ren and I meant to each other amongst the chaos, because it would have been given unselfishly. And that is the type of love I gave and sought from a mate, one that is unsparing.

We hung out a lot with his best friend, Sean. Often, we'd run errands for Ren's mom or just simply hang out. Usually, it was just Sean who would be right there with us, but occasionally others would come along too. One time we went to the mall, and Sean's twin brother Keon joined the three of us. Since I was the only girl present, I thought it would be a natural assumption for the fellas to be at least courteous.

Well, as I mentioned before, Rendell could be a bit of a turd, and he showed it this day. Ren opened the department store door and just walked right in with no regard to me. Then, Sean looked back at me, shrugged his shoulders and strolled right along, following Rendell. Now that left only one man standing, Keon, Sean's twin brother; who by the way, was meeting me for the first time that day. So then, before he entered the store, Keon stepped back to hold the door open, so that I could walk through it before he did; taking in consideration that ladies do go first. I thanked Keon for being a complete gentleman, even though his two compadres, one in particularly, was being a total ass at that moment. However, Keon saved the day. He showed me that chivalry was not dead.

Occasionally, Ren and I would have minor situations as that, but I never made a big deal about it. Overall, that was nothing compared to all the good he brought to me. Rendell created new experiences for me. And with him being by my side on a regular basis, that created a bond between us.

Rendell was a romantic too. We would take walks in the park while holding hands. One night we went to a club called the Brown Sugar. It was our first time going to a nightclub together. Rendell played pool, but I wanted to dance. Everyone who knows me knows I love to dance. And I adore having endearing moments made by dancing with my man. After repeatedly asking Rendell to dance with me, he went to the jukebox and selected a song; then he went back to playing pool.

He told me to wait and I did disappointedly. Seeing that everyone was on that dance floor but me was frustrating. I leaned on the pool table watching Rendell finish his pool game and stood by. After a while, the club began to shut down, and that song that Rendell requested hadn't even played yet—leaving me still without a dance and now sulking.

The crowd in the room started lining up to exit the club. Shortly after, Rendell and I stood in line too, now waiting to leave the club. Suddenly, this song starts to play, "You're My Lady" by DeAngelo. Rendell never said anything more about the song, once the club started to close down. But I knew in my heart that was the song he chose for our first dance that didn't happen. A dance, ironically, like everything else between us, seemed to not fully manifest. We never got to enjoy that song or have our first dance together as a couple.

Despite those shortcomings in the relationship, overall Rendell was incredibly fun and exciting to be with, which fascinated me. He was very spontaneous and contained so much wisdom. In addition to that, he was handsome and had a body built after a god, Atlas to be precise. Plus, he had nice feet. He was everything nice that I didn't know I liked until he came into my life. He was a bag of treats all wrapped up in one. I was so crazy about him, and I didn't care who knew. I even put it on my voicemail for all to hear who called my cellphone, saying his name with his own special greeting. Ren liked that too a lot, as I knew he would. The vibes were good, and the feeling was mutual.

I remember the first time when we made love. It was so mesmerizing. It was as if his body was glued to mine. I felt every thrust as he kissed my cheek, neck and lips.

His whole body massaged my entire body with every push inside of me. I loved every bit of it and he must have too, because he whispered in my ear, *"Olivia, I have saved all this love for you."*

The next morning, he got up and went to work as usual and left me in the bed asleep. I was sleeping good too. When I had awakened from my slumber, my mind was blown. I stumbled out the bed and all around the room trying to gather my balance. My legs were still weak from the night before. I screamed to myself, *"What has this man done to me? ... I'm sprung!"*

My first thought was to grab my red lipstick out of my purse and write big across his dresser mirror, "I'm sprung!" to express my enthusiasm and for him to see it as clear as day when he came home. However, that second thought caused me to do otherwise. I later thought, *What if he gets upset at me for writing on his bedroom mirror?* So, I did nothing and went about my way.

However, looking back, I really wish I had written it. It could've made for another memorable moment, one that would have made Rendell aware of how much I truly enjoyed being with him. Oddly enough, that night never repeated itself. For whatever reason oblivious to me, he decided to switch up the technique, making that night the last time he would create such sexual harmony with me as his lady.

The rest of our sexual encounters were still pleasant, because I cared for him, but not anything like how he put it down that first time. But to be real with you, that one enthralling night alone, in addition to all the other grand qualities Rendell carried as a man, was all he needed to keep me. From that day forward, I was his to love and treasure. Yet, I still secretly longed and anxiously waited for that endearing, mind-boggling sexual experience to repeat once more. But just like all the other missed noteworthy moments between he and I, it didn't happen.

Being at Rendell's apartment was cool, but sometimes I got bored sitting there waiting for him to come home. One day after Rendell came home from work, I was determined to get out of the apartment and enjoy some nightlife with my man. So, I asked him, "Can we go out somewhere to eat?"

"No," he said. "I'm tired, I don't feel like it."

Disappointed, I sat there on the sofa, pouting, getting myself, all worked up. "Why can't we? I'm tired of always being inside. I want to go and do something!"

He just sat there in the chair, totally unmoved by what I was saying. Getting highly frustrated and being hotheaded, I grabbed my jacket and stormed out the apartment, slamming the door behind me. Now, where I was going, I couldn't say, but after driving around Riverside for an hour, I started to miss him. That feeling calmed me down quickly. I felt bad for my misbehavior and I drove back to his apartment.

When I pulled up, to my surprise Rendell's car was not there. I looked at my watch; it was a quarter past midnight. I sat in the parking lot for hours waiting for Rendell to drive up, but it became apparent that he wasn't returning home that night. Although I had the key to his apartment, I didn't like being there unless he knew about it, but after I had stormed out, he wasn't even accepting my calls. Therefore, I drove to my aunt's place and crashed on the couch.

The following day, I called Rendell's home phone and surprisingly he answered, behaving as if he never disappeared or ignored any of my calls recently. I told him about how I stayed up all night and into morning, waiting for him to come home. He listened to everything I had to say and very calmly said, "Yep." I could see that he was proving a point, and a point he made. I never stormed off like that again in anger, at least not by my own initiative.

I also realized that within relationships, everything is by choice. You choose to love, you choose to be hurt, you choose to be who you are within that relationship. Rendell chose to be with me, and just the same, he could choose not to be. Just because I fancied him, it didn't mean that he was obligated to love me automatically. He had to choose to be with me, no matter how much I desired him. That experience for me was a real eye-opener.

There were similar state-of-affairs that surfaced later. One in particularly involved his best friend London, who dated this nationally known singer, Shanice, back in the day when his mom, Mrs. Driver, taught my ninth-grade Algebra class. I remember distinctively, because Mrs. Driver had this huge seven-foot poster of the singer on her classroom wall for all to see. Fast forward, London and Ren were good friends. London stopped by while Ren wasn't home, so I invited him in to wait. When Ren got there, he made the situation very awkward.

Rendell walked in from work and totally ignored London. I told him that London was there to visit him and Rendell assertively said, "That's your company, not mine!" London sat in the living room and could clearly hear and see Rendell. I was totally caught off guard by Ren's actions toward the situation and embarrassed for us both. London was really cool too, I felt like he would be the one friend of Ren's that I could truly mesh and become good friends with, but that night I was without words.

After that experience, I never again opened the door for any of Rendell's visitors unless he was there. When I was at his apartment alone and someone knocked at his door, I didn't even ask who it was or even walk up to the door to even see who it was. It didn't matter. I just shouted from the couch, "He ain't here!"

Despite those few intense, touchy moments, Rendell and I still bonded more and more with each passing day. Once comfortable with our nakedness and becoming sexually fluent with one another, Rendell wanted to introduce another phase to our relationship. He said, "Olivia, if you kiss me down there, I'll lick you down there too."

Tickled by his heartfelt approach, I said jokingly, "Oh, you want to lick it, huh?"

His response, "Yep, I'll lick it like a lollipop!"

Tickled again, I chuckled, but envisioned him going downtown with his long, thick, wide tongue—the thought alone made me warm and cozy inside. *Mmm*, I thought, *how many licks would it take to get to the center of the lollipop*—as that classic commercial stated? I was very eager to find out. However, I wasn't going to be the first. Having sex orally for me was more sacred than having it vaginally. I mean, my head would be below his waistline. No way was I going to initiate that. So, I kept my cool as I naturally do and waited patiently for that moment to arrive. Ironically though, Ren and I did not graduate to that level.

One Saturday night, on the weekend I had my son, Rendell invited me to stay over. I hesitantly agreed to, but first I had to get some things in order. I asked Mara if she would watch DeLon for me. She had nothing going on that night, so she said she would. I packed an overnight bag. Before I left, I told her to call me if anything changed or went wrong. She agreed.

At that point, Rendell and I had been seeing each other for about three months. However, I still wasn't totally comfortable with having my three-year old son spend the night. Even though DeLon had done so once or twice already. Sometimes Rendell would have company, and they'd want to do legal adult things like drink. Other times, they might do a toke. Either way, I wanted to shield my son from that as much as possible. Satisfied that he was in good hands, I kissed him goodbye and left for the night.

The next morning, I get a call from my Aunt Armostean, telling me that Mara had left that night and she was the one who had to keep my son overnight. She also told me, my son had disturbed my Uncle Mike's sleep. And for that, I had to pack my things and get out.

Now, this wasn't my first rodeo when it came to being put out with my son. My mom had done so four times already for the love of money, once my cousin due to her boy-friend not wanting us there. Big Mama even put us out; her reasoning was that I had left a soiled pamper on the floor on the side of the bed, and I even paid Big Mama rent to stay there—$70 a week—that I honestly didn't mind paying. With my aunt Armostean, this would be her third time putting us out. However, this time unlike any of the other times of being forced to leave a secure place, I was not afraid. Now nineteen, I had gained some independence and had some outside support from friends and Ren, who had left their family home in a natural course. And that made this last forced exit a lot more bearable, because now I had some direction of where to go.

The whole ordeal was still unnerving. I was annoyed because this could have been totally prevented if Mara had just done what she agreed to. I could have easily driven over there to get my child no matter the time. I was just one phone call away, but she never called. In retrospect, that would've been too much right for her. Nonetheless, I was aware that I couldn't stay with my aunt and uncle forever, and there would be a time for Delon and I to leave, but I had hoped that this last time would be by my own accord, unforced.

I told Rendell about the situation. I knew that since he was freshly into his own place for the first time, he'd want to experience the thrills of that being in his early twenties and not have an instant family. But I still asked, "Can we come stay with you? Just for a little while until an apartment comes available."

His response was, "Olivia, you need your own place."

It was true; I did need my own place. But to immediately leave my aunt's place, I first needed a temporary spot until an apartment came available.

Rendell had moved into some apartments on the southwest part of town, and there were other apartment complexes in its proximity, so I knew where to apply. It just so happened that my best friend and second cousin, Tina, had recently moved with one of her older sisters to an apartment complex out west, up the street and around the corner from where Ren stayed. Therefore, it was a no-brainer to apply to those apartments. But unfortunately, once the application was accepted, there was no immediate occupancy. However, I was able to convince my aunt to allow us to stay there until an apartment came available for DeLon and me.

It was good timing too, because when the apartment became ready, I had furniture for it. Big Mama was getting new furniture, so she generously gave us her living and dining room sets, and that was a blessing. Other furnishings included an end table I had gotten from Armostean, and my Aunt Mae let me get a wood-framed single bed for a hundred bucks that I paid to her in installments of twenty dollars, but she only required me to make one payment. DeLon and I would have to share a twin bed until I was able to fully pay for a queen bedroom set that was in lay-a-way. However, that was still better than using crates as chairs or sleeping on the floor. DeLon and I had what we needed to move into our very own space and I was delighted.

Getting things together, I suddenly could visualize the benefits of having my own place, the independence of it all. There would be nobody around calling the shots but me. I could come home whenever I wanted to and so on. With Rendell, I figured either I would be at his place or he would be over to mine. Just the thought of it brought a huge smile to my face. I very much looked forward to sharing this newly found freedom with Ren in my life.

A week later, the wheels were in motion for the huge transition of DeLon and me stepping into our own place to call home. Any day now, I would be getting that call to go pick up the key to our apartment, and it was very exciting. In the meantime, I would lay up at Ren's crib too, at least for a short while after he left for the day. When I got ready to leave, I would lock the place up. On this morning though, I decided to stay at Ren's place and put in a movie, one of my top five favorites of all time, *Scarface*.

I was watching the movie for the hundredth time when the phone rang. Without thinking, I picked up the phone receiver and said, "Hello." It was a female's voice, and she asked if Rendell was there. I said, "No, he isn't" and hung up. Before I could bat an eye, seconds later the phone rang again. Still distracted by the movie, I answered, "Hello?"

It was the same voice. "Is Rendell there?" she asked again.

Once more I responded, "No, he isn't here."

Just as soon as I hung up the phone this second time, she called right back again. I recognized the voice, then realized who it she was. It was Cathy. I thought, *This woman is too old to be acting like this.* Cathy was much older than me. Besides, she and Rendell were only friends. Ren hooked her up with his best friend, Sean; and that lasted for a hot minute, because Sean said she was basket-case. Therefore, I knew she was calling just to screw with me simply for being at Rendell's place.

The phone rang again and again, and every time she would ask the same question, "Is Rendell there?" Now, if I had known better, I would have just unplugged the phone and called it a day. However, since it was not my place, I refrained from doing so, but after the tenth consecutive call, I was getting aggravated, because this halfwit was interrupting my movie. When she called again, I answered sternly. I wanted to get my point across, but at the same time keep my cool. I didn't want her to think she was getting to me, when in actuality that is exactly what she was doing.

"Is Rendell there?"

This time, I took longer to respond because thoughts were circulating in my head. I didn't want to say anything too out of the way, like, "Bitch! Stop calling over here!" or "Bitch, if you come between me and my man, I'm a fuck you up!"— Which at that point, I very much wanted to say. But I chose to keep a calm demeanor. My aim was to get her to stop calling, plus get under her skin a little, but absolutely avoid getting Rendell involved. Despite all that, in some crazy way, I still ended up doing precisely what I intended not to do.

Feeling highly irritated from the multiple calls, I said "No, he isn't. He's at work."

"Oh, he's at work?" she replied.

"Yes, he's at work," I responded firmly. Then I asked

with a dare-like mentality if she was going to call him at work, because Rendell made it clear to everyone not to disturb him at work unless it was urgent.

However, she seemed unphased and replied, "Yeah, I'll call him at work!"

So, I said, "Oh, ok. Well, while you're at it, remind him to bring home some pots and pans." And I hung up in her face.

Now I had been asking Rendell to get some pots and pans ever since he moved in to his apartment. He only had one skillet to cook with that he loved to watch me cook scrambled eggs out of while in the nude. But I wanted more to cook with, and he knew it. So, I aimlessly told Cathy to give him a message as a jab to get under her skin, but mainly I wanted her to stop bothering me. Honestly, I didn't think she was really going to call up to Rendell's job to tell him about some pots and pans. And if she did, she would most certainly get cussed out.

All the same, she did stop with the nonsense and didn't call back again.

Finally! I thought as I got back situated comfortably in my seat and continued watching my movie. After a while, her whole meddling act totally slipped my mind until I was rudely reminded.

It was around five o'clock that evening, and Rendell usually got home a little before six. I was sitting in the chair when I heard his keys rattling to unlock the door; I anticipated his arrival as usual. I wanted to greet him with a hug and kiss. However, to my surprise when he unlocked the door, he slammed it open.

"GET OUT!" he demanded in a firm, loud voice. "Get yo' shit and get out of my house!"

I stood there bewildered, because I didn't understand where all of this aggression was coming from. I had never seen him like this. But then I thought, *Cathy*! So, I tried to explain what had happened, but I couldn't get a word in. His voice was so strong and overpowering, it trampled over my soft-spoken voice. I had been caught totally off guard and I felt helpless in the situation, because I could not get through to him.

He furiously said. "You had that girl calling me at my job, talkin' bout, 'bring home some pots and pans!' Get out!"

Unsuccessful at my attempt to get him to hear my side of the story, I stood up and thought to myself, *well, at least he didn't ask for his key back.*

And as if he had read my mind just as soon as I thought that, he yelled, "And leave my key!"

The words tore right through me. Every bitter note that he spoke shattered my hopes for us and our future together. How could this have happened? Ren's reaction was extreme and totally unexpected. I had no idea that he would be this livid or could be so angry, because up until that moment, we never had so much as an argument. Perhaps at worst, I thought he would be upset, say a few cuss words, but then we'd mend and go about our evening. All those thoughts

149

ran through my mind as I looked onto him and watched, seemed like in slow motion, as his hands waved in the air expressing such rage. With every word, he yelled angrily at me; it felt like Ren was shattering every aspiration of a flourishing life together with him.

This unanticipated turn of events completely zapped my high energy. Stunned and in complete disbelief as to what had just taken place, I finally mustered up enough energy to make a plea for our future together. With my voice trembling, I managed to bypass the knot that had formed in my throat. I took one big, dry swallow and said in a low, faint voice, "Rendell, baby, please... Please don't do this... Don't let that crazy bitch come between us."

Unfazed, he still roared, "Get out of my house!" A hurtful phase of rejection that I was already too familiar with.

Again, I pleaded. "But... but I'm about to move out on my own... Please don't do this; don't do this to me." Hoping that my plea would trigger something inside him to settle down, I put more strength behind my tone and firmly stated, "Don't do this to me... Don't do this to us!"

My heart was beating so hard, I felt it pounding out of my chest and heard it through my ears. In dismay, it had appeared that I only made a few steps, because I was still near the recliner where I'd been sitting prior to him storming in to confront me about the foolishness. But as Ren continued to roar "GET OUT," I began to slowly gather my things. I laid his door key on the breakfast bar and exited his apartment.

Devastated and heartbroken, I closed his apartment door

behind me, went to my car and slumped down in the seat. I sat there totally crushed, but not a single tear rolled down my face; my eyes were dry. I leaned forward and dropped my head on the steering wheel to gather myself. Feeling energy-less and shattered, I put the key in the ignition, but lacked the strength to start it. As I saw Rendell's apartment door in my front view, I released a long exhale and thought to myself, *He didn't even get to eat my pussy. Damn*!

I shook my head in utter disappointment; then I started my car and drove off. That would be the last time I saw the inside of Ren's apartment.

The Aftermath

CHAPTER TWENTY-FOUR

I allowed a few days to go by before I reached out to Rendell. My heart started to long for him, and my mind became uneasy. After all, we spent every waking day together for three whole months. That may not seem like a long time, but it created such a bond in me toward him, and I believed the feeling was mutual. Of course, he bonded with me. How could he not, right? Yet still, no word from Rendell since that dreadful day he put me out.

I was over at my aunt's house, sitting on the bed. Staring at the phone, contemplating calling him. I needed to hear to his voice. Something inside of me told me not to call. I understood that if I were to gain control of the situation, it was best for me to wait until he reached out to me first. That's what I should have done.

But instead, I went against my better judgment and caved into the temptation. I had this insatiable desire to reach out to him, to find out where we stood. Still devastated and hurt, I picked up the phone and dialed the number to his job.

"Skyline!" A manly voice greeted me, answering the phone.

Hesitantly, I asked, "Is Rendell there?"

"Hold on," he said.

I overheard Rendell having a conversation with someone at the shop. Still amused from the conversation he was having, after a few minutes he picked up the phone with laughter in voice. "Hello," he said.

"Hey Rendell, how are you? This is Olivia."

"Olivia?" he repeated, and in a low tone with subtle laughter, he said, "I got me a new woman." And he hung up in my face. With the phone receiver still in my hand, my head dropped down and my heart sank even further.

Days passed, and I didn't know what to do with myself. I tried to go back to my old routine before Rendell came into my life and swooped me up. So, I called my girl Marjorie to find out how she was doing and ask if she wanted to hang out like old times. Before I could get the chance to invite her somewhere, she went on to tell me about her guy friend Ricky. How he had taken her to his apartment and invited a bunch of guys over. One of the guys made an advance at her, which she gladly accepted. She told me they started having sex, and the next thing she knew, she was lying in the center of the living room floor, encircled by half-naked men rubbing their scrotums, looking down on her as each one of them took turns going inside of her.

My mouth dropped open in dismay as she described it, sounding as if she had just accomplished the greatest achievement of her life. Her voice was filled with such exhilaration. She said she felt powerful with all those men falling weak to her womanly possession, the vagina. She continued to say that one of the guys with long wavy hair, in the heat of passion, went down and performed oral sex on her in front of everyone. Marjorie explained how she wrapped his long wavy hair around her hands and gripped it tight as she thrusted his face deeper inside of her until she plateaued to a climax of sexual excitement. Marjorie punctuated her story with giggles.

I couldn't say Ricky exploited her. Clearly, she enjoyed the rendezvous just as much as the men involved. I couldn't say anything; I was speechless. I mean, Marjorie was being herself, the free-spirited person she was. She was being true to herself and doing what she wanted. Who was I to pass judgment? I mean, I knew she liked sex immensely; however, even I was surprised to find out as to what extent. From her conversation, Marjorie seemed to be overly occupied with Ricky, so I didn't even get the chance to extend an invitation for us to hang out somewhere. After that earful, I didn't know what had become of my best friend during those three months of being all about Rendell.

I did miss our times together though, because besides her shortfalls, Marjorie was really a genuinely kind-hearted person. She was second to oldest of her all siblings. Her mom died of cancer when Marjorie was just in grade school. Her oldest brother and youngest sister, a twin, both died at a very young age. Quinshell was eighteen when her body succumbed to breast cancer. The youngest person I had ever known to be diagnosed with that disease. And Marcus, her eldest brother, had moved to Texas to live. During an attempted robbery to steal his gold necklace, he had gotten stabbed and ended up losing his life.

So, Marjorie had endured her fair share of loss and pain before the age of twenty-one. And because of that, I felt she tried to mask her pain by intoxicating herself heavily with alcohol, marijuana and oftentimes, sex. She chose the temporary fix, like most people do when they're internally broken. However, despite all that, Marjorie was so much fun to be around and was truly a genuine person with a bubbly personality. We always got along. And I never saw an ounce of hatred in her eyes. When we did hang out, it was usually with buddies we'd just recently met. We'd listen to music, joke around, smoke a little pot and just enjoy our summer nights. Everything was always innocent fun when I was around.

But after meeting Rendell, Marjorie and I didn't hang out like that anymore or participate in our usual routines. Our close friendship gradually became distant. And Marjorie had gravitated in another direction. One of which I didn't want to be a part of. The conversation with her ended, and we hung up the phone.

Going on about my day-to-day, I found things to keep me occupied. Staying busy helped me give less thought to Rendell and distracted my mind from that heart-wrenching breakup. As time went on, I eventually grew accustomed to not having him around. And I was cool with that. I still collected my unemployment check and had come across a side job. I began working at a minor emergency clinic run by the former CEO of Morton, Dr. Mikel. He paid me cash from week to week for helping out any way I could with patients. Working there, I ran into other old faces from Morton too, because Dr. Mikel had started offering dental treatment as well. It wasn't much in pay, but I was content in more than one way. I had a little more money coming in, and my obligation to the new job definitely diverted my attention from the heartache.

Ironically, just when I stopped hurting over my loss in love, our paths crossed again two months later. I had pulled up at a convenience store, and right when I was about to push open the door to enter it, I heard someone call my name. "Olivia!"

I paused, then took two steps back. Surprised, I responded, "Rendell?" The convenience store was located inside a shopping complex adjoined to a barber shop that Rendell just happened to be walking out of when he spotted me.

"Guess what?" he said as he walked over to me and grabbed my shoulders with such eagerness with his big, manly hands.

Still astounded, I asked, "What?"

He continued to say, "I'm throwing a party, and you're the guest of honor!"

Hearing this, I initially gave him my poker-face reaction, with one raised eyebrow. But shortly, the expression of a very confused person openly showed on my face, because I hadn't even spoken to Rendell since he hung up on me months back. Therefore, I was completely flabbergasted, but on the inside, somehow, he still was able to tug on my heartstrings again. On the outside, I had this confused, but cool expression, however, on the inside my heart was screaming, "Happy, happy, joy, joy!" with a big smile and handclaps.

But I kept my cool demeanor, showing little excitement

and said, "Ok, I'll be there."

Now, I can't even remember if I went into the convenience store, bought something or just made a dash back to my car. However, what I do recall vividly is flying home and looking in my closet for something cute to wear for this party. Counting down, I had my eyes set on the clock. What time would be too early or too late to show up? The thought went back and forth in my mind. Fully dressed to his appeal, it was about ten p.m. when I headed out. Elated just to be in his presence again, here I was invited to Ren's party as his "guest of honor," and I couldn't wait to get there.

Rendell's apartment complex was gated and required a code to enter, or you could dial for the tenant to buzz you in. Driving to the entry gate, I dialed his apartment number. It rang, but there was no answer. I thought, *Maybe the music's too loud and no one can hear the phone ring.* So, I pulled off to the side and waited until another tenant or guest entered using their code; then I followed right behind before the gate could close.

All smiles and excited to be back in the presence of my Boo, I drove around to the back where his apartment was located. When I pulled up, I was expecting to see his apartment lit up, cars all around and people going in or out of his door, but it was totally the opposite. I saw Rendell's car, but there were no other cars near his apartment, and the place was dark. Baffled, I slowly walked up to his apartment door. Was I too early, I thought?

I gave three knocks to his door, and Rendell opened it in dismay, with a confused expression. Dazed myself, I asked,

"Aren't you having a party tonight?"

Rendell stood there and was silent for a moment, then shouted, "Get away from my door!"

Befuddled by Ren's unreasonable behavior, I responded, "Huh?"

He came outside, persuading me to move back toward my car. His cute little pit puppy that we shared fond memories with followed him out of the apartment and paused by his side. "Sic her!" he ordered. The puppy didn't make a move, and I stood there, taken aback by Ren's bizarre behavior. This was not the greeting I had imagined as his "guest of honor." Plus, to add insult to injury, he reached down to pick up some pebbles from the ground and started pitching them at me to shoo me away. At that point, I'd had enough of his absurdities, so I got in my car and drove off. I was dressed all up with no party to attend and mind completely baffled.

I was in disbelief about what had just taken place. This man popped up out of nowhere, invited me to a party that wasn't there, sic'd his pit puppy on me, then topped off the night by throwing stones at me. This dude had totally flipped the strip. No matter how I looked at it, I couldn't make any sense of it. Rendell's actions were completely illogical.

But somehow, peace remained in my heart for him, even after that very rocky night. Pun intended. Nonetheless, my mind was now troubled, and I became engrossed with trying to figure this man out.

Drawn Back In

CHAPTER TWENTY-FIVE

Seeing Rendell at the store that day brought him back in circulation. My care for him resurfaced to the top of my heart. The next day, my mind was flooded with questions about him. What was his deal? Had he always been crazy, but I was the last one to know? I was so bothered by his actions; I had to understand the logic behind them. An overwhelming sense of curiosity began to stir within me, and I had to investigate.

However, now a problem had arisen. Since that night of Ren's bizarre and irate behavior, I was very discouraged and highly hesitant to go directly to him with my concerns. At that point, it would have been the perfect moment to turn to Sean for some answers, but Sean had gone back to college for the fall semester. I could have visited Ren's mom to inquire about her youngest child's conduct, but I didn't have enough nerve built up to be comfortable in doing so.

I wracked my brain trying to find some type of connection within Rendell's orbit, someone who could give me some background info on him. Besides Ren's best friend and mom, there was no one I could turn to, at least not right off the top of my head. Nevertheless, I felt impelled to find out more about him.

Along with my curiosity about Rendell came the sadness of missing his love. I still very much wanted him, but the energy he now was releasing pushed me away rather than cause me to gravitate toward him. It felt completely out of order, and I thought perhaps I could somehow put us back together. After that rocky night, much was a blur. However, I do recall that weeks passed, and I heard no word from Rendell. And I most certainly did not reach out to him, yet he stayed on my mind every single day.

The Park

CHAPTER TWENTY-SIX

One sunny, beautiful day, I was riding with my cousin Mara down the Tisdale Highway on the way to her house when I got a sudden urge to have her take a detour by Cheyenne Park. I knew that Cheyenne Park was Ren's hang-out spot, like most of the kids who grew up in that neighborhood. I hoped to see Ren there, but as we drove by, I saw that he wasn't. However, I noticed a few guys there and their faces looked familiar, so I decided to stop.

This would be the place where the most divine and life-altering decision would take place. Cheyenne Park, a location for years, since I was a kid, had been rumored to have been built on sacred Indian land, along with its surrounding houses. Cheyenne Park; the place where even my dad and his siblings, as a youth, hung out and lollygagged at. And with all these passing years, this park was still a main hang-out spot.

Cheyenne Park carried some fond memories for Ren and me. It was the place where Rendell invited me after meeting him for the first time to get better acquainted. Cheyenne was the park Ren and I raced around at, when he set the backseat of his 5.0 Mustang on fire, trying to shoot Roman candles back at me around the Fourth of July. One of the fireballs fell in the bag of fireworks that Ren kept in his backseat. It sparked a flame and set off an array of mini-explosives that burned the seat. With all those fireworks going off in a moving vehicle, Ren nearly wrecked.

I laughed so hard, I had to pull over too. Fooling around with him, I could have been in a laughter-induced car accident. I fell out of that car onto the ground in a momentarily physical weakened state from laughter. Rendell's car swayed, and he frantically got out of his car to put out the fire that resulted in his backseat being charred. That is a memory I will never forget and one that Rendell would always be reminded of, for as long as he owns that car.

Stopping at that park with my cousin, I saw that those familiar faces were passing around a blunt. And that looked highly tempting to Mara and me, so she turned off the Bronco and we got out. Walking toward them, I recognized the guys sitting there —Stokes, Big Hen and Draco. They were friends of Rendell. We walked up, and I asked if they had seen Rendell. They all shook their head, no. Stokes passed the blunt to me. I gave it a quick hit, and passed it on to Mara.

I was classmates with Stokes' younger, half-brother, Diggy, which meant he and I had a common interest outside of Ren's friendship. So, I focused on talking mostly to Stokes in hopes of finding out some things about Ren. I chatted some with Big Hen too. To the other guy, Draco, after a courteous greeting, I didn't say much.

My goal was to have friendly conversation with the guys, hoping my agenda would not be too obvious to them. I did, however, mention Ren's name sparingly to originate some sort of conversation about him. I wanted any information I could get that would aid me with some insight, but nothing worked. The fellas were tight-lipped about anything concerning their friend. And while I was trying to keep my objective low-key, I think they got the impression that Rendell and I weren't as close as we used to be.

In an attempt to stay on schedule, I looked at my watch and told the guys we had better be going. I stuck out my fist and gave each one a dab, a gesture of appreciation, starting with Stokes and working my way down the bench. When I reached Draco, he said, "If I give you my number, will you call it?" He reached in his pocket, pulled out a pen, a piece of paper and wrote his number down.

I really didn't know what to make of Draco's suggestion; however, I saw it as a link that could possibly help reunite Rendell and me. Therefore, I said yeah, and took the number.

Now, I recall only seeing Draco about two times during my three-month run with Rendell. The first time, Rendell was having a gathering at his apartment. People were in the dining and living area. Rendell was talking about opening up his barber shop, Black Ink. And Draco commented about allowing him to sweep the shop's floors. I wanted to ask Ren who he was that night, but it slipped my mind.

The other time, my friend Tina and I were going out to the club. We were all dressed and ready to go, looking cute and dolled up; we stopped by Rendell's apartment first to invite him to join us. Rendell opened the door, stepped outside the apartment, grabbed me and practically stuffed his whole tongue down my throat. That kiss was way overly compressing. In order to keep myself from choking, I had to take a step back and catch my breath.

Rendell then took a step back and looked me up and down, as if I was this gorgeous, glowing specimen. The next thing I knew, he grabbed my hand hastily as if protecting me from some sort of danger. Jerking my neck slightly, he pulled me into his apartment. My hand encased in his, he took me around to the kitchen and pinned me against the wall next to the refrigerator. His manly hands were all over me, from my head to my feet. His excitement was apparent as he hemmed up on the kitchen wall, groping me. I could feel all the sharp and bumpy textures of the kitchen wall, which was very unpleasant.

I had to do a switcheroo, from the kitchen wall to refrigerator door, which was cool and smooth. After that transition, I thoroughly enjoyed his groping, until Rendell got more excited and pulled out the blades, his nails. He started scratching me with his thick-ass nails. Feeling those bad boys made my hair stand on end; I wanted to run for the hills after that. When he started cutting flesh and leaving welts on my skin, that was usually my cue to exit. Therefore, I reminded Ren that Tina was in the car waiting on me still, and he let me up off the fridge door and walked me out to the front door.

Leaving out of Ren's apartment is when I noticed Draco along with a couple of other guys. That was the second time I had ever seen him and even then, there was never any eye contact until presently at that park. Other than saying, "what's up" to him there, I had never even spoken a word to Draco, and he had never said a word to me either.

With my focus back in the present, looking at that number in Draco's hand, I paused a bit with further thought. Perhaps Co could help give me some insight as to what was going on with Rendell. At most, I knew they were acquaintances and perhaps he could be useful in getting us back together. Since that last encounter with Rendell, I wanted to avoid any direct contact with him. And perhaps Draco, aka Co, could be the mediator. He stuck out his hand to give me that piece of paper with his number written on it. And after a short deliberation in my head, with nothing but hopes of getting back to Rendell, I reached out for the piece of paper and took it.

The Warning

CHAPTER TWENTY-SEVEN

I turned away from Draco and started walking toward the car. Mara was already about three feet ahead of me. As I took those steps away from the park bench, I held that little piece of paper in my right hand between the grasp of my thumb, index and middle finger. I recall passing by this huge, thick tree on the left side of me when I felt it. An instantaneous jarring of my body, as if I had been struck by lightning. A sudden force of energy that was so strong, it migrated from my head all the way down to my feet. The jolt was so strong, I wasn't even aware if I was still standing...

Did I fall? I thought to myself. I looked down to see if I had fallen, but I had not. I was still standing. I looked to see if my legs were still moving, and they were. That surge of energy was so strong, I could not tell otherwise; my motor skills were discombobulated. But my spirit knew what this was. Without any words spoken, I knew from the surge of power that shocked my body; something was sending me an evident message to let that paper go. To hold on to it would be the wrong thing to do.

I continued to walk toward the car, still unable to distinguish at what pace I was going. I was not even aware if I was moving extremely slow or at a normal pace. My brain was not yet comprehending what my motor skills were doing. I raised my right hand that held the piece of paper, and thought *Why is it still in my hand?* After all, I could barely feel my hands along with the rest of my body. Why didn't the piece of paper with Draco's number on it simply slip out of my fingers?

That enormous surge of energy that inundated my body was heavy and lingering. It stayed with me for a good while, but the more I walked, the less effect it had on me. That feeling was wearing off.

As I walked, though, I began to hear this random voice. At first, I ignored it and didn't focus in on what I was hearing. With every step, the feeling in my limbs were getting stronger, but now this voice? I blew it off at first, because I thought it was all in my head, but it continued as I walked onward. After a while, I zeroed in on what I was hearing.

I heard the voice say, "Your son will never have a father."

I thought, *DeLon has a father; he's locked up, but he's still got one.* However, I did get the impression the voice was warning me of what could happen if I did not let that piece of paper go. The things I heard were so random; it just didn't make any sense to me at that time, plus the voice was faint. It was difficult for me to discern if this voice I was hearing was a reality or my mind playing tricks on me. Regardless, I still knew I needed to drop that paper, but somehow for some reason I kept making excuses to hold onto it for a little while longer.

My senses came back to life; I was getting back to my normal self. I was about three feet from the street curb, and I told myself I was going to let that piece of paper go when

I got to it. But when my foot hit the curb, I told myself that when I got in the car, I would let it go in the wind. I was trying to understand why it was so critical that I needed to let the piece of paper go. What was the big deal? I stepped down from the curb and onto the street where the car was parked. Before I got to the car, I heard that voice again, still random, but these words I heard much clearer than all of the other randomness. This time I heard it say, "You're going to get abused by a big, black dick!"

Unsure if I was conjuring up this craziness in my head or indeed, I was actually hearing these things; I shook it off and made my way into the car. Whatever the case, making it to the car, I made a mental note to avoid all the big, black guys.

Mara started up the ride and began to drive off slowly. I held my right hand out the window and watched as that piece of paper waved in the wind. Gradually, I began to let it ease away from my grasp. The paper rapidly swayed back and forth in my hand as the winds picked up from the acceleration of the car. My plan was to open the palm of my hand and let the wind snatch it away.

But I started wondering why it was a must that I let this piece of paper go. I wasn't attracted to Co, and had no desires to do anything with him out of context, and most certainly nothing sexual. My only interest was to find out what was going on with Rendell and understand why he reacted the way he did toward me. I needed answers. And this little piece of paper with Co's number written on it was my only connection to Rendell.

In a daze, I watched that piece of paper dangle in the wind. One by one, I slowly began to lift my fingers off of it, leaving only my index finger and thumb to retain it in place, preventing it from completely flying away. Then finally, I began to release the pressure of my index finger and thumb. The more my grasp weakened, the greater it seemed the winds became. That little piece of paper wiggled and rattled, eventually working itself away from my fingertips.

Then, just as it got totally free from my hold, suspended entirely in the air, as it was released from my grasp, I quickly reached and grabbed that piece of paper in midair and snatched it back securely in the palm of my hand.

I recall looking off, not focused on anything really, just gazing at whatever objects went by. Then in my peripheral view, moving alongside the car as we were moving, I saw an angel, appearing like a small, fluffy cloud. Its head was shaking, Nooooo, in slow motion. I could see its facial expression—sorrowful and distressed. It was so close to me, floating alongside the vehicle, as if it provided the wind that was tugging that piece of paper from out of my grasp.

Realizing what I was seeing, I didn't turn around toward it, to fully face it head on. Instead, I dropped my head down lifelessly to my chest, feeling helpless and hurt, I thought to myself, *But he did NOT appreciate me.* The thought of Ren alone transformed those feelings of hurt and disappointment into anger.

I knew without a doubt I should have listened to my Heavenly Father's angel and obeyed those warnings. I knew I should not have kept that little piece of paper. However, I didn't understand why. Along with the many emotions I had felt leading up to that point, I became rebellious. Confused, hurt and upset by the way Rendell had treated me without any logical explanation. I had to find out why he'd done it. I thought, if God intended for us to be together, then we would be together no matter what. What did it matter if I kept that little piece of paper?

Well, it mattered and significantly... Angels don't warn for nothin'!

It was evident that this angel was warning me for a reason beyond my comprehension. It was also evident that in keeping that little piece of paper, I was being disobedient to God's warnings. However, at that time, I didn't envision how drastically my rebellious and disobedient behavior would affect my life and those around me. I couldn't possibly foresee all the deception and hurt that would lie before me through the years to come.

Proverbs 3:5 tells us to trust in the Lord with all your heart and lean *not* to your own understanding. Well, despite my knowing better, I did exactly what I should not have done. I leaned to my own understanding.

Looking back, the angel's warnings were for my benefit. Why didn't I realize that it wasn't just about me and how I felt for that moment? Well, the answer is simply, it was beyond my comprehension. However, I will make no excuses for my actions, because it was more than apparent what I should have done.

It was a sure mistake disregarding those warnings. Despite my intentions, despite being confident with how I felt when I accepted that piece of paper, I was completely ignorant of Co's true nature or how things could be perceived mistakenly. I was oblivious to my future or what circumstances would take place. Furthermore, I didn't think of how my child would be affected, if what the voice had said was true, that he'd never have a father. For those reasons alone, I should have not relied on my own understanding and simply obeyed the warning.

But I was completely wrapped up in Rendell. I could see or hear no other. It was all about him, the one I adored. I had never been so open spiritually to a man, only to have that cord cut so abruptly. So, I was unaware of how those feelings of dismissal or rejection could affect me. Unable to foresee the future, I was oblivious as to the levels of detriment that one decision, I had just made, would cause. One that would involve such depths of disarray, confusion, deceit and even more heartache.

I will tell you who did know, though—God. And He sent an angel to warn me in an attempt to save me from my own foolhardy doings. And I am here to tell you that because of my disobedience, I suffered dearly in more ways than I can say.

My narrow-mindedness, foolish and stubborn behavior cost me more than I could have possibly known, more than what that faint voice at the park had warned me of. I could only see how I was affected at that moment and what I was being deprived of, blinded to the fact of how my choice would affect my son, my siblings and my future. As the eldest of four maternal and nine paternal siblings, whether you think they do or not, your siblings look up to you. I didn't take into account the ill intent of others and how my disobedience would allow the wrong people to enter my circle and cause distractions and havoc in my life.

No, that was not at all in my mind frame as a nineteen-year-old young lady. All that consumed my thoughts was how badly I needed and wanted Rendell back in my life again. And that little piece of paper with Co's number written on it was my roundabout way of getting back in route with Rendell Schwann—or so I thought.

From that day forward, it would take many years for me to understand the significance of the detriment I would cause myself. And all due to that one foolish and rebellious mistake; held within the grasp of my hand.

As time passed, I would see things and feel emotions I never thought I would. It is true that God knows you better than you know yourself. He knows your weaknesses and your strengths before you yourself have an inclination. Therefore, when angels warn, listen and obey—because they are not doing it for nothin'.

What happened after that day in the park, was a blur. I don't recall how long it took for me to call that number, or even dialing it for that matter. But one thing is for sure: I called it.

My initial conversation with Draco was brief. I made it clear that I wasn't trying to get with him. I just needed him to do me a favor, to find out what was going on with Rendell. Draco understood the assignment and said he would look into it for me.

A week or so later, I heard back from Draco. He met me at my apartment to give me the scoop. Co knocked on my door; I greeted him and invited him in to have a seat. Getting straight to the point, I asked, "So, did you get a chance to see and talk to Rendell?"

"Yes," Draco replied.

Anxious and impatient for him to elaborate more, I asked, "Well, what did he say?"

"He said he got him another woman," he replied.

My heart sank. I let out a deep sigh as my back leaned deep into the chair. *Well, Co must be telling the truth*, I thought, because those were the exact words Rendell used when I called him at the shop that day before he abruptly ended the call.

Although I hadn't really shed many tears on the matter, I was still deeply distraught. My emotions must have been apparent through my body language, because Draco asked me over and over, "What did he do to you?"

As if it was something that I could explain. My mind was still trying to wrap around the fact that I felt lost without this man in my life; a feeling I was so unfamiliar with. I really didn't know how much Ren affected me until we were torn apart. I felt crushed, as if something was missing from me, but I could not explain how or why. So, when Draco asked me that question repeatedly, all I could do was lower my head, because I had no words to explain, just an overwhelming sense of loss and sadness.

I did find it therapeutic to have someone to talk to

though. I had always been better friends with guys rather than girls. My best friend growing up was a guy and he was just that, a friend. So, I didn't see any harm in talking to a mutual acquaintance of Rendell. A part of me was hoping that Draco would go back and tell Rendell what we talked about and how I felt, because 90 percent of our conversations were about Rendell. Being on my own for the very first time, it was comforting to have company and have a male opinion, so I kept in touch. Plus, if there was a party going on, I had hoped that Co would be cool enough to invite me along, creating an opportune moment for me and Rendell to run into each other.

But come to find out, that was only wishful thinking. After weeks of confiding in Co, nothing went as I had hoped.

On another visit to my place, Co made his move. "I'll kick it with you," he spoke. After I had just finished telling him about all the time Rendell and I had spent together.

Surprised and taken back, I hesitantly responded, "You? But aren't you and Rendell friends?"

"Well, I see him from time to time, but we ain't like friend-friends."

I leaned back in my chair and stared into space as I thought about it. I don't know how or when my frame of thinking got distorted, but in my crazy little brain, I needed that connection to Rendell. And if it couldn't be directly with him, then perhaps I could be connected at a distance through a mutual acquaintance. Besides, what could be the harm in hanging out or just socializing with this guy, right?

After some self-deliberation, my mind drifted from contemplating plans of action and my attention turned back to Co. And, so I agreed, "Yeah, I'll hang out with you."

Vulnerability

CHAPTER TWENTY-EIGHT

I can imagine there comes a point in everyone's life when they feel vulnerable — defenseless, unguarded. And due to those areas of weakness, it could cause some unwise and thoughtless decisions to be made. You never know how or what could affect you in such a way that would provoke vulnerability. That's something that you learn by living and cannot be humanly foreseen until it is done.

After dealing with my son's father, Eric, I became utterly aware that my weakness is my heart. When I love, it is with such depth that it reaches my God-given soul. The love I share is pure, passionate and relentless. All my barriers are down once my love has matured within that relationship. I trust that person entirely with my heart and perhaps foolishly with my life. In the case of my first love, Eric, he taught me the deeper I love, the weaker I become and the more profoundly the heart aches when it is broken.

Broken-heartedness is a feeling that can literally impact your whole well-being. It can affect a person's physiological mechanisms. It can disrupt the stableness of the mental and physical state. Your focus is thrown off; the body is momentarily weak. For me, my soul feels drained and oftentimes the weeping is unyielding, or so it seems. Inevitably though, for my love to flourish, I have to let down my guard, which in turn, makes me defenseless against the one

I love. I'm sure you can relate. Thank goodness, though, the Good Lord made our bodies to adapt and endure. Therefore, with every disappointment I feel and every tear that falls down my cheek, my defenses get a little stronger, and the love less flowing.

Overall, through my experiences of recovering from a broken heart, I can honestly say that love is a weakness for me. Not love itself, but the manipulation of it. The way it breaks you down and exposes you completely. To love truly makes me defenseless; it is a total kryptonite. And as people who come from different backgrounds and have different belief systems, it can be harmful to truly love a person whose love is not equivalent to yours. The action of love and the definition of it could have varying denotations depending on who it is you fall in love with. But quite simply, not everyone loves the same.

My first two loves in life were also my two greatest weaknesses. With Eric, my first at everything, I loved without precaution. I didn't know to do otherwise. I loved him to the point to where I couldn't even raise my voice, even when he was totally out of line and inappropriate, which became more frequent as the time passed.

In retrospect, with Eric and our history together, it was a blessing in disguise that he got locked up. At that young of an age, sixteen, to bear a child and have the father of your child be as cluelessly impressionable as he was, I'm sure our relationship would've headed down a less purposeful road and certainly off my life's fulfilling path. Due to those experiences with Eric, it's not a decision that I've made consciously, but I've never loved that hard again. Especially to the point to where I became steadily passive and mute.

With Rendell, a lot of confusion took place after he abruptly ended it. However, prior to that I had bonded with this man and didn't even know it until he tore himself away from me. During our relationship, I hadn't told him that I loved him and neither did he, to me. I don't even think it got to the point where we were in the "in love" phase. As far as I knew, we were still on the level of being "very fond of" one another. However, we developed a bond that linked our souls. With our day in and day out routines together, we had no arguments or anything to disrupt the flow of us connecting.

It was like we were on autopilot with our relationship, because we unconsciously developed a routine. Everything just flowed so naturally between us. I was uncontrollably and undeniably tied to this man, but was unaware of the magnitude of it until the relationship was no more.

For in my mind at that time, Rendell was the fundamental piece to my life's puzzle that linked all the abstract parts into a masterpiece. He held the key that unleashed the boldness within and could set me free. So, when that critical piece was removed from the core of my vision, everything got distorted and somehow, I lost my way...

Angels don't warn for nothin'.

The Outing

CHAPTER TWENTY-NINE

The first time Draco and I went out, we grabbed something to eat, smoked a joint, then he took me back home. I recall Co entering the apartment, sitting down, then suddenly rising up, meeting me in the hallway. He was tall, taller than what I was used to, so it was somewhat intimidating when he came at me as if he was cornering me in. My back was pressed flat up against the wall as he towered over me.

He said something that insinuated we cross that buddy line and have sex. That, I remember clearly, because I stood there and thought to myself, *Sex*? Sex hadn't even crossed my mind with this guy.

But then I recalled a past conversation that took place with an older cousin in-law. She was more sexually fluent than I was. This cousin advised that the best way to get over a man is to have sex with another one. And that night, being backed up against the wall, that notion came to mind. It had been over a month already with no word from Rendell, so it was apparent that he had moved on. Now, I needed to get him out of my system, so I took the plunge and had sex with Draco.

The sexual experience with Draco was awkward at first. My body was so used to Rendell's touch, Rendell's body. Having someone other than Rendell felt, well, indifferent. I instantly felt claustrophobic when Co placed himself upon me, because of his height. I was partially covered with a sheet and had to keep turning my head away from him, just so I could feel like I could breathe. After it was over, the sexual act for me just so-so. Perhaps my nerves and the uncomfortableness of the initial sexual encounter took away from the experience, which I really wasn't into anyway

Afterwards, Draco got up, put on his clothes, and I walked him to the door. He said he'd call me. I said ok, then closed door behind him and proceeded about my day. Although we'd had an act of sex that took place between us, I didn't expect the dynamics of the friendship to be any different. I wasn't trying to be his woman, nor did I want to be. He was a guy who presented himself to me and in hopes of getting over my heartache, I accepted the offer. There were no feelings that manifested after our encounter. However, if Co said that he would call, I expected him to do that.

After a whole day of not hearing from Co, I got concerned. No matter what type of feelings were absent from our involvement, no girl or woman wants to feel like she's been used for sex, then dumped. So, I called him. Draco didn't pick up. After several unsuccessful attempts to get a hold of him, that initial feeling of concern turned into panic. Then suddenly, I began to regret what I had done.

Distressed and needing the comfortably of a familiar voice, I backtracked and turned to Rendell. On the phone with tears in my eyes, I explained to him what had taken place. After he realized the gist of what I was explaining, he sharply cut me off and said, "Oh, now that Draco fucked and left you, you want to come running back to me!?"

Stunned by Rendell's words, I was at a loss for mine. I was coming to him simply as a friend; not with the notion to run back into his arms, because as far as I knew, his arms were already filled by another woman. Immediately the tears stopped, and a drastic state of confusion draped my face. Baffled, I held the receiver to my ear in silence as I wiped away the tears that had dampened my face. Then suddenly an indignant feeling came over. Like a match to a flame, Rendell had struck a nerve, a deep one. The feeling of discontent for Draco had now turned into anger and strife for him.

Holding back the fury, I responded in a firm tone, "You're wrong." I kept my temperament under control, but the heat inside of me was rising. After a few other words that were spoken, I hung up completely confused and upset. Why would Rendell think that I was running back to him, when it was he who rejected me multiple times? I am not that person who insists on being with someone when I unwanted. And Rendell made it crystal clear that he did not want me anymore.

The next morning, I lay in bed trying to wrap my head around what Rendell had said. DeLon was in the living room, driving around in his foot-pedaled toy car and playing with other toys. I knew that because I could hear his key ring with a hundred keys that he'd collected over time, rattling around. I don't know what it was about keys that DeLon was so fond of, but he got a kick out of collecting them. He would drive around the apartment all day in his plastic car, using various keys to open his car door, start the engine, and shift the gears. As my baby was in the living room playing, the doorbell rang.

Who could that be? I thought. I got up to answer the door with my shorts and t-shirt on, looked through the peephole and to my surprise, it was Rendell. It was the first time he'd visited me at the apartment since I had moved in. I unlocked the door, not knowing what he was there for. Excited to see Rendell, DeLon ran into his arms. Rendell picked him up and sat him over his shoulders. Witnessing the joy in my son's eyes, my heart sank further.

I had always felt that Rendell would be an awesome father. I very much wanted him to be for my son. At that time, Rendell didn't have any kids and as we got closer to each other, I knew he had all the right qualities that would make any kid happy, especially his own. When we were together and talked about having kids, I knew without a doubt that it would be a special experience for us both. Regretfully though, we never got to that place in life with each other.

Seeing Rendell and DeLon have their moment reminded me of what could've been between us. Without saying a word, I retreated to my bedroom. Rendell followed, still with DeLon hanging around his neck, the majority of his weight supported by Rendell's forearm. I didn't understand why, but I wanted to capture the moment that could very well be the last I had with this man, so I grabbed my camera and took the picture. Rendell looked into the camera with a sense of sadness and disappointment. After the picture was taken, he placed my son back on his feet and Delon went running back into the living room, playing with his toys.

Leaving Rendell and I alone, facing each other.

Rendell closed the bedroom door for privacy and started in. "Out of all the niggas to fuck in Tulsa, you had to fuck my best friend?" he said.

Puzzled once more, my mouth dropped. "Your best friend?" I repeated after him. "Rendell, Co told me that he just saw from time to time and that you two weren't close. He made it seem like you both were just cool with one another and not close friends."

"Man, that nigga got me kicked out of kindergarten!" he shouted.

"Kindergarten? Rendell, I had no idea! Co told me—"

"You're a liar!" he shouted, cutting me off before I could finish my sentence. "Olivia, whatever life we could've had together, we can never have! You fucked my best friend!"

Staggered by the words I was hearing as he stood before me, waving his big hands in the air, intensifying every word that he spoke, all I could say was, "Rendell, I didn't know." But there was no convincing him. Rendell did believe me.

In haste, Rendell walked out the bedroom. I heard the front door shut behind him as I remained sitting there on the edge of my bed. I got up to lock the front door. DeLon was still just playing away, occupied with driving his toy car, like he was actually going to work and driving home. Those hundred keys just a jiggling. He was completely oblivious as to what had just taken place. Utterly devastated and feeling drained, I leaned back on the front door and watched DeLon drive his little toy car up and down the living room floor. Shifting the gears when he went in reverse and stopping at every imaginary traffic light.

When I gathered enough energy, I pulled myself off the door and retreated back to my room. I threw myself on the bed and buried my head deep in the pillow, so that all I saw was darkness. I lay there, feeling so weak and just disgusted with myself, thinking, *how could I have let this happen*?

I really couldn't defend myself, because I had broken my own rule. I never wanted the men I had sex with to even know each other, much less be mutual acquaintances. I didn't want any knuckleheads sitting around, talking about how good my stuff was or comparing sexual experiences. And look, what did I go and do? Broke my own rule. Then come to find out these two are best friends? As far as I knew, Sean was Ren's best friend and Draco was a random person that Ren happened to know. But apparently, according to Ren, what Draco led me to believe was far from the truth.

I never thought to even question Draco about their friendship. I didn't think to find out how long they knew each other or inquire about how they met. I just mistook Draco's word as being truth, and it wasn't.

I couldn't even envision having a friendship that lasted for as long as Ren mentioned theirs had. As a kid, I moved around a lot growing up. And in the process, I attended multiple schools. My friendships ended when I moved out of the neighborhood or switched schools. Never could I fathom having a friendship from kindergarten all the way up to adulthood. *Really*?

All those thoughts scoured my brain, but what really haunted me to the core were those words Rendell had spoken: *Whatever life we could've had together, can never be.* It echoed hard through my mind and touched my heart, until all I could do was sob... Angels don't warn for nothin'.

Discovering Intentions

CHAPTER THIRTY

The next day, I got a call from Draco. He assured me that he didn't have any intentions to not call or come by anymore, but just got busy with doing things. Ironically, I did find comfort in knowing that. However, he did have some explaining to do.

Later in the day, Co came over and immediately we sat down to talk. I expressed how I felt, that his avoiding my calls made me feel like he did a hit-and-run, basically. And that did not sit well with me. I also mentioned to Co that I felt so bad about it that I confided in Rendell regarding the matter.

Hearing that, Co got quiet. When he did open his mouth, he said, "I wasn't going to tell him."

Surprised by his random response, I repeated, "Wasn't going to tell him? Why would this be a secret?" Co must have forgotten how he played down his and Rendell's friendship, because I thought at best, they were just acquaintances from how he talked.

Draco then proceeded to say, "Man, I wasn't even looking at you until you came over to his apartment with that black dress on." Referring to the time when I went over to

Rendell's place to invite him out dancing with me and Tina. And Rendell pulled me inside exposing me to the company he had sitting on his sofa. One of them, being Draco.

Listening to Draco, I felt an irritation come over me. Apparently, Co had an ulterior motive from the beginning, and he executed it by lying. Then to make matters worse, his comments insinuated that it was my fault for capturing his attention by wearing a dress that was never intended for him to see. I wore that dress to lure my man into going out with me; for only his eyes to adore. It was not at all my aim to capture the likes of Draco, but apparently, I inadvertently did. The nerve of him.

I was in a perplexing situation. Rendell did break it off with me initially, and it was a strong dis. And prior to seeing him at the store that one day, months had gone by with no word from him. Plus, it was confirmed that Rendell had another woman, by his own mouth. However, now that Rendell was aware of me and Co's interactions, he wants to jump up and say, we can never have this life that we could have had.

Honestly, I thought that life that "we could've had" was done with. When Rendell slammed that door behind me after he told me to get my shit and get out- over a phone call about some damn pots and pans. It evident to me that we had ended then. Still yet, knowing that a line had been crossed between Co and me, I couldn't help but think, that did seal the deal on top of adding insult to injury. Co knew how I felt about Rendell. And with all these sudden surprises, I don't think Co even talked to Rendell about me, as he said he was doing. Nonetheless, the circumstances disconcerted me and I had to figure out what would be my next move.

Draco, looking at me, interrupted my thinking. He said, "I don't care what you two had going. I still want to kick it with you. I do like you."

Digesting what Co had said, I sat in my chair as he looked on and waited for a response. I stared ahead past him, looking out of the living room window. Co cleared his throat, directing my attention back toward him. At that moment, I couldn't give him a definite answer. I needed more time to think. I explained that to Co, then asked him to leave.

He said, "Ok," and left.

I sat there in my chair, staring up at the ceiling, still pondering what I should do. I thought to myself, *Ok, Olivia, it's apparent that you ruined it with Rendell, although he did cause the division. However, the whole point to all of this was to move on, get past the heartbreak.*

Co for sure did not compare to Rendell, not even a little bit. Yet, it was Co who was still open to sustaining a friendship. And as for Rendell, well, that was a done deal; the life I had once envisioned for the two of us was no more. I felt horrible about it, because not only was he a refreshing change for me; Ren was also the apple in my son's eye. Although Rendell may have shattered that picture perfect life for us, I unknowingly set it ablaze.

That dreadful mistake I made was irreversible and inconsolable; it weighed far more than a simple misunderstanding. Knowing that I couldn't undo what was done consumed me and made me even more sorrowful. I found myself once more in the bedroom, crying into my pillow. "I didn't give us a chance," I said as cried myself to sleep.

It was crazy too. Our last moment together even haunted me in my sleep. I was having dreams about this man and those last words Ren spoke to me—We can never be! Hearing that in my head, I would abruptly wake from my slumber. It was like I was reliving that moment over and over again, and there was nothing that could be done about it. That caused me to hit a new all-time low, and I for real felt that I had ruined my life.

Co didn't hear from me for a few days. But then I got tired of being sad. Things got lonely around the apartment when DeLon would leave for the weekend to visit his grandmother. I needed a pick-me-up and wanted some company to get my mind off things. Therefore, I called up Draco.

At that point, I thought, *What else do I have to lose?*

Caught Up

CHAPTER THIRTY-ONE

Draco knocked on the door and I invited him in. He sat on the sofa and we began to chop it up. He said he had some weed and asked if I wanted to smoke. I responded, "Hell, yeah." The way I had been feeling, I needed a lift. Co pulled out his stash and broke it down to roll up a joint. I decided to turn on some music, Tupac's *All Eyez On Me*; that was the album that stayed in rotation at my place. When I returned, Co already had the joint rolled.

"Dang," I said, "You must be a professional." Co laughed. When Rendell and I smoked, we had to use a cigarette roller to roll our joints. Co took out a lighter and lit the joint up, took a hit off it and passed it over to me.

I felt so chill. The music was going, with smoke clouds floating around in the room. By the time we finished the joint, we were cracking jokes and laughing at all sorts of silly stuff. I think I even got up and danced for a bit. It was nice to not feel down and depressed. I enjoyed his company. As the night went on, we got deeper into conversation. It got really late and I became sleepy. I told Co I was ready to turn it in.

He made a joke, saying "Oh, I can't turn in with you?"

I laughed and said, "No, I'm walking your ass to this door."

He laughed and got up off the couch to make his exit. I told him to have a good night. He stepped outside the door, wished me the same and left. I locked the door, and that was the end to a good night.

The next day, I got a call from Co. He asked how I was doing. We talked about the day. He asked if he could come over later, and I said he could after DeLon was asleep. De-Lon was usually in bed by 9:30 p.m., so at about ten, Co was knocking at the door. I let him in. This time we had to be much quieter, because I didn't want to wake up my son. However, we did light up a joint.

I don't know what is about smoking a joint, but if it's a good grade, I thoroughly enjoy it. it makes me feel relaxed. I'm more social after a few puffs, and it really helps to liven things up. However, if the atmosphere is not kosher, toking a joint can also make you highly paranoid, no pun intended. I start to think irrationally.

One time, I had fired up a joint, smoking alone. I was driving around in my car and stopped to go into Walgreens. When I came out, I noticed for the first time that one of my hubcaps was off. I stood there looking at my tire, then started looking suspiciously around, like somebody took my hubcap off after I left to go in the store. I hopped back in the car and drove, steadily looking in my rearview mirror as if I was a target of some sort and being followed. I drove around most of the night, cutting corners and driving into neighborhoods, taking the long way home. Trying to shake off whatever imaginary person I thought was following me. That was so silly and not a good feeling.

However, that night hanging out with Co, there was no paranoia. It was just chill. We laughed and talked, then talked some more until I got up to walk in the kitchen. And that's when he made his move again—or should I say, his demand. He walked up on me and posted himself behind me as I reached up in the cabinet for a cup. He said in my ear, "Go to the room and take off your clothes, so I can make you feel good."

Surprised by his sudden and unexpected assertiveness, I jumped; then turned around to face him. "But my son is in the other room asleep," I responded.

"So? We won't make a lot of noise."

I turned back toward the cabinet, reached up again for a cup and got some water out of the faucet. I stood there and drank it as I looked on, Co stared back at me. After I finished drinking my water, I put the cup down and went down the hall to my bedroom. Loosening his belt, Co followed right behind me and shut the door once entering the bedroom. The music was already playing. I just changed it to something softer, so I could get in the mood.

I looked around and Co was already naked, with nothing but his socks on, pulled all the way up just under his knees. His clothes were shoved off in a corner in a little pile as I stood there fully clothed surprised by his speediness.

Gat dang, I thought, *how did I get myself into this mess?*

Nervously, I started to get undressed. A smile formed on Co's face as he looked at me; then he instructed me to lie on the bed. Feeling somewhat stiff and self-conscious, I lay on the bed. Although we were two consenting adults, I still wasn't totally comfortable. But that soon changed. Co meant what he said about making me feel good, because he did exactly that.

I won't go into all the specifics or tell you what it was, but I will share what it wasn't. He was not a minute-man. And although there was a lot of movement going on, he did not empty the bank. I didn't have any out-of-body encounter, nor was it anything like the mesmerizing love-making experience I once had with Rendell. However, I did have to bite the pillow a few times to keep from being too vocal. And after it was over, I was left yearning for more.

It was about three in the morning, when I woke from dozing off after being worked over. I wasn't thinking anymore about Rendell after that. I looked over at Co to wake him up. He was snoring a bit. "Hey, wake up," I whispered in his ear. He woke, then popped his head up to ask what time it was. I told him, and he got up out the bed and started putting on his clothes. My legs were a bit weakened afterwards, so I lay in bed as long as I could before I had to get up. Then I grabbed my housecoat and walked him to the door.

"I had fun," he said.

"So, did I," I replied. I unlocked the door, and he left. Then I rushed back in the bed to grab a few more hours of sleep before having to wake up DeLon for school.

Mixed Feelings

CHAPTER THIRTY-TWO

Later that morning after I got DeLon off to school, I was sitting in the living room watching TV when I heard a knock at the door. I looked out the peephole, then opened the door to see Rendell standing there before me. What was he doing here? I thought as I stared at him speechless. I guess I stood there looking puzzled too long, because Rendell bypassed me and let himself inside my apartment.

"Olivia," he said in an anxious type of way, pacing back and forth on the living room floor.

"Yes?" I responded, standing there with the door still open and the knob in my hand. "What do you want, Rendell?" *What in the heck was up with this dude?* I closed the door and sat on the cough, facing the TV. Rendell stopped pacing the floor and sat down next to me with anxiousness.

"Olivia," he said, "guess what? I have a ring for that finger right there!"

"What?" I said in disbelief and confusion. "A ring? What?!"

"You heard me; I have a ring for that finger right there." He was pointing down and touching my marriage finger.

Where's the ring at, then?" I asked in a sharp, stiff tone.

"Uh, I don't have it right now," he said with hesitation in his voice. I sat and looked at him in astonishment.

As Rendell kept touching my marriage ring finger and talking about a ring he didn't have yet, my mind drifted in thought… *What is it with this guy? He devastates me with the notion that we could never have a life together, but now he wants to pop up, talking about a ring?* And of course, Ren had perfect timing, because he did all this after Draco had slithered back in and put it down this time. I was totally confused.

"Rendell," I said in a calm voice. "You broke up with me. You threw me out of your apartment; you threw rocks at me. You told me that you had another woman…"

Rendell interrupted and said, "I know, I know, Olivia; I was just going through menopause."

"Menopause?! Menopause, Rendell?" I repeated. Hearing him say that made me fume. All the emotions, grief and sorrow that he put me through…the misery I put myself through…and he wanted to sit here and say he was going through menopause? I became livid.

"Well, you're too late," I said in an elevated voice, then I got up from sitting next to him. I stood in front Rendell and looked him in the eyes as he remained seated, and I said, "I don't want you anymore."

By that time, I got another knock at the door. My attention turned away from Rendell to see who it was. Still annoyed from all the confusion, I walked over to open the door without even looking through the peephole first. It was my home girl, Kay, and her cousin Poo. They were in the neighborhood and decided to stop by. Rendell was still sitting on the couch when they walked in.

Kay said, "Oh, are we interrupting something?"

"Nope!" I sharply responded, keeping my attention toward them.

Rendell, after feeling the cold shoulder, got up to leave. He looked at me and walked out the door. After he left, I turned toward the other guests and said, "I don't know why he was here."

Kay's cousin Poo said, "Oh, you two aren't together anymore? So, you don't mind if I holla at him?"

"Nope, go right ahead," I said. Then I flopped myself right on the cough with no qualms about it.

Kay and Poo left shortly afterward, leaving me there in my apartment alone. I sat back on the couch, thinking about what had just transpired between Rendell and me. Throughout all the heartfelt emotions I had for that man, the one emotion that stood out the most right then was anger. I was furious at him for tearing us apart and causing me so much grief over the lack of our togetherness. I wanted to be over him and finally at that moment, I was—or so it felt. The other night with Draco definitely affected my feelings for Ren. Whatever genuine fondness I had in my heart for Ren was now masked by anger and lust.

Intricate Love

CHAPTER THIRTY-THREE

A week or two had gone, and I hadn't heard from Rendell since that day at my apartment. I would see Co from time to time. He would come by during the day to visit and we'd just talk, but usually he'd return later that night when my son was asleep. Co was a cool guy, but I had no intentions of having a relationship with him. Our friendliness toward one another was purely sexual. And for a change, I was no longer heartbroken mentally over Rendell.

That following Saturday was warm and sunny. I love the sun and being outside in it; the heat just warms my soul. Consequently, I was out enjoying the weather by myself, walking home from the Riverside trail which was nearby my place. Right in front of my apartment complex was a small shopping center with a convenience store. I noticed Rendell's car parked outside the store. Shortly after, I saw Rendell walking out with his usual fast-paced, pepped up steps, looking just scrumptious as always.

I paused a bit just to watch him from afar. Then who did I see coming out of the store, hot on his trail? It was Poo, Kay's cousin! Now, I hadn't yearned for that man in a while; it had been weeks. And for that short moment, I thought he was totally out of my system. But seeing them two together pierced my heart and shook my soul. In that instant, I was reminded of what I missed, of what I adored so greatly. It made me want Rendell back again, and I wanted him badly.

I stood there and watched as they hopped in the car, one after the other, then drove off. It reminded me of how Rendell and I used to ride around together. What I witnessed there practically mirrored what Ren and I used to do. However, I was not Rendell's girl anymore. Someone else had taken my spot on the passenger side of his car. Seeing them pierced my spirit. The heartache I thought was behind me had resurfaced its ugly head and encumbered my soul. And just like that, I found myself back in that sorrowful state; desiring, missing and loving Rendell Schwann.

It's funny how life evolves. The things you never thought you'd do; you end up doing. And the life you intended to have; you end up living the opposite. I never intended to get involved with Co, but with the circumstances that took place, I found myself caught up. Just like the famous quote of Walter Scott, "Oh, what a tangled web we weave."

Despite being totally honest with them both, I had indeed gotten myself entangled in a treacherous web. And from that point on, the cobwebs would get mystified and very sticky....

From the Gate

CHAPTER THIRTY-FOUR

Now, as I have mentioned before, I did not understand the depth of connection Rendell and I shared. However, on the surface I could visualize us building an empire together. For I always believed couples who progressed together created stronger bonds between one another. And I could foresee that for Rendell and me. He was the type of person to give me just as much support as I gave him. That bright and prosperous future that was in the works for us, along with having a slew of beautiful kids, so regretfully did not happen.

I adored everything about Rendell. There was nothing I disliked about him, with the exception of his thick, sharp nails that he liked to use to take skin samples from me. Besides that, I felt that I could endure anything with that man by my side. I knew early in our connecting, without doubt, he was the one for me. The one being who made every particle of me feel whole.

Shortly after meeting him, I recall repeatedly writing down my future marital name on a sheet of paper. Olivia R. Schwann, Olivia R. Schwann... Olivia R. Schwann, I wrote that name down several times. Like millions of other young girls, I too dreamed of being married with kids and having that white picketed fenced yard with a two-story home. And Rendell fit the bill on every level. With my multi-syllabized first name, I thought, for my marital name to have a good ring to it, my future hubby's last name would have to be a one-syllable name. And ironically, Rendell's last name was just that.

I found significant connections between Rendell and me in every way. I read into zodiac signs too and looked at numbers, like birth dates. It's a personal belief of mine is that the universe and everything within—the stars, moon, man, animal, trees—all are creations under God. In addition to that, I believe that somehow, man and the universe are intricately associated by design. For instance, water tides or ocean waves are created by the gravitational pulls between the Sun, Moon and Earth. The earth's body is made of 70% water, likewise for the human body, that averages a percentile slightly lower than that. Furthermore, just as those outer attractional forces affect the earth's bodily water, then so it does for our moods and behavior, the word lunatic is originated by the word, lunar. Man is made up of matter and water, just like the earth. We were originated from the dirt of this earth, specifically African dirt. Beings, Godly sculpted by His personal touch; molded from the deeply enriched dark African soil, bronzed by His light- the sun; and given soul/life from His breath which is defined as a spirit-soul.

On a Biblical note, even God used the stars, as well as other elements, to direct the path of man. For it was the Eastern Star that shined so brightly in the heavens and led the wise men to baby Jesus and Mary. For it is read in Matthew: after Jesus was born in Bethlehem of Judea, wise men from the East came to Jerusalem, asking, "Where is the child who has been born king of the Jews? For we observed his star at its rising…". And in modern times, it was North Star that burned bright in the sky, aiding Harriet Tubman in freeing hundreds of slaves.

Coincidence? I think not.

With Rendell being a Libra and I, an Aquarius, according to the zodiac stars, our signs made the ideal couple. Moreover, it was true. We got along great up until that dreadful day. And even more evidently, he had the same heart-shaped birthmark as me. So, I knew we were kindred spirits. With our birthday numbers, my date of birth is 2/11 and his 10/14. What I saw in that was the number two. For mine, one plus one makes two, and the eleven, two ones put together also make the Roman numeral II. The number 14, of his birth date, divided by seven is two; seven being a prime number with only 2 factors, 1 and itself; just like 11. Farfetched? Perhaps, however, perceptively, it all made sense and certified things for me.

Rendell had my mind, body and heart. With every day spent together, he gained access to a portal within me. Slowly but surely, I would reveal those deep feelings for him and had every intention in doing so with time. However, our time together was cut short. We were over before we could barely scratch the surface.

What happened? Did I take all those signs for granted, or was it that I lost faith in what I knew in my heart? I allowed my internal feelings to be overshadowed by the hurt and abandonment caused by Rendell's actions. And instead of taking my troubles to God in prayer, I attempted to handle things in my own way, creating a tangled mess.

I can be tough as nails to anything and everything in this world, but when it comes to my heart, that is another story. Love is my kryptonite, and Rendell Schwann was just that. This man had enchanted my heart in every way, then in turn created such heartache in me with his erratic behavior. I felt lost, literally like a piece of me was missing. I attempted to reach out to him, but after the damage was done, I thought that there was no turning back. This man could never love and adore me in all the ways I needed him to. In all the ways a King should love and admire his Queen.

Therefore, I thought, what choice did I have but to move on? That's not an illogical thought process. That's what one does, when moving on with their life—stumble across someone new to build and grow with. That is a natural course in life, especially when the previous relationship doesn't work out, right? Well, unfortunately, for me it wasn't that simple.

At nineteen years of age, I knew Rendell was my soulmate. Nevertheless, I was ignorant to the fact that no one else would even be capable of quenching that unknown thirst within me as he did. At that tender age, I could not even fathom how he and only he could fulfill me as a mate. So, once again, I found myself feeling that spirit of emptiness and had to reach out. I called him.

And Ren responded.

What Next?

CHAPTER THIRTY-FIVE

Rendell came to my apartment. DeLon was up, and it didn't bother me if my son saw him there. My son adored Rendell and was always excited when he came around. And I must say, so was I. Now at this point, I didn't know what Co could have possibly said to Rendell about me. I was trying to feel Rendell out by his body language, but physically he wasn't telling me much. DeLon and I were in the process of having dinner and Rendell may have eaten too, because he stayed for some time. The mood was pleasant, yet still there was this awkwardness between us.

Rendell and I got more at ease as the night advanced. The time had gone by so fast, before I realized it was past my son's bedtime. I got DeLon ready for bed and laid him to sleep for the evening. Afterwards, I went back to the living room where Rendell was watching TV. I sat next to him and smiled, secretly hoping that tonight would be the start of making a new life with each other.

Although there was this uneasiness between us, it felt good to be in Rendell's presence once more. We had small talk, but neither one us dared to bring up Co's name. I wished to God we both could forget about it all, but that wasn't our reality. Co was very much the sore thumb in our lives.

I knew that Ren could still be involved with Poo, but that didn't make any difference to me. My heart was reopened and my mind was reminded of what I once felt for this man; and I knew that he still cared for me too. I'm not really sure what I was expecting when I invited him over, but Rendell leaned over to kiss me, and it was on from there; I was all in.

My heart, my love, my baby—it didn't matter how the sex was. I got to feel his touch once more, my skin up against his. His big, soft hands caressing my body. Those lips—oh God, how I'd missed those lips... There was no doubt I was in love with this man. He had my heart in every way, and there was nothing I could do about it.

It saddened me though, because the downside of it was, I knew he had insecurities now; I could see it in his eyes. Only he didn't realize that he had nothing to be insecure about. He was all I wanted and required in my life. Rendell did not understand just how much he touched me. He didn't comprehend how deeply his actions affected me. He still meant everything to me and I truly desired him as an eternal mate.

The next morning, we got up, Rendell got dressed and kissed me goodbye; then he left. All that day, I waited for him to call. Perhaps Rendell would ask if I wanted to ride with him somewhere, like he used to. Maybe he would even invite me out to eat. But disappointingly, nothing happened. Rendell did not reach out to me at all. I was ghosted.

Back to Work

CHAPTER THIRTY-SIX

After that, I decided I had way too much time on my hands, so I sought part-time employment. One thing about being in the health field is that you have a network of well-known professionals. Back then, in the black community amongst the professional circle, everyone looked out for one another. Word got out that the resigned CEO of Morton was in the beginning stages of starting his own health care practice. I heard about this too and went to the clinic to apply for a job.

The name of his practice was EM Minor Emergency Clinic. At that time, he had a physician's assistant named Bill and his wife Angie, a nurse, working with him. Although I was a trained dental assistant, Dr. Mikel hired me as a medical aid for Bill while Angie oversaw everything else.

I loved working there. It was exciting being an assistant in the medical field, because there was no telling what one might see. It gave me a purpose during the day when my son was at school; in addition to earning some extra cash on the side. It didn't pay much at all, but I wasn't too pressed for cash. Working at the medical clinic was the experience of a lifetime. I was blessed just to be a part of it and happy that I could provide the extra manpower that Dr. Mikel's needed to keep things afloat.

I remember one time, a black woman in her mid-forties came in to see Bill for treatment. She was a Type II diabetic and had a huge abscess on her left buttock. Now, this woman would be classified as obese for her height. She was short and wide, but very nice. She could easily be anyone's favorite aunt. However, that day, she was in a lot of pain. I had her follow me into the room, then gave her a gown to put on, so Bill could address the issue properly. Bill tapped on the door and she gave us the okay to come in.

She moaned and groaned as she lay there. Bill lifted up that gown, and what I saw blew my mind. This woman had about a sixty-inch width in hips, and what comes with wide hips, wide buttocks. That abscess took over one whole booty cheek, and it was green with a red lining surrounding it. Bill asked for a surgical blade and some medicated gauze strips. I hurried to grab what he asked for and rushed back to the room where he and the patient were.

Bill took that blade and lanced that boil right in the center. The lady let out a scream as all this green fluid came oozing out of that boil. More and more came out of it, as Bill kept applying pressure to it. Then to make matters more uncomfortable for the patient, but to her benefit, he took the medicated gauze strips and pushed them inside the boil, further removing more of the infectious pus. That lady screamed some more.

By the time Bill removed most of the infection, I had a medical pan full of green, pus-saturated gauze. And it gave off a foul odor. I cringed at the sight of it, but thankfully held my composure. Bill gave her a round of antibiotics and sent her on way.

Needless to say, when she left, she was much happier than when she came in. And as for me, I couldn't wait to come back and see what the next day entailed.

Regret

CHAPTER THIRTY-SEVEN

To be back amongst the working society was a good feeling. It distracted my mind from the troubles that waited amidst the shadows. Those daunting life's turbulences that lingered about and would resurface in mind when I had too much spare time. It was in a state of mental turmoil that I could not easily shake. Every day, I felt as if I carried around an invisible cloak of shame that weighed me down heavily. However, when I was productively working, all that went to the wayside.

Once on the radio, I heard counseling advice from the late Dr. Joy Browne, aka Dr. Joy. She recommended waiting a year to date another person, after one had undergone a serious breakup or divorce. The reason being, a person would feel better about themselves mentally and less likely to be vulnerable or have low self-esteem. Not giving yourself healing time could result in making choices you wouldn't normally make in a healthy state of mind. And I felt that.

I absolutely could relate to what Dr. Joy was saying, because that's where I stood presently. The decisions that I had made at that time were against my better judgment, and I would not have normally made that decision if I had been in a healthier mental state. As a result, I had gotten myself into a dreadful entanglement. On one end, my heart and soul were intertwined with the likes of Rendell Schwann.

And the opposite end of the spectrum, my flesh was riveted in lust for Draco. One, I wanted for a lifetime and the other, only for the moment. Unenviably so, I found myself torn between the two men, who also referred to themselves as friends.

When I say angels don't warn for nothin', I mean that wholeheartedly. And at that point in my life, I was aware of the mess that I had gotten myself into. The travesty of it all distinctively reminded me of that warning, I had experienced at the park. That angel knew how drastically my future would be affected by keeping that number. It was trying to save me from myself, and I was too foolish, selfish and stubborn to take heed to that divine warning.

I overlooked that angelic, rare intercession, and instead leaned to my own understanding. And because of it, everything got displaced. My support system was disrupted, and the chain of command interrupted spiritually, especially for those close to me. Therefore, it was not just me who was affected by this grave mistake. The chaotic repercussions lasted for a season, but it would still have a pending effect for years to come.

Therefore, when I say angels do not warn for nothin', please believe that they warn for an absolute reason.

Gathering Myself

CHAPTER THIRTY-EIGHT

Even when prematurely dating, I have always been a one-man woman. I was never the fast type, and I was only attentive to that one who captivated me. Wherefore, this whole ordeal that I had succumbed to, floored me. Not in a million years would I have ever thought that it could be me stuck in the middle; entangled by the heart's desire for one and the intense sexual fancies of the other. On the contrary, it very well was me who was embraced by these two men and stood in between them, torn.

At any time, Rendell could have had me all to himself. Although my involvement with Co severely complicated things, it never took away from the love I had stored for him. If Rendell had come by the apartment with that ring as he spoke of, invited me out on a date, or openly expressed his true feelings for me, I would have dropped Co in a heartbeat. Those concrete steps would have been vital to the reinforcement of my devotion to him. With all the up-and-down emotions Ren previously caused me prior to Co, I needed something solid from him to assure me of his intent for our future together, if there was ever one.

However, those things never transpired. Consequently, I knew that I was at a point of no return; and for me to openly express my heartfelt feelings to this man, I first had to let go of Co. That meant separation by time and space. There was no way I could go to Rendell pouring out my heart to him, knowing that I still had desire for another man. I had to first undo the fleshly tie that was formed between Co and me, which was more easily said than done.

Days would go by before I heard from Rendell. That would sadden me, and I would need some cheering up. There were times, as well, that I resisted the temptation by ignoring Co's calls, and I would avoid calling him as well. However, on those days where I wallowed in self-pity, those would be the moments that I required some relief. I would give in to those sexual impulses and answer Co's call. Usually, after some small talk, Co would knock at my front door. When he arrived, the anticipation alone would elevate my heart rate and after receiving a night of pleasure, the sorrows were alleviated, but that was only be a temporary fix.

I knew things were out of control when one day, out of the blue, this sexual urge came over me. I called Co. No answer. Annoyed, I paced the living room floor, giving Co time to return my call. Thirty mins went by, and still no word from him, so I called again. By that time, my body was shaking. I had to mentally focus just to steady my fingers in order to correctly dial his number. And when Co finally answered, I had so much aggression in my voice. I let him know I needed to see him ASAP.

Jeez! I thought, after I hung up the phone with him. I was acting like a crack-head; only it wasn't drugs that I was pheening for. Lust had overtaken me and I felt so ashamed by it, but I could not help it. I needed a fix and I needed it speedily.

Behaving in that manner was so unlike me. I knew all this going back and forth between the two was getting way out of hand. I had to gain control of the situation, and of my flesh. Therefore, I made the decision to cut it off with them both. Things were getting very complex, but most importantly, it was disrupting my natural course of life. And the irony of it is, I wasn't sure if either of the two men were aware of the full picture. I assumed they were not discussing amongst each other their dealings with me, but I wasn't for certain that they weren't either.

Regardless, I needed peace of mind to return to me; and that was in contingent upon getting my flesh in check. Therefore, I made the decision right then to stop smoking marijuana and discontinue all interactions with both men. And that's exactly what I succeeded in doing.

A New Leaf

CHAPTER THIRTY-NINE

Making a new start, I avoided both men. I resisted the temptations of my flesh and those of my heart. Hence, all forms of communication were cut off. I wasn't accepting any calls or doing any calling to either one of them. I didn't see them out in public or anywhere else, for that matter. It was like I had completely vanished. However, Rendell's bizarre past behavior still troubled me.

With each day that went by, eventually turning into weeks, I found myself getting back to my normal self. By not succumbing to those sinful desires, I felt I had reclaimed my power. I was back in control of my circumstances, and that made me feel good inside.

I began hanging out with a close friend of the family, Monique, which helped me to maintain my mental clarity. Monique and I were the same air signs, so we had similar personalities and got along great. That usually consisted of us acting silly, dancing and having fun. When we would go out to the local clubs, we normally spent all our time there on the dance floor, tearing it up.

On a night she and I were hanging out, I met this guy named O'Rian. He was cool, taller than me, about 6'2". O'Rian had a nice smile and gorgeous eyes, which caught my attention. His lovely brown pigments were a russet brown, and he was in shape too, because his biceps flexed through his sky-blue colored long-sleeved shirt as he reached to shake my hand, introducing himself.

We had made small talk, then afterwards before going our separate ways, we exchanged numbers. Taking his number, there were no expectations, but I did hope to at least gain a friendship. I found that being around new people brought about different energy, and it was usually positive. Plus, having a change in scenery definitely helped me regain a coherent state of mind.

Getting Comfortable

CHAPTER FORTY

O'Rian called me the next day. We talked on the phone for about an hour. After we hung up, I thought, *Now this is the type of guy I wouldn't mind getting to know better.* Plus, O'Rian didn't waste any time over who would be the first one to call. He let his presence be known, and I liked that about him. In addition to him giving good conversation, he seemed like a cool person.

It has always been a thing of mine to wait and allow the guy to make the first move. I like for the man to openly show his interest for me. Naturally, it would intensify my attraction for him. After O'Rian and I talked, he certainly sparked some curiosity; he made it very clear that he was much intrigued with me. I already knew he was a lot of fun too, because he danced a few songs with me at the club the night we met. Therefore, he had already gotten started on a good foot literally, because we both enjoyed dancing.

Now, I am a horror movie buff. I grew up watching scary movies, but I damn sure never want to feel like I am in one. Luckily, O'Rian was not psycho, but a decent catch. He was a couple years older than me and a recent college grad. He lived with his mom and her husband at their home on the Hills. Like Rendell, he didn't have any children yet, which was an added bonus. O'Rian seemed to be laid-back and level-minded too, so I wasn't concerned about him being a stalker or causing any terror in my life.

The more we talked, the more my fondness grew for him. O'Rian spoke about his aspirations and plans for achieving his goals, which inspired me. I love a man with a vision and a plan. Every woman wants a man who can complement her and vice versa. I was feeling this dude a lot. I could almost envision us being a power couple. Of course, we would both be starting from the bottom. However, quite honestly, I preferred it that way. There is nothing better in a relationship than to be with your mate whom you have fought, loved and grinded with from the ground to all the way up. That's the kind of thing I was into, and with all the riffraff behind me, I could finally focus on leveling up.

The multiple phone conversations we had led up to our first date. It was the usual dinner and movie; but afterwards, he took me over to his mom's house to hang out a bit more. O'Rian had a room separate from the other bedrooms, downstairs adjacent to the kitchen. The arrangement was cool; it was like he had his own separate living area that provided much privacy.

In his bedroom, O'Rian had a dresser, bed, TV and a desk with this cool-looking chair to go with it. The desk chair stood out to me in more ways than one. It was huge, yet elegantly made. It certainly appeared to be the most expensive piece of furniture in the room, a beautifully polished wooden chair accented with tannish brown leather that was soft and plush. It was a grand chair, one fit for a King and when you sat in it, you felt like royalty. All that it was missing were the gold trimmings.

O'Rian and I went out quite frequently, and we thoroughly enjoyed each other's company. One night over at his place, we both had some drinks and were feeling good. He and I were laughing and talking about random things. O'Rian was sitting in that big, nicely built chair that I fancied; facing me as I sat on his bed. All of a sudden, his lips captured my attention; an urge came over me to kiss them.

I leaned forward off the bed and mounted myself onto Rian's lap facing him as the hefty chair fully supported us both. I tilted toward him for a kiss. O'Rian kissed me back, and it was nice. After that, things got a little more heated. O'Rian took the lead, kissing my neck as he unbuttoned his shirt and unbuckled his pants. I quickly slipped off my shirt and tossed it on the bed and helped O'Rian out of his shirt as well, leaving us with just our bottoms on.

We had a brief intercession to remove all our garments. Then I pushed him back in the chair and reclaimed my position on top. Securing his thighs within mine, I went in for more kisses, and we quickly regained our momentum from where we left off. O'Rian took control again, but this time with no clothing restrictions. He kissed my neck, down to my shoulders, and lower. My hands had a full grip on those leather, plush arm rests as the chair cradled our bodies and I rode O'Rian like he'd never been rode before.

After getting fully acquainted with my new guy, things were coming along pretty good. I still had no contact with either Ren or Co, and I was all right with that. O'Rian and I were learning more and more about each other with every passing day.

With the steadiness of our relationship, the idea of becoming a family, a unit, was churning in the air and close to being a reality. Becoming very serious with each other, it was due time to turn it up a notch. I knew the moment would come where I'd have to reveal to O'Rian the most intimate part of me. This called for me to be vulnerable. Which meant I'd have to put my mind at ease, let down my guards and expose the most delicate part of my heart.

So, I did. After many relaxing deep breaths, I was able to gather my thoughts and make the decision. I decided to introduce O'Rian to the most precious treasure in my life, my beloved son, DeLon.

DeLon

CHAPTER FORTY-ONE

DeLon was a great kid. He was advanced for his age, having full adult conversations at the age of two. When we lived with our Aunt Armostean, she would go to him for information about what was going with Mara and me, labeling him "the informant." Therefore, we had to be selective about the words we spoke around him, because DeLon quickly caught on to things.

On top of that, DeLon was very well behaved on every level. He required little disciplinary action. He never threw temper tantrums. DeLon never really got too much out of hand to where he needed many spankings, and I seldom recall doing so. If he was sick or his head hurt, as opposed to crying like typical two-year-olds did, DeLon would just say, "My head hurts" or "I don't feel good," and he'd go lie down on the bed or sofa so I could tend to him. I adored my child tremendously, but sometimes his advanced capabilities were a bit eerie.

I remember the time when DeLon caught me doing something he disliked. And he made it clearly known. We were staying at my best friend's place at the time in her two-bedroom apartment. DeLon and I shared one room, and Keneitha and her child had the other room. That one night I, Keneitha, and both our boyfriends were in my room passing a joint around. The kids were all in Keneitha's room watching TV. At that time, DeLon was about eighteen months old and was no taller than the lower-level kitchen cabinet doors in the apartment.

I left the room to light up a joint on the kitchen stove. DeLon must have heard me come out and left Keneitha's room to find me. As I was lighting it, I looked up and to my surprise DeLon was standing next to the kitchen cabinets. I was caught red-handed. He gave me a glare, as if he was annoyed by what he saw. Then he opened the cabinet door, slammed it shut, then stormed back into the room with other the kids.

I stood there in disbelief for a while, the joint still in my hand. Eventually, I went ahead and fired it up, but when I got back into the room, I passed the joint off to the next person. No more did I have the urge to hit the joint, at least not for that night, too spooked about what I had just witnessed from my child.

My son was an exceptionally great kid that I had been blessed to have. He was a favorite in a lot of people's eyes, and he most certainly stood out amongst the crowd. He possessed such charisma and was a gorgeous child. So much, in fact, that for a short while I tried to get him into acting and modeling with the Langley Modeling Talent Agency, a local talent search business. But the photo shoots were too expensive. It was way out of my budget and required traveling, which posed a huge obstacle for a low-income single working mom who was just starting out.

All my friends liked DeLon. He was just that likable kid. There was never a reason for anyone to dislike him, and

O'Rian was no exception. Therefore, when I introduced the two, O'Rian stooped down to DeLon's eye level, shook his then little, three-year-old hand and said, "Nice to meet you, fella."

Seeing that brought a smile to my face as I watched at a distance with my arms crossed. I could see that DeLon liked O'Rian too, which was a plus. With the way O'Rian interacted with my son, I could tell he wanted to be with us for the long haul.

Not Worth a Quarter

CHAPTER FORTY-TWO

Being in a relationship with O'Rian, my mind was clear. I had regained my couth, and it felt great. Even though we were sexually active, it did not take over the relationship nor have my flesh in an uncontrollable state. One day though, I was over his mom's place, and we were in his room just chilling. O'Rian was cleaning his tennis shoes with this shoe foam cleaner. After seeing how clean his shoes got, I asked if I could borrow the shoe cleaner. O'Rian, without thinking twice, said no!

Taken back by his response, I said. "What do you mean, no? It's just a can of shoe cleaner, I'll bring it right back once I'm done with it." But O'Rian still refused, and that did not sit well with me.

Yes, it was just a canister of shoe cleaner, but I was bothered by the principle of it all. I wasn't asking this man for two hundred bucks. After all this good loving that O'Rian was receiving from me, and I wasn't even good for a nine-ounce can of $5 shoe cleaner that I only wanted to borrow? That was an immediate turn-off, and I became very annoyed. For one, I cannot stand a stingy man. And two, I'd never asked O'Rian for anything, not even a quarter, so for him to deny me this one small thing; it pissed me all the way off, to say the least.

Although I was fuming inside, I did, however, manage

to hold back my tongue and declined to thoroughly express my disappointment with him. I felt so let down, because I thought we were better than that. The whole ordeal was a for-real Debbie Downer, and the relationship suffered because of it. With someone like me, a genuinely giving person, I hardly ever ask for anything. Therefore, with the rare times I do ask my lover for something, the word "No" should not be in his vocabulary. If anything, when I asked to borrow that shoe cleaner, O'Rian should've been like, "Here, baby… anything else you need?" However, that was not the case; O'Rian chose to do the opposite.

The dynamics of O'Rian's position in my life altered. I no longer viewed him as a focal point to thrive from, due to his selfishness over a measly can of leather shoe cleaner, especially at that stage in the game of our relationship. I knew then that this man could not love me with the depth of sincerity that I required. He could not possibly be able to reciprocate the levels of affection that I am capable of. If I wasn't even worth the hassle of separating from a five dollar can of shoe cleaner, then I could only imagine the one-sided disappointments that waited in the future.

I eventually got over O'Rian's shortcomings and returned to my good-spirited self. However, that piercing ache of disappointment never quite dissipated from my mind. Seeing that O'Rian was unlike me in the giving department brought thoughts of Rendell back to the forefront. Rendell was very giving. He would give the shirt off his back if he had to. And although Rendell was in the past, I found it challenging not to compare the two.

The Interruption

CHAPTER FORTY-THREE

One night, my bestie-cousin Tina was over to my apartment, visiting. I had cooked us a steak dinner that we had just finished eating. Sitting at the dinner table, we were just talking and laughing about family and classmates. My son was playing with his toys in the living room, going back and forth from the kitchen. In between conversations, we would stop and play with him. We were all having a nice night when we heard a knock at the door.

Who could that be? I thought. Tina and I turned to each other and shrugged our shoulders; neither of us was expecting anyone. O'Rian was with his family and didn't mention anything about coming by, so I was clueless as to who could it be. I got up from the kitchen table and walked over to the front door. In front of my door stood Draco, and behind him was Rendell with this uneasy look on his face. Neither one of them had been invited.

Stunned, I looked back at Tina and said in a low voice, "Girrrl, it's Draco and Rendell."

Tina asked in a whisper, "What are they doing here?"

"I have no idea," I responded.

I had cut off all communications from them both, and it had been a good two and a half months, if not more, that had gone by. My car was not even parked in front of my apartment, because it had broken down a couple nights before and had gotten towed. Therefore, just driving by, a person would think no one was home. Rendell was infamous for snapping at anybody for popping up unannounced at his place, yet here he was doing that very thing to me.

If it was only Draco standing outside my door, with no hesitation I would have completely ignored his knock. However, Rendell was standing there too. And somehow, I still had a weakness for him. Seeing him outside my door through the peephole made my heart thump harder.

I then looked to Tina again and questioned, "Do you think I should open the door?"

Strange Things

CHAPTER FORTY-FOUR

I opened the door, and the two men walked in. Draco was the more vocal one, acting very casual, as if I had just spoken to him yesterday. Neither one mentioned anything about dropping in unannounced or asked to be pardoned for their interruption. Rendell came in and sat on the sofa, while Draco followed his nose and went straight to the kitchen and scarfed down a slice of steak that was left in the pan. There was too much commotion going on initially, and it prevented me from centering in and gaining control of the situation.

It was about 9:30 p.m., too late for my baby to be up. I grabbed my son, took him into the back, and began to run a bath for him. DeLon may have spoken to Rendell. In the process of preparing my son for bed and peeking in the living room from time to time, I noticed Co in the kitchen talking to Tina. Ren was still sitting on the couch. Ren had this awkwardness about him and was just sort of being in the background of things. After I had bathed my son, he was ready for bed and went directly to sleep when I laid him down.

I wanted to touch base with Tina, but I couldn't because Co stayed in the kitchen with her. Therefore, I waited until I could get her alone. Then I noticed a marijuana smell in my house coming from the kitchen. Now, I hadn't smoked weed in months, and I really didn't have a strong desire to start back, but when the blunt was presented to me, I took a hit. I looked for Tina again, but she was still in the kitchen.

Feeling the sensation of the hit, I went back to the bedroom and straightened up a bit, and then headed to the bathroom to clean out the tub. While I was cleaning, Draco came back there, invading my space and said, "You down with having a ménage a trois? Tina's cool with it."

Startled, I quickly responded, "What?! NO!"

Draco was still running his mouth, trying to convince me when I pushed him to the side, moving him out of my way as I exited the bathroom. I was on my way to kitchen to confront Tina and find out if what I had just heard was true; but then Draco grabbed my shoulder to get my attention, stopping me in my tracks. The tension was already building from his outlandish suggestion, but now Co was trying to deebo the situation with his malevolent ass, which heightened my irritation even more.

"All right, everybody out! Get out of my apartment!" I said with sternness. I tried to keep my voice halfway under control, because my son was in the back, asleep. I wasn't sure if Co was telling the truth about Tina being down for that nonsense or not; but suddenly I felt uneasy and uncertain about all of them being in my apartment, so I asked everyone to leave.

Before that night, Co had mentioned something about a threesome on two separate occasions. I would always nonchalantly blow him off and dismiss the idea. One of the times was outside of Ren's barber shop, Black Art. In passing, he stopped me to get my attention, said a few words, then brought up that idea out of blue. I glared at him like he had shit on his forehead, and walked off without saying a word. The other time he brought it up, I do not recall where I was, but Co got the same shrewd response every time. The whole notion for him to even consider that offended me. Draco knew I cared deeply for Rendell. I utterly regretted ever getting involved in such a mess, so why would I ever agree to that?

After everyone left the apartment, I was occupied with straightening up the place, when I got another knock at the door. It was Draco and Rendell again. *What do they want?* I thought to myself.

I opened up the door and again Draco just walked in, claiming that he forgot his keys. Then here came Rendell trailing behind him, not saying much of anything. Draco went to the couch and shuffled a few pillows. Seeing that, I returned to the kitchen to finish cleaning up, turning my attention away from them. I was still very much under the influence from the smoke earlier. I came out of the kitchen and saw them both sitting down across from each other, one on the sofa and the other on the loveseat.

I looked at them and said, "What's going on here?"

Draco was doing all the talking, while Rendell kept quiet in the background. I began conversating, but I was speaking in parables. Draco couldn't comprehend what I was saying and asked for me to take it down a notch. Usually, under the influence I would get creative with my lingo, but it was going completely over Draco's head. From time to time, I would look over to Rendell, but it was like his body was present, but his mind was somewhere else. After so much small talk, Draco brought up again the suggestion of having a threesome.

I don't know why, but every time I heard that word threesome mentioned, it would always take me by surprise. Draco knew I wasn't that type. Hell, most of our conversations in the past, post-Rendell, were mainly about me trying to encourage him to stop his illegal activities and fly right. I had never in any way come across to Co other than being a positive influence. However, for whatever reason, he kept bringing up this ridiculousness, even after I had already said no, several times.

I sat there in my chair, thinking, looking to my right at Draco, then to the left at Rendell. Rendell was still nonexistent in his own way. He looked very awkward as he sat there mute. If he felt uneasy about being here, then why did he agree to come here with Co? Lord knew, if it wasn't for Rendell being at my door too, neither one of them would have been sitting in my living room. Therefore, it baffled me why Ren was acting so strange. It made me wonder, what were their true intentions for knocking at my door?

As I sat there facing the two, an unusual occurrence came about. On one shoulder, I had a little devil pop up and on the other I had a little angel, literally, and having full dialogue with me. Now, I have seen this in movies, and like most viewers, I thought it was fictional—but no; it was just as real as you and me. Like in the movies; the devil was trying to convince me to go along with the idiocy. The angel sitting on my right shoulder was telling me to not go along with it.

The little devil countered that by saying, "Aww, what's the big deal? It's not like either one is unfamiliar territory." When, actually, it *was* unfamiliar territory. Although I had been with each one at one point or another, never was it concurrently.

In addition to that, it had never been a fantasy of mine to be with two men at the same time. And in this case, one man, I longed for; and the other one, quite frankly, was able to hit the skins by default initially, due to me being in an immensely vulnerable state when he came into the picture. Therefore, combining both men, with very different roles in my life, into one sexual experience would totally be foreign to me.

Now, I'll admit, I was wrapped up by Co in the beginning. But at this stage in the game, I was done with that and over him.

Insight

CHAPTER FORTY-FIVE

I was very much aware of what was at stake if I gave in to this foolery Co was suggesting. Whatever hope there was between Rendell and me would surely be kaput. My light had already been tarnished for overstepping that boundary with Draco in the first place, breaking my own rule. Now, if I were to cross this line that was presented, all the chances of Rendell and me rekindling our love would most certainly be burned to ashes, irreparable and subjected to a realm of hopelessness.

Even now, I have solely just wanted Rendell to view me in the highest light. If I could become a born-again virgin for this man, I would. I desperately needed him to know without question that God intended me for him and him for me. It was vital for Rendell to comprehend with all assurance that his love was meant to surround and protect me. I wanted it to be affirmed in his heart with all dignity in place that the one he held in his loving arms was his most precious gift— me. That's how pure and loving I only wanted his thoughts to be of me.

Rendell, for me, was truly a breath of fresh air and he moved my soul. I could breathe with all ease when we were actively together. There was no feeling of doubt; I never felt boxed in or smothered by him. I freely was able to be myself, and that was so refreshing. Rendell had a profound effect on me; so much, in fact, that if I were to choose a soul mate with every life I was given, I would choose him in each and every existence. I adored him and could love him a million times over. Everywhere I was weak, he was strong, and my areas of strength were his weaknesses.

He was the yang to my yin, and vice versa. With him by my side, I knew I could spread my wings as wide as what was required and thrive in all areas of life—as his wife, a mother and a successor within our community. He was capable of making me whole in every aspect of the matter. And with that solid foundation affirmed within our circle of love, I would be able to direct my attention toward other affairs in the world; because I have always known that my life would be an astute testimony—however, it was unknown to what extent.

Rendell was that missing abutment to my life that enabled me to bridge the gaps. That solid connection as a people to the Holy Trinity. For when a man and woman with the same vision, same spirit and respect for God come together as one, their union is in alignment with the Lord as their head. With that type of anointing, a couple could uphold all types of awesomeness. If Rendell and I were together in that way, I undoubtedly believe our lives would be filled with unwavering faith and favor. As for myself, being a God-fearing and spiritual woman, knowing that all the pieces of the puzzle in this life had come together as was intended, I could not help but give God all the glory and His due praise!

Bringing my thoughts back down to earth in the living room of my apartment, I was facing these two men who were looking at me. I sat in my chair, all majesty poised in front of them, with the understanding that one was genuine and the other was a thief. I could obviously see that one really didn't want to be there and the other had deceptively plotted. Yet, my curiosity was still stirred. Why did Rendell choose to come here with Draco? I was mindful that the other was beneath one, and envied his friend's good nature. As I looked at the two, I knew that one shared my heart and the other desired it.

However, I was only ever meant for that one.

Crown Compromised

CHAPTER FORTY-SIX

I continued to listen as Draco rambled on about nothing and observed Rendell's caitiff behavior. My mind would occasionally drift off into my own thoughts. However, Draco managed to direct my attention toward him. I would look over at Rendell from time to time; he was still not engaged at all; not to me or to Co.

After a while, Draco fixated yet again about his absurd idea of having this ménage trois. Didn't he see that I wasn't interested in any of that nonsense? Why couldn't he get the drift after the fourth and fifth time I said no? I sat there and heard Co prattle on, as did Rendell, sitting to my left just five steps away. Rendell didn't have the slightest courage to speak up for what was in his heart. He just sat there like a puppy with its tail in-between its legs, and I observed his cowardliness with my chin resting atop my balled fist.

With the ridiculousness of it all, I laughed out loud. It must have been a forceful laugh, because it caused my bladder to leak and I ended up with soiled britches. Having a leaky bladder was a noticeable change that had occurred after giving birth, and it would seldom happen. However, for this to be the time for my bladder to act up was a complete inconvenience. I immediately jumped up and awkwardly rushed into the bathroom to clean myself up.

Now, my first thought was to keep those soiled drawers

on as a safety net in case Co got any bright ideas. Just in case he felt a little frisky, he'd think twice about it if his hands touched some pee-pee soiled undergarments. On the other hand, I didn't want to be walking around smelling like urine either. I knew I would feel much better if were to clean myself up. Therefore, I started to run myself some bath water.

The bathroom door was closed as I sat down into the water. I thought that the two of them would get the hint and leave, but they didn't. Co came to the door and cracked it open to get a peek. I quickly shielded myself with the shower curtains, asked him for some privacy, and hurried up out of the tub to put on some clothes.

Feeling refreshed, I went to confront the two guys again. "Hey, look, it's late and I'm ready for bed, so will you both please leave my residence?" Co looked surprised and Rendell was emotionless still, neither one responding as quickly as I'd hoped. "Yes, please go," I reiterated. Then Draco got up to walk to the door, and Rendell followed. I opened the door to let them out, and once they were completely outside, I shut the door and locked it.

Walking away from the door, I remember feeling a sense of internal warmth, a strong positive energy that radiated within me. That inner joy made me feel at ease, with a sense of assurance that my life would be back on the right track. I walked over to my sofa and dived into it, face first, and landed completely flat with my hands and arms to my sides. The sense of relief and joy, I was feeling at that moment was so intense, it felt like I was glowing.

I reached up for the remote control to turn on the TV, but could not find it. So, I got up from my comfortable spot to search for it. I lifted up all the pillows, looked underneath the couch, dug in the crevices of the sofa and the loveseat. I searched on and around the TV, the end table, but that remote was nowhere to be found. Then I thought, *Draco stole it!* The paranoid effects of smoking weed had taken over, and I charged outside. To my surprise, Ren and Co were still parked outside my apartment. A good ten minutes had passed already since they had left. And there they were still here, just sitting in Co's El Camino, right in front of my living room window.

Without getting too close to the car, I yelled, "Do you have my TV remote?"

"What?" Co said.

I repeated, "My remote control to the TV, do you, have it?"

Without answering, Co stepped out the car and walked toward me, and Rendell followed him. Seeing the two, I walked back toward the apartment and stopped just behind the front door threshold. Co and Rendell came back to the apartment and met me where I stood. I asked again, "Did you take my remote control?"

"What, your TV remote?" Co responded with a strange look on his face.

"Yes, I can't find it anywhere, and I left it lying on the couch where you sat."

Draco looked at this as another opportunity to bring up

the threesome. "Are we going to do this or not?" he said with irritability in his voice.

Still standing by the door, I said, "No! Now, stop asking me!"

Draco, in frustration, turned to Rendell and said, "Man, fuck this bitch!" Stunned by his choice of words, I took a step back.

Rendell then grabbed me, shuffling me behind him, putting himself between Co and me, saying, "Co, don't do her like that."

My mouth dropped, and a sense of annoyance came over me. Now, Rendell wanted to say something in my defense? The entire time he had been here, listening to Draco consistently badger me about this damn threesome. And there he was, in the middle of it all, and never said a word against it. At any time, he could've stepped up and made the decision to leave or tell Co to lay off it, but he didn't.

I got so upset, the rebellious side of me got to fuming. I felt that I wouldn't even be in this situation if Rendell hadn't been that tag-along friend in the first place. If it was just Co standing outside, my door would have stayed closed, and I would have remained unbothered. However, Rendell did agree to go along with Co; there we stood.

And I got angry, so I said, "Fuck it!"

D.D. Ways

CHAPTER FORTY-SEVEN

Now, it has always been in me to be somewhat of a daredevil (a D.D., as I like to call it). To take risks or challenges that did not suit me was just a part of my nature. I was not a thrill-seeker. However, when the opportunity presented itself, at times I would pass on the urge, but most of the time, I wouldn't. When I gave in to the instinct, I did feel a sense of eagerness; and when I succeeded in the task, beating the odds only added to my excitement. Those thrills stirred inside me even as a small child.

Depending on the type of dare, for the most part, I have managed to come out unscathed. However, there have been times when I've simply bit the dust. Luckily though, that's all it's mostly been, never breaking a bone or even knowing what it's like to have a nosebleed. Just me brushing off the dirt and healing from a bruise or two, or a cut. Nonetheless, in spite of my agility and quick reflexes, I have been left with scars. Some have been superficial ones, but as I've gotten older, I have found that the deeper and more profound scars are the ones you cannot see. Scars created from challenges that went beyond bodily ones.

My very first daredevil experience happened when I was about five years old. I remember it just as clearly as it was yesterday. It was a school morning, and my mother was up early gathering our clothes and preparing them for the day. She was getting herself ready for another work day, and me for kindergarten.

That morning, I recall sitting near the headboard when I detected the danger. I was positioned upright, with my legs crisscross on top of the bed. Observing as my mom paced back and forth down the bedroom hallway, grabbing this and that. I patiently and quietly sat there, with my chin in the palm of my left hand while resting my elbow on top of my left bent knee. My head swayed from left to right, back and forth as my eyes were fixated on my mother's every move. In one hand she had her blouse; in the other hand she had one or two of my garments. In the midst of her scurrying about, I noticed the iron positioned upright in the center the bed. And I knew that it was scorching hot. Mother had been ironing our clothes and forgot to turn the iron off as she scurried about.

Suddenly, I got this bright idea. I'd see if I could do a complete circle around the heated iron plate without tipping it over. In my mind, I would go around the iron as if I were a crouching, ferocious panther hunting my prey. Fully aware of the risk of getting burned, I was still excited by the challenge. Therefore, I committed myself to the daring attempt of encircling the steaming hot iron.

I got on all fours, with only the palm of my hands and knees touching the bed. My feet were tilted upward, making no contact with the mattress. My hands and knees acted as my paws. Then I set out on my quest as I cat-prowled toward that iron like a ferocious jungle cat that had only to feed on its mind.

Taking my time with every move, I curved my body around the scorching object. As I turned and arched my body encircling it, I could feel the steaming heat coming off the iron plate, yet it stayed in place. I kept an eye on the fiery object with every methodical step I made. Just two paces away from achieving my goal, I got a sudden burst of confidence—or you could say cockiness—and thought to myself, *this is easy-peasy.*

At that moment, I was so close to making a complete circle around the hot iron when something shifted. I laid my right palm down, which supported most of my weight, then leaned my left shoulder downward, and pressed forward in preparation of making that last step. Consequently, the weight of my body indented the mattress and caused the heated iron to fall forward. The tip of its soleplate came right down on my left shoulder, and I heard a sizzle. Immediately, I turned from a prowling panther to a paralyzed, hurt cub and let out this screeching cry.

My mother ran right in, quickly removed the iron from my shoulder and picked me up to comfort me. Aggravated from the intense, burning pain, I was inconsolable. Her cuddling made it hurt worse. I looked over at my shoulder and saw the top of it was oozing blood; I cried even harder. With my face drenched with tears, my mother steadily held me in her arms as she rocked me from side to side. Exhausted from crying, but still in a considerable amount of pain, I lay my head on her shoulder, and I recall thinking, *mission failed.*

My mother tended to my wound, got me dressed and sent me off to school. I remember playing that day with limited abilities, not my usual rambunctious self on the playground. I didn't play hard or run fast during recess as I normally would.

I was a wounded warrior. Unfortunately for me, that powder blue, long-sleeved, buttoned blouse my mom chose for me that day had no give to it. That tight sleeve pressed on that wound, constantly reminding me of what I had done. No matter how I tried to loosen or stretch that sleeve from off my injured shoulder, nothing worked; so all during that day, I tried just not to move it.

As the days went by, I looked forward to being fully healed. The perpetual shoulder discomfort made it difficult to forget about all this agony that my daring act brought me. It took some time for that shoulder to mend too. It was tender for weeks, even after the scab was formed. It seemed like as the pain subsided, I would start back roughhousing and reinjure it. Not being careful, I'd fool around and scrape that scab right off again, and there I'd go, starting the healing process all over again.

I eventually became very mindful of that impaired shoulder of mine. It continued to bother me up until the scab was completely dried and the underneath skin had formed. By that time, I was highly protective of that delicate area. I let that scab be, to the point where it just flaked away. When the burn did heal fully, it left me a scar to remember it by; a perfect triangle, the precise geometric size of the tip of that iron soleplate. I got branded for life.

Even to this day, that scar is present. It is slightly darker than my normal skin tone. When I was six, the scar stretched across my entire arm, whereas now, less than half of it, but it's still smack dab in the center. Occasionally, the inconspicuous scar still manages to catch my eye, reminding me of that fearless and daring task which caused me such agonizing pain over 35 years ago.

Another D.D. moment of mine was when I was about seven. Big Mama had all her grandkids over. And like always, when we all got together, there was no telling what crazy things would transpire for the sake of having fun (good times). On this particular day I do not recall what happened to have caused us all to get in trouble, but somehow we managed to do just that.

What I do remember is that all the grandkids were standing in line to get their whipping, with me included. I think I may have been fourth in line, anticipating that dreadful moment. I recall my two older cousins, Pedy and Anthony, were first up. Big Mama had that shoe in hand and stood in front of the door with it wide open. The sunshine was beaming through as she was tearing up their butts up with that shoe. I looked on frightened as they screamed and hollered. Their faces were glistening with tears, each one gyrating around in one spot, trying to avoid the blows.

One by one, they took their lashing and stepped aside for the next to go up, making it closer for me to encounter the agony. I stood there, plotting how I was going to get myself out of this predicament. Finally, it was my turn. My heart was beating so hard, it felt like it was outside of my chest, and I could feel it through my eardrums

Big Mama said, "Come on, your turn." I took a giant

gulp and made a step forward. I looked to my right where Big Mama was waiting for me with the shoe in her hand. Then I turned my head to the left, and there was the doorway to outside. I took another step onward as if I was going toward Big Mama, and then made a sudden dash out the front door with no clue as to where I was going. Running out of the yard, I didn't know how far I had to go; all I knew at that moment was to run, and as fast as I could.

Big Mama must have sought Pedy and Anthony after me, because I looked back and they were hot on my trail. I had a good distance between me and them until I stepped into the water meter hole and fell straight to my knees. I quickly got back up, but didn't have enough time to achieve that same momentum, and before I knew it, my cousins had caught up to me. Each of the boys took an arm and dragged me back to the house. Big Mama stood in the doorway waiting for them to bring me back. When they finally got me back in the house, Big Mama took that shoe and gave me several lashes with it. I took the blows and remember thinking it didn't hurt all that bad. I certainly was crying up a storm though, but mostly out of fear.

Later that evening, my cousins were in the den and talking about how I ran from Big Mama. They couldn't believe I did that. In their eyes, that was a bold D.D. move. Although I didn't find anything funny about it, my cousins joked and laughed for hours in disbelief on what had taken place: "Olivia ran from Big Mama!"

As an adult, I realize that those daredevil mannerisms were somehow correlated to the rebellious side of me. The other part, that does not play safe, gives me such a rush; but also provokes insubordinate thinking at times. On that day at Cheyenne Park, despite those clear warnings to discard that piece of paper with that number written on it, when I chose to keep it, I was being defiant against God. Leaning to my own understanding, doing the opposite of what I should have—that was me subconsciously challenging God. This resulted in me having multiple scars, heartfelt ones. Of all the risks I've taken, that one by far was the most critical and daring choice I have ever made.

I remember thinking that day, *What's the worst that could happen? If Rendell and I are meant to be together, we'll be.*

At that moment, my nineteen-year-old mind could not possibly fathom all the heartache and betrayal that waited for me in the future. However, the Angels knew. And I later, would find out the hard way what they were attempting to safeguard me from.

You see, when I kept that number in my hand, I was no longer under God's divine protection regarding the matter. By doing the opposite of what He directed of me, I exposed myself to the evil snares of this world. And it first began when I invited that snake into my home. Completely oblivious as to what scheme Draco had already hatched under his sleeve before I even called. I thought if I was honest and upfront with everything, he would be too but ... Angels don't warn for nothin'.

That Night

CHAPTER FORTY-EIGHT

That night as I stood on the floor of my living room, infuriated by my surrounding conditions, I became defiant against my own regard. I put myself at risk. Convinced that I needed to see this man prove he had love for me. It was critical for Rendell Schwann to act upon what was truly in his heart. So, I let my D.D. ways take hold; and my contrary nature reared its ugly head on that night when I said, "Fuck it."

That was the first (and last) time I ever resorted to anything like that. It was like I threw all the playing cards on the table, with nothing to lose. Knowing good darn well, I had a whole hell of a lot to lose. Along with my dignity, favor, and true love, there was a host of things that I was chancing. Everything was on the line. My neck was out there, and I needed Rendell to save me that night.

I desperately wanted Rendell to speak up and do what was right in his heart. If he truly cared at all for me, at that moment on that night, I needed for him to show it—make it be known how much I meant to him. Let me hear his voice be vocal about the sincerity he had in his heart for me. I needed to be reminded that his heart was made to love me. I wanted Rendell to outright refuse to allow me to go through with this. I anticipated that he would pull me aside and say, "Olivia, don't do this!"

But he didn't.

After I agreed, Draco looked at me, then back toward Ren, and a smile crept onto his face. I looked at Rendell. He was quiet again. He had that deflated look back on his face. That same expression he had all night, like someone had burst his bubble. I saw no heroism in his eyes, as if there was no war left to fight. If that manful attempt to save the day was all Ren had, when Co disrespectfully called me out, then why did he let it get this far?

As that rebellious nature of mine revealed itself, it pitted out the grounds I stood on. And despite the words that were blurted out of my mouth, I still had no earthly desire to do such a thing ever with these two men. Although I was vexed with confusing thoughts and emotions that night, I had to be shown where I stood in the heart of this man. Rendell had to show his want through body language and verbiage.

Even though I was toying with it, my life was not a game. However, I wanted Rendell to make me understand that he was serious about me. Regardless of all the baseless grief he caused me with his indefensible and irrational behavior, I wanted Ren to confess his feelings. I needed to see the emotion in his eyes, that he truly cared for me. I wanted to feel the passion of his embrace protect and surround me.

But he didn't show it that night.

Therefore, I put myself out on the ledge. In doing so, I was indirectly challenging Rendell to stand for what he wanted while simultaneously jeopardizing my crown. Putting at high risk the threat of my dignity and respect being lost in the eyes of the man whose love and embrace I only yearned for. This was a daring showdown that could go incredibly right or extremely wrong.

If Ren did not step up and intervene, he could potentially become nothing to me. Just as his angry actions made me feel that I was nothing to him, when he wigged out on me for no justifiable cause. Those demeaning and unnecessary feelings of resentment weighed heavily on me. Because this very man had once whispered in my ear that he saved all his love for me, while making endearing love to my body. This exact one, who created a deep bond between us in ways unknown to me and perhaps even to him, had also caused us to rupture.

This same man with his own seething tongue, in an instant and with no regard to my heart feelings, turned his back to me and shunned my presence repeatedly. As if what we shared was a figment of my imagination, unshared by him.

So, I placed Rendell in a position of scrutiny. I wanted him to attest to his feelings for me. Therefore, I placed myself in an uncompromising situation, a daring move that put our future hopes, love and togetherness at stake.

That Night II

CHAPTER FORTY-NINE

Defying a clear and present message sent from the Lord got me caught up and led to that night too. If I had not kept that number, Draco would not have had a direct point of contact to me. There would not have been a way for him to interfere between Rendell and me. It did not matter that I was noble or my intentions were innocent for Draco in the beginning. And regardless of my feelings for Rendell, Draco already had an agenda, which is why he offered his number to me in the first place. Calling that number gave Draco access to me, enabling him to plot his motives.

It was completely foolish of me to think, I could control a situation where I was totally oblivious to all outside factors involved. This triangular web that I had gotten myself tangled into was a clear example of confounding variables. Draco was the lurking variable that influenced the state of affairs between Rendell and me, the independent and dependent variable. The association that Draco had with us both, caused the correlating bond that Rendell and I shared, to be distorted. The connection between Rendell and I was now permeated with confusion and shame. It shook up the authenticity of our relationship; provoking a spurious union. Concealing our true feelings for one another.

Prior to that night, I thought that Co and I could at least be cool with one another. However, I learned that you can't be cool with snakes—and that's how that night, too, came about. I stood there in between these two men, one who had my heart so strongly, it pierced my soul, and the other a regrettable tie that had been newly undone. Yet, I was annoyed at Rendell for coming over to my home with Draco in the first place. The thought of it, got me angry even more, releasing that rebellious side in me, and so I gave them what they came for. Sort of.

Draco took things a step further. He said to us, "Ok, well, you two go in the back first, and I'll join in a little later." Like two deer in headlights, Rendell and I looked up and without saying a word, we walked back into the bedroom. After entering, I closed the door behind us, still thinking that Ren would stand up and put a stop to this. But he didn't.

I sat on the bed in front of him, and what did he do? He unbuckled his pants and whipped it out. I sat back and pushed his narrow behind to the side, like, *get out of my face*. In our relationship, we didn't even get the opportunity to explore each other in that way, and he thought it was about to be that kind of action now? No sir! Besides, by the looks of things, it was evident that Rendell really didn't want to be there either. Yet, instead of speaking from his heart and doing what was right, he conformed to the fiasco.

The room was quiet. I sat on the bed fully clothed and looked at Ren, who just stood there with his pants unzipped and head drooped low, looking sad. I thought we meant more to each other than this. His heart was obviously not in it, so then why didn't Ren step up to the plate to save the day? It was obvious that he didn't want to be in that situation, yet there he was anyway.

Then Draco barged in to have his way. "Ok, now it's my turn," he said, rubbing his hands together, like he was in the woods, trying to start a fire. I stood up and stepped away from him, and ended up by the corner wall. Draco, excited, went around to the side of the bed. "Now, you know I like to feel that pussy!" he said, taking off his clothes and laying on my bed.

I stood in the corner, watching. Then Rendell reached for me, pushed me toward the bed and pulled off my pants. Now naked, I stood there, numb and unresistant, not sure what to do or think.

Rendell gave me another shove. "Go on," he said. "You know you like that big dick!"

At that moment, I thought, *Well, it's not like I am a stranger to it.* So, I got on the bed and climbed onto Co. I sat on top of him motionless, which was very unlike me. Somehow, I was unphased by what was happening. Then, Rendell put his weight on my shoulders, pressing my body down on Co's dick, as if he wanted me to be hurt by it. Draco, laying horizontally beneath me, had intercepted us once again.

Shortly after, I quickly got off of Co and told them to leave. "Ok, get out," I said boldly. I grabbed my robe to put on, and watched them scurry out my room and walk to the door. At that time, I felt no emotion. No feelings of anger or shame, even though I had acquiesced to that little red devil that sat on my shoulder. There was no guilt. I felt nothing. It was just like, *Ok, you got what you wanted. Now get the 'F' out.*

Reaching for the door, I opened it and they both stepped out, then turned to face me, standing shoulder to shoulder as if they were waiting for me to say something. I closed the door in their faces. Still standing at the door, I thought about what had just transpired. Then I turned around and fell back against the door as if it was catching me in mid-faint. I rested my right hand on my forehand, and said, "Now, I'll never get back with Rendell."

Then I walked over to the sofa and flopped myself on it. And lo and behold, I found the remote control after all that. It was a spiritual setup.

Day After

CHAPTER FIFTY

That night when I agreed to that foolishness, I didn't feel any kind of remorse. It was as if I had no conscience, or a hardened heart. However, the next day was a different story. It was like God had clenched His fist a little bit tighter. I was pressed with so much guilt and shame, I could barely lift my head up. If I had thought the glass had been cracked before that night, it had most certainly been shattered now. With shards of glass scattered everywhere. I cried in sincere remorse and pleaded for God to forgive me yet again.

Devastated and deeply ashamed, I stepped outside my apartment for some fresh air to aid with my mental process. I looked up to the sky. It was filled with dark clouds. I felt the sky was displaying God's disappointment in me. I could feel that He was frowning down upon me with every step I made. The weight of the shame loomed over my shoulders as if it was physically weighing me down, and it literally made it hard for me to even look up.

The confidence and stamina that I was slowly rebuilding had now been all stripped away. Again, I was back feeling stuck in a hopeless situation, where I could not see the light of day despite it being all around me. Pondering on everything that had taken place within the last twenty-four hours, I didn't know how or when I'd be able to hold my head up high again, much less come face to face with Rendell.

Feeling the guilt of my actions to the core, I knew that I had made another huge blunder. I let my Holy Father down yet again, and as a result, I let myself down too. Moreover, due to my rebelliousness, I'd managed to create burdens deeper than I had been presently dealing with.

Still outside, I decided to walk over to Tina's place. I had suddenly felt an irresistible urge to disclose what had happened on that night after she left. The guilt was weighing on me, and I needed some sort of alleviation. When I got to Tina's place, we stood together by the stairway. She could tell by the way I was looking that I was terribly disturbed by something.

"What's wrong?" she asked.

Feeling defeated and devastated, it took a moment for me to gather myself and speak. In a low tone, I said, "We had a threesome."

"Huh, who?" she responded with a woolly expression on her face.

I answered, "Me, Ren and Co." I then sat down on the stairs and dropped my head in my lap. I went on to explain to Tina how I could feel God's disappointment with me. I said, "Look! Look at the sky."

She looked up; her gaze went from side to side, then back fixated on me, a blank look came on her face. "What is it? What about the sky? Liv, it's just a cloudy day."

Which it was; the sky was covered with greyish-black clouds. However, what I felt at that time— I could assure those dark clouds was exemplary of God's discontentment with me. I could feel it through and through.

Nonetheless, I refrained from elaborating more on the subject, because I could tell from her confused facial expression, Tina really didn't get it. She would have deemed me temporarily insane if I had spoken more on the matter. Although it helped somewhat to divulge my darkest secret to a trusted friend, I knew that this was a situation that I would have to get through all on my own.

Imbroglio

CHAPTER FIFTY-ONE

Hours turned into days and days turned into weeks, as I dwelt in my apartment mentally beating myself up. The troublesome thoughts of what had taken place filled up every corner in my mind. I wasn't answering any calls. I wasn't out visiting anyone. And my poor child—I can't even recall if he was over to his grandmother's or at home with me.

During that tumultuous season, I was still very much involved with O'Rian. Although he knew neither of the two other men, or what had transpired that night, our relationship suffered severely. Due to the depth of shame, I felt after that disgraceful night; I could not openly and wholeheartedly look O'Rian in his eyes and genuinely smile. I was guilt-stricken from my destructive actions, so much so that it ate at my conscience. And that caused me to be very withdrawn and unhappy within that relationship.

The days O'Rian came around, he saw that I was extremely reserved, certainly not my usual self with him. He asked questions, but I avoided any conversation that would lead to me revealing the horrendous truth. He asked if it was something he had done. I'd look at him with a stale expression on my face and shake my head no, then walk away. Leaving him where he stood, which was absolutely clueless on every level, and I'm sure emotionally hurt too. But what could I have said to him?

Either way I was in the wrong. If O'Rian had known the entirety of what happened that night, he assuredly would have left me anyway. Therefore, without the truth being said, the dynamics of the relationship significantly declined.

The third week in, I was still in a funk. O'Rian and I were at odds still, which was no surprise. I still felt stand-offish and shamed, but I decided to get out of the apartment for a change. My upstairs neighbor had moved into a house, and she invited me to her housewarming party. We became friends a couple months later when I moved into the apartment. The neighbor's name was Mo; she had a son around the same age as my son, and his name was Delorean. Mo was super tall, slim and highly fair-skinned. She kept her hair cut short, like Mia Farrow in the movie, *Rosemary's Baby*. The hairstyle suited her very well.

Being the small world that it is, Mo's boyfriend happened to be related to Rendell. Go figure. I thought to self, Rendell and I could have been kickin' it with them as a couple, if things had not taken a turn for the worse. I didn't even know of their relation until after the chaos, but despite how I was feeling, I went ahead and accepted the invitation.

Getting out into the sunshine, I headed over to Mo's new place. I pulled up alongside the curb and parked on the street. Walking up to the yard, to my surprise, I saw Rendell standing on the side of his car that was parked in the driveway. He was talking with his best friend Sean, who was sitting in the passenger seat with one leg hanging out of the truck. Seeing Rendell for the first time since that night, my heart dropped. I took a deep breath and continued to walk toward the house.

Sean, looking excited to see me, yelled my name, "Liv!" He had returned home from college sooner than everyone expected. I walked over and paused in front of them, causing Rendell and me to come face to face; neither of us said much at first. Sean blurted out, "Where have you been?"

Still not feeling like myself, I couldn't really give him an answer due to the circumstances. Then suddenly Rendell uttered, "We ran the train on Olivia!"

I raised my head so quick to yell, "No, you did not!"

Sean, with this now shocked and confused look on his face, gazed back and forth at the both of us and said boldly, "What happened!?"

Then Rendell went on to say, "Co fucked Olivia!"

I countered his statement by saying, "You broke up with me!" Then I turned away from them both, leaving them where they were and vigorously walked away. While doing so, I allowed the steam to ease off of me as I entered Mo's home.

Despite the fact that Rendell brought that trouble to my doorstep by accompanying him, I placed all the burden and fault on myself. I too had a simple choice in the matter. Instead of doing the noble thing, I submitted to the anger, mischief and inevitably that little devil that sat on my left shoulder. As a woman, that decision cost me enormously. It led me to being momentarily stripped of my rightful crown. It shredded my pride and severely altered my state of worthiness for myself and in the eyes of the only man my heart and soul deeply desired. I felt very low about myself for what I succumbed to; it was in fact, the lowest point of my life to this day.

Several weeks went by, and I still felt down in the dumps. I found myself in a lost and hopeless state. I looked to man to console my grief as opposed to staying firm within the Lord. I felt the need to confide in another who knew of my conviction. Like in the past, I wanted something or someone to mask the pain that I felt stirring up inside. That weakened mental state caused me to feel dispirited, which eventually led me to returning to desperate measures.

Which in turn, reopened the door to Draco Scoria, and he gladly waltzed right back in.

Weaning

CHAPTER FIFTY-TWO

There I was on the living room sofa, sulking and wallowing in my catastrophic actions, when I got a knock at the door that diverted my attention from the television. "Who is it?" I yelled from the couch, trying to avoid getting up. The voice was muffled, but I could distinguish that it was a male. I got up to look through my peephole.

Draco?

If I had been in better spirits, I would have avoided him altogether. However, because I felt so low, like I had nothing else to lose, I yielded to that weakness and unfastened the door.

Draco entered the apartment and sat on the loveseat across from where I was sitting. I slumped back on the couch and just looked at him. I wasn't in any mood to hide what I was going through. And Draco could clearly see that I was going through something. He asked how I was doing. I gave him a lackluster response.

Then he said to me, "What happened that night, that don't bother me."

I asked him, "What do you mean?" I repositioned myself to be more attentive to what he was saying.

"You know, that shit don't make a difference to me. I

know you're cool. You ain't a hoe or nothing."

From that comment, I knew he was implying that he wanted to start back where we left off. He may have talked some more; I do not recall what he said. However, for some reason, the feeling of acceptance despite of my shortfalls comforted me. And just like that, Co eased his way back into my good graces once more.

Draco and I got reacquainted with each other very quickly. He was cool on the surface, but I knew there was a dark side to him that drove his actions, which was totally opposite of my nature. Like before, amongst our many conversations, Draco would plot a scheme to rob one of the doctors I worked with. Flabbergasted at his thought process, I would of course decline his outlandish plots and instead persuade him to go about things the right way.

One day, one of our conversations was about him and me becoming a couple. We were talking about something, and Draco brought it up again about being his woman. Now before, the answer was an instant no. However, this time, the question took up a little energy. I actually thought about it.

I knew Draco was a street guy and apparently a thief too, which in both cases led to nowhere. I knew that he had four kids already with multiple baby moms, and he smoked cigarettes. Draco was nothing remotely like the ideal kind of man I wanted in my life or could see myself with for eternity. The only positive was that the sex was good.

With deep consideration, I gave Draco a proposition. He sat across from me and listened attentively to what I had to say. I looked over at him, sighed and said, "I will be your woman, but only if you stop with the fast-money, street business. You can go back to school, get a job or do whatever you have to do to survive the right way, but you cannot be my man and be about those streets too."

Co gave me a blank stare and said, "I'll think about it."

I said, "Ok, I'll give you some time." Then he got up to leave for the night.

I may have given in to foolish ways, but I wasn't a fool or that crazy. I knew of the uncertainties of that lifestyle along with the risk, the dangers of losing my freedom and well-being. If I got into a relationship with Draco, for it to have any hope of being a successful one, Jesus would have to be all in it. That meant he had to leave the street life behind and start flying right as well as occasionally attending a church service. If he was serious about being with me, at least I gave him a fair chance and a choice in the matter.

After about a week or so, Co gave me a call. He asked to come over so we could finish the discussion we started the week before, and I consented. He arrived less than an hour later, came in and sat on the edge of the sofa. He said, "You know, I thought long and hard about what you said; and I came really close to deciding to the leave the streets, but I can't do it. I'm not going to stop selling… I can't give up my money."

I said, "Ok, the choice is made." I wasn't hurt by his decision or bothered the least bit, because I knew Draco and I weren't meant to be with each other to begin with.

Spending time with Draco only alleviated the heartache

momentarily, and what I needed was a permanent solution. The urge of desiring something with substance made its way back to the forefront of my mind and heart, but most importantly I wanted my peace to return. I understood that to achieve that, I had to first clean my slate once again.

Therefore, I decided to cut out everything bad in my life. I stopped drinking alcohol and smoking weed. I enrolled myself in school, and cut the cord with Draco.

The Light in Darkness

CHAPTER FIFTY-THREE

Amongst the haze, I still had to push through, maintain everyday life and take care of my child. At that time, De-Lon was dealing with a skin condition. He had these little bumps that caused his skin to be irritated and itchy. I had an Rx ointment that I was applying regularly, but sometimes that wouldn't help the itchiness. Although DeLon's problem was just on the surface, it still bothered me naturally. As a mother, you don't want your child to undergo any pain or hurt whatsoever, and my son was miserable that night.

On a night that I was treating my baby's condition, something out of the ordinary came about. His skin was more irritated than normal. After I rubbed the topical ointment on his skin and put him to bed, I went into the living room, feeling overwhelmed with all that was going on. Right where I stood, I started to pray and said the most unusual thing. With tears in my eyes and a very sincere heart I asked the Lord to heal my baby. I said, "Lord, just touch him with Your big toe."

Now, I don't know why I said big toe of all things. I could have said thumb, finger or pinky; however, instead I said, "big toe." I'm not sure, perhaps I was thinking it would be more convenient for God to extend his leg and tap us with the tip of His toe as opposed to Him bending over to stretch forth His arm.

Amazingly enough, I got a response.

I went to bed around the same time as usual. DeLon was sound asleep as I got into bed right next to him. I situated myself underneath the covers in our queen-sized bed, making it comfortable enough for me to close my eyes for a good night's rest. Not long after, I heard this noise that sounded exactly like electrostatic. As I opened my eyes, I was astonished to see this glorious, massive beam, brighter than the sun. This vivid, radiant energy filled the space from ceiling to floor and stretched forth about four feet from the corner of the room. I had turned off every light in the apartment yet this divine, luminous energy lit up the entire room.

In shock at what I was seeing, my first reaction was no reaction. My head was already down, due to being curled into a fetal position when I fell asleep. Therefore, I did not look directly into the radiant light. However, I was able to see the luminous rays in my peripheral vision as I gazed at the object that was in my direct view when initially opening my eyes. I was completely riveted by what I was witnessing.

The next thing I noticed is that I was feeling completely naked. Lying there, my body felt entirely exposed. I spent the next thirty or forty seconds trying to cover myself up. Laying on my side, my left arm was reaching down for covers, but although I was going through the motions, I could not get a hold of anything to cover my bare body. Then I finally realized, although it absolutely felt that way, I wasn't naked. I had my pajamas on, and I was underneath the covers.

I lay there stunned by what I was encountering, and I wanted to look up, but I was afraid. I thought that if I did, I would see in the center of this light had a lion's head with fire surrounding it. Also, I was fearful that if I looked straight into the lucid beam, my hair would turn totally white; like Moses's hair did with the burning bush. However, I started to feel ashamed, because I did plead for my son to be touched and healed. And there I was, more concerned with covering my nakedness and mentally psyching myself out with fear instead of staying focused on the matter at hand—my son's skin condition. During that moment, I could have at least reached into the beam and allowed the light to touch me; however, I did not. I remained still and only said a silent prayer for healing and after so long, the gleaming light disappeared.

After that phenomenon, I immediately checked DeLon and me for any changes. I looked over at him; DeLon appeared to be asleep still, so I didn't want to bother him too much. However, I did examine his skin, and the rashes were still there. I got up and looked in the mirror; I appeared and felt the same too, no white hairs. However, I would later find one white hair in the corner of my right eye adjacent to my nose. Horrified by that small finding, I tried to pluck the hair out, but it hurt trying to remove it, so I left it alone.

Still in awe of that supernatural encounter, the next day I went to work and shared my experience. I confided in two of my coworkers at the medical clinic where I worked part-time. One was Angie, a nurse there who later became a good a friend. The other was Dr. Algie, the part-time, older doctor who really didn't see any patients, but rather lent medical advice.

When I told Angie about it, she did not believe me. She

said, "Maybe it was a headlight of someone's car that shined through the window." It was a rational response. However, there was no window on that side of room in the corner by my headboard.

Then I informed Dr. Algie of what I had seen; he believed me. He replied, "Sounds like you had something there," and I did. Dr. Algie was right. I encountered something extraordinarily amazing.

I would later find out that I wasn't alone with the experience either. My son, DeLon, witnessed it too. Later on, when I found myself telling him the story, to my surprise, DeLon revealed that he saw it too.

Looking back, though, I wish I had at least reached into the light. Although the beam was so intensely bright and I felt so piercingly bare in its midst, I could have at least tried to touch it. I could have kept my head down and extended my arm towards it, instead of being stiff with fear of the unknown. After that divine experience, for months my mind wondered. Was that God's big toe?

Enlightened Testimony

CHAPTER FIFTY-FOUR

Besides those two co-workers, the only other time I shared my story was at a Bible Conference. A friend of mine, named Shaina, invited me to it. She asked me to come along, so I accepted. The church revival was out in East Tulsa, if I remember correctly. It was held underneath—what else—a huge, white tent.

Shaina and I both needed some Gospel rejuvenation. While you already know of my troubles, Shaina's issues were something totally on a deeper level. She was a cute, but very mouthy girl who had a reputation of being loose. Shaina was a hairstylist, a very talented one, I might add. She fell in the category of being young, ignorant and misguided, like most of us. She was going through her daily drama with her baby daddy, men in general, and female jealousies or what have you. Plus, it didn't make matters better that she was a beautician working in a salon, because that was a central location for all the latest gossip to be exposed. If you wanted to be up on the news in the streets, you went to get your hair slayed. Furthermore, being in that environment daily, Shaina seemed to always be ruffled about something.

On the outside, Shaina looked like the type of chick I'd want to kick it with. She was some years older than me and appeared to have some assurance about herself, which

ANGELS DON'T WARN FOR NOTHIN'

I liked. I wanted to go out and be part of the club scene, which was her thing too. I loved to dance, which was always my motivation to go, and basically, I wanted a friend to be social with. After a few times of asking to hang out with her, Shaina finally agreed. We clubbed a few times, went to parties, drank Seagram's 7 and 7 Up on the weekends and just had fun.

On the flip side, Shaina seemed to always be tied to unnecessary drama. That, in turn, led to her feeling burdened and in need of some spiritual uplifting, which is why she invited me to attend this revival with her. And I gladly accepted.

It was a perfect day for an outdoor revival meeting. The sun was shining, and there was a nice, cool breeze that pervaded the tent. I don't recall feeling sweaty or uncomfortable; the sensation of being there in that weather was wonderful. The evangelist was a tall, slender Black man. Regretfully, I do not recall his name, but I do remember he wasn't bad-looking. Shaina and I sat there and listened to this man give everyone his insights on life and how it correlated to the Biblical scriptures he read.

A couple of things stood out to me. After the evangelist read a few scriptures from the Bible, he broke it down and said, "Sometimes to maintain progress, you have to go about things the unconventional way."

The other thing that stood out was when he started prophesying over a handful of people. He randomly would select people out of the crowd—and I was one of them. The evangelist pointed to me and instructed me to come in front of the congregation where he stood, and I did. I got up there and he said to me, "You must be with someone on your level or higher."

At the age of twenty, I did not fully comprehend what he was saying. At first, I thought, *Ok, I'll date a doctor or someone educationally advanced than me*. However, living throughout the years, I would later realize that the message the evangelist gave me was deeper than what I initially understood.

Listening to the evangelist and how he prophesied over people propelled me to want to share my divine intervention encounter, the best way I could at the time. I gathered the nerve to get up and volunteer with sharing my experience. However, my delivery was not the best; in fact, it was just borderline ok. I was so nervous being in front of all those people and speaking, I was extremely jittery. (Even as I write about the recollection of it, I feel a knot forming in my throat).

As I began to tell my story, an uncontrollable nervous laugh started to interject after so many words of me describing my experience. I couldn't even speak a full sentence, much more verbalize a complete thought. I'm sure hearing me speak of my encounter, that evangelist was like, *Ok, anyone past high school level will do for her*. Eventually I finished my story and went back to my seat next to Shaina.

Shaina looked at me and said, "Were you serious about that? Why were you laughing so much?"

All I could do was take a deep breath of relief, shake my head and shrug my shoulders, because I did at least complete my task. Although my delivery wasn't the best at that moment, it was a start.

In Between

CHAPTER FIFTY-FIVE

I was eager to get my life back on the right track. I would still hang out with friends, but refrained from many extracurricular activities. Rendell and I would see other at various events. It turned out we individually knew the same people and shared friends within our own circle after all. Therefore, there were plenty of times that I ran into him. He still captured my heart. And I could tell by the look in his eyes that I still had his as well. But neither of us took action on the matter during that time.

On the days that we'd see each other, Rendell and I would make small talk. He once asked me out of the blue, "Why do all of my friends gotta fuck my girlfriends?"

Taken aback, I didn't know what to say, because that did happen between me and his friend. Although it was not entirely my fault how things took a turn the way it did, I did; however, I took the brunt of the responsibility. Because, it was I who had been divinely warned and I still carried the guilt of that night, so I just kept silent and put my head down. Nonetheless, I did think to myself, *So, your friends have a history of having sex with your girlfriends? Who knew*? I sure didn't!

Perhaps that moment was an opportunity for me to be transparent with Rendell and share with him how deeply I cared for him and that I never intended for any of that mess to take place. However, the guilt from that night still taunted me. I felt like I was scarred with the scarlet red letter tattooed on my back and I couldn't speak up for anything concerning a relationship with Ren. Hearing him ask that question made me want to break down and cry, but I was all cried out. Those words were heart-rending to me. Nonetheless, how could I speak up and do so confidently with that shame lurking around me still? After a while of silence and no response from me, Rendell went on to another subject.

For a while, it seemed like Ren and I both could be content with just being friends, supportive ones at that. Once during school, Ren came up to check it out and see how I was doing. We chatted for bit and I walked him out. I could confide in him about certain things, and he'd give me his best advice. If I needed help with something, he'd make himself available to aid in whatever it was. He was just that type of guy.

Shortly after graduating from Platt with honors, earning my certificate in dental assisting, I got a job at a dental office. The same dental position that an instructor wanted another student to beat me out of; because I wouldn't go along with the grain. In the dental aid course, we had a small class, maybe about six or seven of us. We had the chatty Asian, the rich white blondie, the bitter divorcee with child, and a few single moms with multiple kids. Then there was me, the chill, quiet, single mom of one.

I chatted with everyone in the classroom. Everyone except Tessa, that is; she was the single mom with five kids and was oddly quiet. Her facial expression usually looked like someone had made her face the corner and sit there for about five hours. In class, Tessa just frowned about 80 percent of her 50 percent attendance rate. However, for the most part, everyone was respectively cool to one another. There was never any bickering of any sorts until that one day.

It was the day that Amanda, a single mom of two, disclosed to everyone in the classroom that she was dating a married man. Once those words drifted in the air, the atmosphere totally changed. It became anti-Amanda Day every day. Everyone in the classroom had their two cents to say about it, except me. I felt that although it was wrong, that was her business.

Now, I certainly did not condone that behavior at all, because if my husband cheated, I tell you, it wouldn't be nothin' nice. I'd beat a woman's head in and my dude's too, if I walked in and found my spouse being unfaithful. With that said, I preferred to stay in everyone's good graces and not cross that line. Nonetheless, it was a consensus amongst my peers and instructor to shun Amanda. As for me, I just kept my treatment of her as it was prior to me knowing of her adultery. I would later find out that even that was an issue.

Torri, the instructor, pulled me to the side one day and strongly suggested that I disassociate myself with Amanda. She made a sturdy claim as to why I should separate myself, making sure I knew what Amanda was doing on her own personal time. I nodded and said something like, "Yes, I am aware of what she does."

Still, I kept our friendship as it was. Why should I be judgmental? Besides, I kind of felt sorry for her, although she was the one who opened her big mouth and said something. Nobody else socialized with her. Amanda was totally ostracized, and I didn't feel that was right.

Well, because of my decision to go against the instructor's advice, she tried her damnedest to block me from getting that job where I applied. Torri sent another student, a white girl and supposedly the top student in another graduating class, to interview at the same location. When I went for my second interview, they told me the girl Torri sent over didn't even have her high school diploma. Hearing that shocked me; I didn't know it was possible to be a student there and not have a diploma.

Although Torri tried to intercept my employment with the office, I still got the job. When she found out, I could tell she was feeling some type of way about it, but that didn't make any difference to me. Torri couldn't control my employment status. However, she did have power over my student-of-the-year award. That award was presented to Tessa, the one who was absent from class the majority of the time. I'll bet even Tessa was surprised to get that recognition.

Nonetheless, Dr. Thorne and Associates seemed to be a good dental office to work at. There was a staff of about six, including me. The ages ranged from early twenties to thirties. Dr. Thorne was an American Indian dentist; about 5'7", nice-looking, and he wore braces. There was one hygienist, two other DAs, and one office manager, who I later found out was his wife. The dental office was in Northwest Tulsa, off West Edison Street. Right behind it was the Gilcrease Hills shopping center, the location of the convenience store and barber shop where Rendell saw me and grabbed me up, talking about how I was his "guest of honor"—smh.

Linked

Chapter Fifty-Six

There is an ancient Chinese belief about soul mates. It is said that there is an invisible red thread tied to the fingers of two people who are destined to be together and married. This thread represents a soul tie. The string can be stretched, tangled and knotted, but it will never be broken. For me, this Chinese folklore is very much a reality, because the bond that Rendell created between us still remained, despite how distant and twisted our connection had gotten.

It's a funny thing about those spiritual ties. Even when the paths are separated between the two, somehow one finds a way to be physically connected to the other and vice versa. I was sitting at the front office desk working at the Dr. Thorne's dental practice when doting Rendell Schwann came strolling in. Seeing him walk through those doors made my heart pound. I smiled at him, keeping my professional face intact, and greeted him.

"Welcome to Dr. Thorne's office. How can I help you?"

Rendell looked down at me sitting in my professional attire, smiled and said he'd like to make a dental appointment. I took down all his information and gladly made him one.

Dr. Thorne had felt that the front office was better suited for me, and I was cool with that. It later dawned on me that the office was primarily built for staff members under 5'6", short people. Being 5'8", I was always hitting my knees or hands on something in that office. Plus, when I got nervous at times, I became extra clumsy. Therefore, I didn't make the best impression as his chairside assistant, and ironically working front office suited me just fine for that moment.

A week later, Rendell made it to his dental appointment, and on time at that. He came from the back to check out with me after getting his teeth cleaned. He got a good report, no cavities, which made me happy. Even though our office didn't push for adults to get sealants on their molars, just because it wasn't covered by insurance, I still advised Rendell to get his teeth sealed. He took my advice and made another appointment to have it done.

At Rendell's last appointment before his six-month cleaning, he came in to have his sealants placed. I explained to him that this was a good investment, because sealants are a protective covering layered in the deep grooves of the teeth to prevent cavities from forming. Back then in 1998, it only cost $25 a pop, and it would last for years. Enlightened, Rendell gladly forked over the cash.

It was close to my lunch hour when Rendell checked out. I knew that it would be some time before I'd see him in the office again, so I decided to walk him out. We talked all the way to the parking lot and parted ways when Rendell got to his car. He stopped to get in his vehicle, while I kept walking, headed to the convenience store behind the office. All of a sudden, Rendell turned toward me and called my name.

"Olivia!"

Startled, I stopped in my tracks and turned around to

see what he wanted. Before I could say anything, he said, "Have my baby!"

"Huh?" I said, not expecting him to say anything like that.

Rendell repeated himself. "Have my baby."

At that moment, so many thoughts ran through my mind. I thought of my mother being a single parent of five children with different fathers; and I most certainly didn't want to mimic that. I once envisioned life having his kids, but that was with us being together as a couple. Never did I think to bear Rendell's children when we were apart.

Then I remembered how heavy the emotional aspect of carrying a child was for me—very depressing, especially with no one by my side. Then I returned my focus to Rendell, still standing there, patiently waiting to hear my answer. I wanted to ask him so badly, "What would it mean to have your child?" But I didn't. Instead, I smiled, sighed and just shook my head no, then walked away.

Days later, that question Rendell had asked still lingered in my head. I was driving down the street, my mind in deep thought, and spoke softly out loud, "Have his baby?" It took some time for it to sink in, because so much had happened between us. I never even fathomed being Rendell's baby mama, due to the fact that I solely was stuck on the natural course of being in a valid relationship with him that would eventually lead to being his wife.

Then a feeling came over me and I got excited. "Yes, I do want to have another baby." I quickly picked up my phone to call Rendell and tell him of my change of heart, but I could not get a hold of him. His cell phone kept going to his voicemail. After multiple failed attempts, doubtful thoughts worked their way to the forefront of my mind. Giving in to that second thought again, I let the excitement of bringing in a new life with Rendell slip away. I placed the idea to the back of my mind and went about my way.

Years would pass before the topic would be brought up again.

Adverse Effect

CHAPTER FIFTY-SEVEN

Working at Dr. Thorne's office was good. However, it would be the start of me realizing how much I didn't have in common with fellow peers. I was twenty years young, a single mom and starting my permanent job number two. Everyone in the office either didn't have any kids at that time, or were in significant relationships, or married. There were no check marks in my box for any of those categories.

Back then, business luncheons or outings were tax-deductible. Therefore, the office manager would pay for lunch occasionally or we'd get-together outside of the office for a business brunch. With the conversations around the table, all I could do was listen. Although I empathized with them fully, my ability to share was limited. I couldn't chime in with my own relatable experiences, because I had none. Perhaps if I were in a steady relationship, I could discuss couple issues or talk about all the couple's trips that were taken. However, that wasn't my reality. I took trips, but it usually involved my son and/or cousins.

Being in that environment, I saw the success of young college graduates, coupled and working together, black and white. However, instead of it inspiring me—it's sad to mention, but it made me regret that I had a child at such a young age. I, too, had aspirations of going to college right after high school. I looked into colleges like Texas Southern and

Prairie View A&M when I was pregnant. I wanted to be out of Oklahoma, but not too far away. However, those things just didn't come about for me.

Now, nothing ever stopped me from loving or caring for my child, of course. Nonetheless, I may have been stricter than what was required. Unhappy with myself, I was unhappy with him. I would fuss a lot and be really stern with my little boy as if he was a grown man. He was my little man, but a three, and a half year old, mini one. DeLon didn't have a clue as to what I was going through. How could he? All he knew was that his momma was mean.

Feeling bitter, it took me some time to shake off the resentment of my life choices. My precious child, during that forlorn period of my life, felt that I did not love him. When, in fact, he was my only inspiration. However, when life weighed on me, DeLon, being the only one and closest thing to me, felt the rippling effects of it. Instead of me loving freely on my baby, and with no hurt in the world, I was very guarded and stern.

Handling all the stressors of life, I either bottled up my emotions or vented in my own way. I had not one person to rely on. Or at least, no one close enough to entrust showing that vulnerable side of myself to. I rarely, if at all, asked for help with anything. What I couldn't afford on my own, I did without. It was a tough life, but I endured triumphantly through prayer, that one vital thing that stuck with me since I was a kid. I wasn't much of a churchgoer then, but I knew how to get on my knees and wholeheartedly pray.

In dealing with the burdens, I couldn't help but wonder

how things could have been. How much easier life would have been for both my son and me if Rendell had not been torn from our side. I recall a time or two where I had to work late, past the time of DeLon's aftercare program, and I called on Rendell to pick him up. No sweat off his back, Rendell gladly did it for me. That gave me a glimpse of how the pressures of life could have been eased with a helpmate.

However, the guilt from the past still was prevalent in my mind. Although the connection remained, with all that had gone down between us, I didn't think Rendell could love and honor me as his Queen as I needed him to. No matter how friendly we became with each other, months after that night, I was aware there was still this void, a black dot, that caused a gap between us that time alone could not bridge. As a result, I didn't want to be too reliant on something I felt would not be consistent or lasting in my life.

Therefore, I distanced myself from Rendell and dealt with all the strains of work, family and personal matters on my own. This left my beautiful child to seldom see his mother genuinely happy, and not in the best light, especially during those trying times.

Coping

CHAPTER FIFTY-EIGHT

After getting settled into my new job, I felt that my son and I had outgrown our first apartment. The telltale sign was when our clothes began accumulating on the backrest of the sofa in the living room, acting as extra closet space. DeLon was a year older, and I wanted him to have a yard to play in. Therefore, after six months of working at the private dental office, I started to look for us another place to reside.

I liked the Southwest Tulsa area, so I wanted to stay within that proximity. The location where we lived was cool: We had nearby highway access; it was closer to the Riverside bike trail located behind Westport, and it wasn't too far from the North side. Plus, on the Fourth of July, we had a clear view of the fireworks ignited in celebration. This grand, annual pyrotechnic display would be set off on the 21st Street Bridge just before sunset, and it would be a block away from where we lived. Overall, I developed a strong liking for the district, and I didn't want to be any-where else.

A year had passed at our apartment in Riverview Village for DeLon and me. And around that time, I had found us a decent two-bedroom duplex just three blocks away from our old apartment. It was closer to the highway. Plus, there was a really nice housing addition right across the street from it and a church a little, ways down. My landlord was named Frank, a strawberry-blond, curly-haired white man with a big, round plumber's belly. Because of my age, I had to convince him that I was a stable, low-risk tenant. He was highly doubtful at first, but within time, he was able to see firsthand that I would be a great tenant. I never threw any parties or had a lot of company. It was simply a place for my son and me, to live in; our personal space to call home; which was a delight, considering our past circumstances.

Transitioning from the apartment to the duplex, I snapped one last photo. I took a picture of the apartment living room in remembrance of our very first place.

After a few months of living out of our packed moving boxes, DeLon and I finally got settled in our new space. Being a busy, single, working mom, I didn't feel the need to overwhelm myself with unpacking everything all at once. I gradually unpacked and organized our things as we needed them, and that worked out fine for us.

DeLon liked his new place too. We had a decent front yard for him to play in. There were kids down the street he could play with. His bedroom and closet were more spacious than his last room and we had carpet in the bedrooms, whereas at the apartment, it only had tile flooring throughout. My son seemed happy about the move, and I was elated to be able to provide a place of stability for my child. And have peace in mind while doing so, because that was the one thing I consistently prayed for, a stable foundation for DeLon and me.

With watching my son grow, I still could not help but

think about the past with Rendell. I knew DeLon would've adored having him as his father figure growing up. Ren would not have been the perfect father figure at first. I mean, it would be a role that he would eventually grow into, because I can recall a time when Ren almost frightened my son half to death. I remember it clearly—all three of us were the only ones at the Westport pool that night. And instead of the gradual process of letting my son get used to the water, because it was DeLon's first time being in a pool, Rendell ups and just grabs my son out of my arms and launches him in the pool; my baby was so scared and he cried. Therefore, in some cases as that, Rendell was a little rough around the edges, but overall he represented a good man. Plus, I am sure being in an environment where a child witness's a healthy love is good for their being spiritually and mentally, because seeing positive energy flow within your life triangle feeds the inner spirit and reinforces the mental strength in preparation to sustain in the outside world. And as adults, we should transfer that same healthy love within our own created life triangle. DeLon needed to see his mother within her own life triangle, but that didn't happen. As young as DeLon was when Rendell came into our lives, if Rendell and me had continued to be, they both would have had a significant impact on each other's lives in a positively enforced way, reinforcing their mental and spiritual strength which armors against the negative influences of the outside world.

Through my eyes, Rendell Schwann would have made the ideal father figure for my son and all of our future children together as a whole. Aside from his radical behavior, he was my perfect mate. And with everything that had transpired between us, I thought that life for us was no more, I had ruined it. My mind was so wrapped up in agony for the loss of Rendell being in our lives that I would have waited years for him to return to us. Well actually I did, but my hopes would be slowly downplayed by the doubts in my mind, and the guilt from my past would spearhead my actions, negating ambitions, and I would get discouraged. I would think to myself: *How can I expect Rendell to only want me, when there are so many other beautiful girls out there who haven't fucked his best friend?* And the sadness would overtake me, and I would break down crying where I stood.

It seemed like somehow, I found comfort in wallowing in my own sorrow. Or perhaps the tears released allowed an egress for the hurt I contained. On the weekends that De-Lon would leave to visit his grandmother's house, I would stay home and grieve. I would put on some love songs and think about the life and love that should have been between Rendell and me. I would just let the music play for hours, sometimes letting one song repeat over and over, as I lay across the sofa and cried my heart out.

After a year, the guilt was still burdensome. At times, it was almost unbearable, simply because I was aware of how drastically different my life would have been if, only I had obeyed that warning. My son would have had a good role model to look up to. I would have been united with my soul mate without guilt or negative thoughts lurking about. The moral and physical support of my mate and son would've been there, surrounding me. The spiritual motivation that comes with love and children would have been super charged within me. Indeed, our life's path had been diverted by separation.

And all I could do was imagine what could have been.

The pain ran deep. It was like I couldn't get away from it. Different guys would try to talk to me often, and naturally none of them would be my type, which saddened me even more. It felt like it was a constant reminder of my wrongs, because how could I mentally move on when my heart wouldn't let go. No one ever came close to Rendell Schwann. His wisdom, his touch and passion were unmatched in my sight. He was really the whole package minus one or two mental glitches, but who is perfect? Anyhow, I couldn't get over him as it seemed.

Unique Observation

CHAPTER FIFTY-NINE

Basking in my sorrows also made for a bizarre occurrence. One night, alone at home, I was outside in my driveway. I rested on the pavement and gazed up into the wondering sky. Looking up at the dark, glowing firmament, I saw the clouds were highlighted by the moon that drifted in and out amidst the stars. It was like watching waves of the deep blue ocean from the beach, but with an inverted view. The sea was the sky, and the waves were the clouds.

I recall lying underneath the sea-sky and making up a melody with only the words, "Father, Son and Holy Ghost." I repeatedly sang those lyrics as I gazed up into the wild blue yonder. After a while, I got up from the ground, dusted myself off and went back inside. Still humming the song, I got cozy on the sofa and ended up falling asleep right in the living room.

As I slept, I felt this cool air blow all around me. Still in slumber, initially I thought it was air from the ceiling vent. However, this burst of wind was substantial. It was like I had absolutely no ceiling whatsoever over my home. The draft was all around me, so much in fact that I had to remind myself I was still lying on the couch. I could feel the briskness of the wind and hear its whisking sounds; however, it did not move a hair on my body or shuffle any of my clothing. I felt no need to panic nor fret in any way. I just lay there, calm and still with my eyes closed.

The phenomenon lasted for a short while. As I continued to lie there, I began to picture in my mind what I could not physically see. Something obviously desired a closer look; I envisioned that it removed the top of my home as if it was a lid that could be unhinged, to gaze down upon me. The room was entirely filled with currents of light, steady wind. It felt as if I was totally removed from my natural environment; and placed in this mystical atmosphere where I was completely swept over by this cool breeze, and absolutely nothing was around me; because all I felt was air.

The supernatural encounter lasted for about three minutes or so. Then in an instant, it went away. As if the roof top had been dropped back down to the house, the experience had halted. I got up, turned on the living room lights and looked around. Everything was still in its rightful place, untouched and unmoved. In awe of what I had experienced, I wondered, was that the Holy Ghost?

Back on the Set

CHAPTER SIXTY

Now, I went back and forth with my sorrows as I pressed my way forward through the struggle. However, sometimes that included being out there on the social scenes too. Once I got out of that sad, solitary, self-confined state of mind, I called on some of my back-in-the-day friends to get me out of the house and into the mix.

Of course, I had to step out correctly—sassy and above-average, classy. That was always me. I'd slip on some high heels, show a little cleavage with a cute blouse, but refrain from displaying all the goods. I didn't go out too excessively, but when I did, I would usually get a lot of attention. I would tilt the room, so to speak, when I entered into a club and receive recognition from the men and even some women. Although, it was all very flattering, I never let any of it go to my head.

Nonetheless, the ones who hollered the hardest were absolutely not my type. They were either too short, too skinny, had a gold grill or missing teeth, but they seemed to always have a nice ride. In the beginning, I would just tell 'em point-blank, "You're not my type," and keep moving. As a result, the guys would respond negatively. They would call me a bitch, a dyke or stuck up. It surprised me too, because my delivery wasn't harsh at all; I was only being honest. However, since I rejected them that would be the response, I'd get on numerous occasions. Therefore, in efforts of avoiding offenses as those when meeting new people that I was uninterested in, I chose other routes to decline their advancements.

Every once in a while, there would be a rough rider who caught my eye in some kind of way. I always had a need for speed, so I got acquainted with some motorcyclists. With only one or two that I regretted getting on the back of their bikes, thankfully though, I was kept safe amongst it all. However, with the ones I did trust to really ride with, we sped up and down those highways, dodging in-between automobiles; and I loved it! With one motorcyclist, we were on the highway going 160 mph. Of course, I stayed prayed up, but on that bike riding at that speed, it was so exhilarating.

If you owned a motorcycle and been riding for years, I would rock wit' cha. Which led me to this one guy named Ronnie. Ronnie had a clique, a set of friends, and they all happened to ride motorcycles. I was out doing me, when Ronnie crossed my path. He was on his bike; it was one of those cruisers; a nice one too. He approached me. His spill wasn't too lame. He talked real slick-like and had a toothpick in his mouth as he lips swayed to the side, trying to talk and keep the toothpick in place. Ronnie was 5'10", a huskily built, mid-high yellow-pigmented brother who wore a five o'clock shadow beard. By his looks, he was a lot older than me, like twenty years, it seemed. Even though he dressed well and smelled pleasant, his body looked tired. Without any noticeable scars, Ronnie looked like he had been shot, stabbed or banged up some kind of way. I suppose that meant he was a real biker.

I wasn't too interested at first until he mentioned that he owned a car dealership. I'm not a user, but I thought it could be beneficial to know this cat. After all, I was twenty years old and driving a bucket. Who didn't dream of rolling in a new ride at my age? Therefore, when Ronnie offered his number, I took it and gave him a call.

Ronnie and I talked for a bit and got acquainted with each other. He's the one who turned me on to my favorite drink presently, Crown and 7 Up on ice; *mmm*, the taste is so smooth and enjoyable. Ronnie and I hung out together quite a bit. Occasionally, I would go over to his house and work out in his home gym or we'd have dinner somewhere. He didn't make my heart pitter-patter, but I didn't mind him occupying my time.

I also got around to test-driving some of those vehicles on his car lot. There was this one Acura he was pressing me to get. On the outside, it was a cool ride, but once I got inside the car, the seat couldn't go back far enough; cramping my lean, long legs. The stirring wheel wasn't adjustable either, so when I turned a corner, the steering wheel rubbed against my legs. Driving the darn thing was very uncomfortable. I am sure I looked good in it, but in actuality if I had purchased that car, I would have been setting myself up for a liable auto accident.

However, I thought strongly about getting it for the low-low price Ronnie was offering me for it. I mean, after all it was an Acura with leather interior. I could probably get used to it, getting some act right, or so I thought. Luckily though, my common sense kicked in and overruled that shallow thought of just owning an Acura, because honestly that car was more fitting for a person 5'4" or shorter in height. My 5'8" statuesque and still growing self, felt like a giantess buckled into that car.

I ended up telling Ronnie the truth: I safely could not drive around in that car. I could barely move my legs enough to press on the breaks, so I ended up rejecting his offer on the vehicle.

Staggered

CHAPTER SIXTY-ONE

Like the rest of the men I'd known, Ronnie appeared to be cool people on the surface. However, when things got down to the nitty-gritty, ole Ron would surely let me know what he really wanted. On one of our many nightly conversations, he finally spoke on it. Ronnie asked me to have sex with him and another female.

Lying on my bed, I was looking at myself in the mirror of my headboard, twirling the receiver cord around my index finger while talking to Ronnie. Hearing him ask that of me stunned me. The sudden surprise felt like the time I was being this curious kid and casually encased within my hands a bee. Outside in the front yard of Big Mama's house, I saw a honeybee rest itself right on top of a yellow-round wildflower. I snuck up on it, stooped down and captured the honey bee with both hands; everything was kosher until I felt that zing—the bee had stung me. And of course, my natural instinct was to let it go. Being startled like that was how I felt when Ronnie propositioned me. I mean, he and I had one sexual encounter protectively, and I wasn't curious about anything more with him, much less a threesome.

I was soon to find out how relentless Mr. Ronnie could be over something he strongly desired. He would chill on the subject for a bit, but then he would bombard me with these explanations of how it could go down. He exaggerated how it could be this "ultimate experience" for us both. Ronnie approached this topic all sorts of ways in an attempt to convince me that this is what I wanted; but I just didn't know it yet.

However, I did not budge at first.

My firmness on the decision began to sway some after hearing ceaseless accounts of Ronnie's antics. I began to be curious about it and ask questions. I said, "Ronnie how do you safely have sex with two women? Do you take one rubber off and put a new one on each time you switch off?"

His reply would always be, "Aww, baby, there's ways around that."

I heard what he was saying; however, I couldn't visualize any way around that. Nonetheless, after I got off the phone with Ronnie that evening, my mind began to ponder on it.

Lazarus's Hand

CHAPTER SIXTY-TWO

Later, I looked at the clock and it was close to midnight. I hopped off the bed to turn off the light and snuggle myself under the covers. However, when I turned off the light, I noticed it was darker than usual. Normally, I could still see my way to the bed through the darkened room, but on this particular night, I couldn't see a damn thing. The room was completely pitch-black. It alarmed me at first, but then I blew it off and laid myself to bed.

As I lay, my eyes rested shut and I took a huge sigh to exhale the day's tension away. I might have whispered my nightly prayers too, for I had a habit to say my prayers every night. I conditioned my son to do the same as well. Anyhow, I was not in bed more than five minutes when I felt this subtle but sharp object graze the top of my left ear. It did it repeatedly, slowly and lightly running up and down my ear. I was so frightened, because obviously something else was in the room with me. Frozen in fear, I did not flinch or move an inch.

This entity lightly brushed what felt to be a long, curved, skinny nail on top of my skin for a good moment. I could feel nothing else but it. No shifting of weight on the bed. No hot breath breathing down my neck or anything. I only felt this long, witchy nail that I envisioned was attached to this long, withered, decrepit finger that grazed my ear frequently as it leaned over me.

My eyes remained closed through the whole experience purely out of fear. The room was so dark; even if my eyes were open, I wouldn't know the difference. My vision would be entirely obscured. In addition to that, this thing's touch felt like it was something resurrected from the dead. If my eyes did catch a glimpse of its image, I would have probably passed out or had a heart attack from intense fright.

The whole experience was weirdly spooky. The mannerism in which this thing touched me was like a mother caressing a child's face to offer comfort. Yet, in that moment I felt no sense of comfortability. As a matter of fact, it was completely opposite of that. This strange being with its motherly stroke was something out of *Tales from the Crypt*.

Then it spoke. In a slothful, eerie manner with this ancient and raspy tone, it said, "Stay with your Father." Then in a snap of a finger, it was gone, and I lay there totally creeped out.

I opened my eyes, and the room was back to its normal lighting, not pitch black as before. If I could describe this encounter, I would say that I had been paid a visit by Lazarus himself. I say that, because an entity of some sort, either undead or temporarily rescued from the torments of hell came to relay that message. What else could it be? The way that thing lightly and creepily stroked my ear; it was like I was being touched by the hand of Lazarus. I doubt very seriously a demonic force would be cautioning me to stay with my Father as this thing did.

Terrified from that visit, I immediately jumped up and fell to my knees on top of the bed and cried out loud for forgiveness. My face was soaked with tears, with snot freely flowing from it as I was begging God for mercy. My heart was open, and I was sincere to the core with repenting from those sinful thoughts. I hadn't rectified myself like that since I'd been an adult and the very first time is when I was overcome with guilt at the young age of six.

Needless to say, I was frightened back to my good senses. The next day, I called Ole Ronnie boy up, told him that I was not doing that, and instructed him not to call me anymore. I didn't give him a reason or an explanation why; I just hung up the phone in the midst of him talking. After my point was made, I wasn't trying to hear anything else Ronnie had to say. Obviously, he was trying to steer me on a path that would have severely altered my perception of life, and God wasn't having that. Even afterwards, Ronnie made a few attempts to call me; however, I didn't care to acknowledge him. I was literally scared straight, and that situation was swiftly nipped in the bud.

Since that creepy night that I was touched by Lazarus's hand, I slowed my roll completely on everything. Other than work and family gatherings, I wasn't trying to do much at all as far as sinning. From then on out, I was back on the straight and narrow and with no regrets. I had my peace and dignity intact, which was more valuable to me than anything the world could offer.

Getting Back Social

CHAPTER SIXTY-THREE

After a few months of being a recluse, I started to get out and socialize again. I met back up with an old family friend and dancing buddy, Monique. We occasionally lit up a dance spot or two. One night after leaving the club instead of going home, Monique and I stayed out a bit. Chatting by our cars, we were simply enjoying the outdoors. It was a beautiful summer evening, and the temperature was just right. It was one of those splendid nights where you felt like you could sleep outside, a perfect evening to return to the social scene.

While still hanging out, because neither Monique or I were ready to go home, a couple of guys leaving the club raised an eyebrow. They were going to their car, which happened to be parked two spots over from where Monique parked. I apparently grabbed the attention of the light-skinned guy, because seeing me, he immediately turned and smiled my direction. He soon approached me to introduce himself and his acquaintance to Monique. He said his name was Evan.

Evan was cute. He was fair-skinned, looked to be biracial; slim built, but muscular. He had a tapered fade haircut with a taller top that naturally curled. He said that he was Black mixed with Italian. Evan had somewhat of a funny shaped head, but had a nice smile and his pretty teeth triumphed over that. Observing his body language as we chatted, I was reminded of the promise I made to myself. I had told myself after my son's father that I would not date any more light-skinned, yellow-boned men—simply because lighter-toned males usually felt they were God's gift to women, instead of it being the other way around. However, after a small conversation with Evan, he had convinced me enough to give him a try and so I did.

Evan was a cool prospect initially. We talked for a bit. I found out Evan had been in the military and presently was a student at TCC, a local college. His plan was to transfer to the University of Tulsa and hopefully get into law school there. After a few regular conversations, Evan invited me out to his mom's place to go swimming and I gladly accepted.

It turned out Evan was a lot of fun too. I got out there to find that we had the whole pool to ourselves. We had swimming competitions with each other to see who could hold their breath the longest under water. I laughed a lot that night, and of course with a little ganja in hand, the experience was more elevated. We took full advantage of our private swim time, and I dug it thoroughly. It was nice a change to enjoy someone's company of the opposite sex and not be reminded of the past.

After our swim, we went back to his mom's apartment to eat dinner. It was an artichoke risotto dish that Evan had made prior to my arrival. The dish had a dull and grainy appearance to it, which made me unenthused to eat it. However, when I ate the food, the taste wasn't as bad as it looked. The dish was very subtle in flavor, which I suppose it had to be in order for the artichoke to be accentuated. Although it really was a sweet gesture, him cooking for me and all, but that artichoke dish was my first and last.

I really enjoyed everything about my shared evening with Evan, with the exception of that risotto dish. None-theless, that amusing night led me into going against my better judgment. I would give into my temptations and get involved with another yellow brother.

Prince, El and Dennis

CHAPTER SIXTY-FOUR

It's unclear how my Achilles heel for exotic-looking men originated. Perhaps it was Prince, the artist, who initiated this distinct attraction. I had an erotic dream about him once; I was only six and got aroused too. I could not begin to tell you what brought that on. All I know is that when my mother disrupted that dream to wake me up for school, I was highly disappointed. I tried my best to recapture that feeling and continue where the dream was interrupted. I lay back in bed and shut my eyes tight in hopes to redream that fantasy again, but nope; that was the end of my erotic experience with Prince.

Better yet, it could've have been the DeBarges who fed into that weakness of mine for mulatto looking men. They were this popular, sibling singing group sensation who had everyone dancing to their tunes in the early 80s. The DeBarges' music rang heavy on the streets; "Rhythm of the Night"—oh, yeah. I adored me some El DeBarge, the lead singer of the group; an absolute heartthrob he was back then. Listening to the Debarges' tunes, I felt like their sounds landed through my stereo speakers straight off the golden-sanded, Caribbean shores, sipping pina coladas, tapping on coconuts and all. Or at least that's how their music projected itself to me.

Another early memory of me being extremely fond of

West Indies looking, light skinned brother was with my old neighbor and childhood friend, Dennis. I may have been about nine; we were the same age. Dennis at that time was as fine as all get-out. I would even go as far as to say, he was even finer than El DeBarge. Furthermore, he was just two houses down from me and age appropriate; so, my chances of getting with Dennis was much more imaginable than with El. Not to mention, I was really good friends with his older sister, Netra.

My crush on Dennis was massive. When we played outside, I would chase him down the street for no apparent reason. I was so attracted to him, I just wanted to be close enough to touch him or smell the clean detergent fragrance from his clothing. Most of the time, I couldn't catch him though. Back then I was a chunky little ole thing, so Dennis could run circles around me, and he did. However, I cherished the moments where I could just lay eyes on him and gaze at his beauty. The sight of him alone simply melted my nine-year-old heart.

Now with Evan's look, although cute, he could not compete with the P.E.D.s. His skin color had paleness to it, like a dark-featured Italian with deep olive undertones. Unlike the P.E.D.s, whose skin tones appeared like sun-kissed ripe mangos, Evan's skin tones would have to be manipulated by a really good tan. Evan wasn't a bad looking guy, but there was no competition when compared to the P.E.D.s

I liked Evan for many reasons. He was knowledgeable of things that were not usually spoken about. He had nice, full lips that kissed me fabulously. That alone went a long way for me. However, outside of Evan's charm and intellect, my rationality for giving the swirl another twirl had mostly to do with my son.

DeLon was six at that time; I knew he was at that age where he could have used a father-like figure in his life. De-Lon had been asking for the whereabouts of his own father since he was at the age of two. I know he would have adored having a male role model to look up to. Plus, it would be a nice change to have some heavy testosterone around the house. So, I decided to go against my better judgment and date this light-skinned yellow brother who I was very skeptical about dating in the beginning.

Although Evan did not compare in looks when it came to the P.E.D.s or my son's father for that matter, he still ranked in my top five of cuties. With my history of having hard-hitting crushes in my earlier years, it was evident that I had a ridiculous soft spot for mulatto-looking men, and Evan was no exception.

C'est la Vie

CHAPTER SIXTY-FIVE

It's funny how life is. The things less appreciated should be highly cherished. Likewise, the life lessons we learn are chiefly from our own mistakes. As Murphy's Law states: anything that could go wrong would, and in most cases it does. So, then why, being knowledgeable of that, as humans, do we put ourselves in risky situations?

Similarly, the very thing you need in life is typically what you're running from. And verily, why do we tend to have the most precious and godly gems right before our eyes, and still, be blinded to its worth? Correspondingly, if life is so priceless to us all, then why do we treasure it most when we fall or fear it slipping away? Yes, indeed; life has an uncanny way of working itself out, and opening up our eyes to the things most valuable.

As for me, I was still going through the motions of life, trying to pick up the pieces. For, I did not fathom what I had until it was gone. At that park, when I was mystically cautioned of the things I would risk, I was clueless about the depths to which I would be affected by that one decision. But now I was starting to see it more clearly. The pressures of being a single, young mom sometimes diffused throughout my two-person household.

In addition to that, the one who excited my hidden abilities was no longer in my life. It had been two years since that forced departure from Ren, and I still felt an internal emptiness.

However, and naturally, life does go on.

Although I did have my reservations about Evan and his light complexion, at the end of the day, I had this little Prince by my side to look after. And as his mother, I did want DeLon to have a good father-figure around. My decision to move forward and accept Evan in our lives was an opportunity to leave the past in the past. Regardless of my heartfelt connection with Ren, I had a son to provide for; and he deserved everything necessary in molding him to be an outstanding young man.

And with that, entailed settling for nothing less than a King to be by my side. Even though Evan was not ideal for me, he had a lot of positives going on for him. Therefore, he and I began dating.

An Unideal Situation

CHAPTER SIXTY-SIX

It was obvious to me that DeLon was not Evan's biological child, despite them both being fair-skinned. However, to an outsider seeing those two interact, one would be surprised to learn Evan and DeLon were unrelated. They enjoyed talking with each other. Evan would be interested with how DeLon spent his day. When he ran to the store, DeLon would ask to ride along. Witnessing the two, it was like they were really good friends. They got along quite well.

I liked Evan too, and it seemed that he was a decent match for me initially. However, as he and I continued to date more, I began to see a different side of him. He became very critical of my appearance, my home situation, and the level of reliance I had on him at that time. To say the least, my first mind was right to think what it did; Evan was no different than what I had expected. The closer we got, the more he would remind me of why I avoided getting involved with another yellow brother to begin with.

Now prior to meeting Evan, I was in the process of overcoming some obstacles. I was without transportation due to a car accident I had a month prior. My hair was fried, because my stubborn self was so set on swimming on a day that the pool was closed. The excessive amount of chlorine in it chemically parched my hair and skin. My whole body was super dry; it took months for my skin to feel normal again. Luckily my hair didn't completely break off, but I was going through the motions.

From Evan's outside perspective, he saw me as this cute girl with potential, but who had dry ass hair and no car. Nonetheless, like everything else, there was more to this story than what the eyes could see. At that period, I was trying to recover from my losses, but from Evan's standpoint, he thought that I was just without grease and wheels.

With Evan in the picture, I did rely on him more than I ever had with any guy friend. He took me to and from work daily. He made trips to the grocery store. Along with dates, he paid for me to get my hair done at the salon once. In his mind, he couldn't understand why I went around with my hair pinned back. Evan felt the need to school me on some things. He gave me this long speech one day, about how his ex was in the military and could keep her hair done all the time and if she could in the Army, I should be able to, too, as a civilian.

I could have explained the situations more thoroughly to Evan, but with his negative attitude, I didn't bother. I just let him think what he wanted to think, what he assumed to be true. Of course, I appreciated everything he did for me, because Evan did come through for a sister. However, with his help also came a lot of judgment.

Being "co-dependent," as Evan liked to put it, allowed me to see another side of him fairly quickly. During our involvement, I did not have solid transportation, which made managing life difficult. I had a son to pick up from school or daycare. I had a job that I needed to get to and from. It was challenging not having my own vehicle. Therefore, what I needed mostly from Evan were rides, and he reluctantly obliged.

Despite that, there was never any kind of financial reliance on Evan. I never asked him for a dime, and other than not having a vehicle, I could clearly take care of my own bills. Yet my lack of transportation seemed to have weighed heavily on him. Therefore, the pressures of it all weighed on our relationship.

Trying to think of solutions to the problem, I reached out to my son's grandmother, Eric's mom, Mrs. E. By this time, Eric had been locked up for four years. Furthermore, Mrs. E had a white Dynasty sedan just sitting in her driveway collecting dust that she said would be for Eric whenever he got released from prison. Now, it was unlike me to ask for anything from anybody, but considering this challenging situation, I thought I could offer her a proposal that she wouldn't refuse.

I asked Mrs. E if she would let me drive Eric's car so I could have transportation to pick up her grandson, my child, and get myself back and forth to work. In return, I would make all the repairs necessary to have her car in tip top shape. Then when Eric got released from prison, I would hand the car over to him. In the meantime, my goal was to save up enough money to pay cash for another vehicle.

However, Mrs. E. turned me down. She said that since Eric and I were no longer together, she didn't feel I should be driving his car. So, it was back to drawing board for me.

Apparently, it did not matter to Mrs. E that I was a

young, single mom who responsibly took good care of my child, her grandson. It did not matter to her that we needed transportation so we could have access to essential household items. No, she was more concerned about lesser things, such as me driving around knuckleheads in her car or even worse, letting them drive it. I don't know where her mindset was at my age, but that had never been my M.O., even though I was just twenty. I have never been the type to allow my guy friends to drive any vehicle of mine. However, that was her reason for not allowing me to drive Eric's white Dodge Dynasty that was just sitting in her yard, being unattended to.

Instead, she offered to keep DeLon during the week, leaving her to be the one taking him to and from school. In turn, I would have my son for the weekends only. I wasn't at all thrilled about the idea, but for the moment, my hands were tied. Mrs. E had no interest in helping me directly. Instead, she chose to minimize my motherly duties and reduced my time with my son to two days a week.

It took some time for me to get adjusted to not having my baby around every day. It was difficult at first, because our usual pattern from work to his school, dinner, and then home was no more. My mommy role had dwindled, and a part of me felt like less of a mother. However, my stress of needing transportation to maneuver around the daily routines had lessened too. Instead of needing a ride for DeLon and me, all I had to be concerned about now was a ride for me. That itself was a strange feeling, because since I was eight, becoming a big sister, I had always had somebody to look after. At the age of sixteen, I had my own little one to provide for. And now at twenty, fleetingly, I only had my-self to fend for.

Getting used to the adjustments came with its ups and downs. The good thing was DeLon was ok with the change. His Grandma E gave him almost anything he asked for, so he didn't have any complaints. I was the one who was most affected by the switch-up. With DeLon not being around and having so much free time during the week, I felt a bit off-balance. Therefore, I directed that emptiness and un-used energy toward sex, which helped me to cope a little bit better.

Evan was cool when it came to intercourse, but he wasn't great. Naturally, he did not compare to that trea-sured first lovemaking experience with Rendell Schwann. Yet Evan was satisfying to an extent. During our sexual en-counters, he would make some unusual requests. His erotic suggestions were something that I was totally unfamiliar with, yet I was consistently aroused by them. His sexual desires made me feel more of an alpha she-male than a sub-missive damsel most of the time.

Our sexual exploits had a downside to it. In those mo-ments of intimacy, I felt invigorated, but after the aphrodi-siac had worn off, a feeling of repulsiveness would invade my senses and overshadow the experience, making the cli-max unnoteworthy.

With all the heightened sexual activities in the bed-room lately, it definitely brought about some changes. On a weekend that I had DeLon, he was outside playing with his neighborhood friends when a strange feeling came over me.

It was like my body was magnetized to the bed. A heavy sleepiness came over me, and all I could do was snooze. In the bed that day, I could not even move, much less keep my eyes open.

I could hear DeLon going in and out the house. And I recall feeling horrible about it, because with me only seeing him on the weekends, I wanted to at least get up and fix him lunch, a snack or something. However, my body was not having it. Come to find out, my body was undergoing some strange kind of adaptation.

Days after that very peculiar weekend, things seemed back to normal. My energy level was back up again. My son returned to his grandmother's place for the school week and I, well, went back to my daily grind. Everything was back to the usual, at least on the surface.

The Little Things

CHAPTER SIXTY-SEVEN

Little did I know then that the extreme episode of weariness, which I'd felt weeks prior, was my body's way of preparing for something special. When it came time for my menstruation, it was nowhere to be found. I was missing it tremendously. Every day after the anticipated day of arrival, I checked for the red tide, every hour on the hour for seven days straight. My mind was even playing tricks on me. At times, I thought I felt a little moisture in my undies and I'd run ecstatically to the bathroom for confirmation, which would be short-lived and overtaken with utter disappointment. After a while, I forced myself back into reality and accepted the fact that I was pregnant.

As fate would have it, in the middle of my private chaos, an old acquaintance decided to emerge from out of the blue. It was Byron, wanting to reconcile our differences and reestablish a friendship. It had been three years since I had even heard from Byron. Yet, here he came trying to get back what he chose to leave. I had thought for sure he'd be married by now or at least close to it. However, come to find out, once a cheater, always a cheater; and it's not always the man either. From what I understood, his girl wasn't trying to be monogamous until after she walked down the aisle, and I suppose even then she might not have totally committed. Anyhow, Byron found out about all her extracurricular activities and called off the engagement. Now, he wanted to reinstate his love affair with me; but first he had to rekindle the friendship, or so he thought.

Later that day, I chose not to tell Evan about the call I received from Byron. I figured it did not concern him, so I didn't bother to mention it. However, I did tell him about our unexpected, unforeseen arrival. Evan was over to my place as usual, and we were eating dinner when I gave him the news. We sat at my quaint, round, five-foot wooden table that compactly seated four. Enjoying our meal, Evan thought it was just two of us eating that night.

I looked over at him, but the words "I'm pregnant" would not come out of my mouth. I was nervous and very hesitant about the whole situation. After my first pregnancy, I vowed to not bring another baby forth out of wedlock, and there I was about to do the same thing twice. We had small conversations at the table, the usual rambling that my ears were accustomed to hearing. I was physically there, but my mind was thinking of how to tell this man about the pregnancy. Then, I got this strong urge for a good, cold glass of milk. I walked over to the refrigerator, reached in the fridge and while doing so, I blurted it out. "*I'm pregnant.*"

I stood in the kitchen drinking my glass of milk, very casually. Evan stopped what he was doing and walked over to me and asked, "*What did you say?*"

I looked him in his eyes and I reiterated, "I am expecting your child," as I wiped away the milk mustache that had formed above my upper lip.

Evan's reaction was mediocre, and hard to read. He didn't seem thrilled about the news, or upset. I knew he was taking classes in hopes of transferring to the University of Tulsa, a step closer to getting into law school. So, as if the struggle wasn't already real enough, on top of every-day survival in trying to get ahead of the game, here I was knocked up. However, it was hard for me to tell where Evan stood with the announcement.

I was relieved to finally get the news off my chest, but at the same time, I knew the situation was not ideal. Evan's lackluster response did nothing to comfort my weary mind. And at that particular moment, any little ounce of reassurance would have been appreciated. I wanted to feel confident of the direction I was heading; and I willingly relied on Evan to strengthen that confidence within, belittling my doubtful thoughts. However, that wasn't the case.

A few days later, Byron called again in an attempt to insert himself back into my space. He asked if I would like to accompany him to the Dallas Cowboys' game and then to the Texas State Fair. The invitation alone was intriguing enough, because it would be my first time going to an NFL game; and kicking it with a group of adult people. The invite sounded enticing.

Obviously, Byron was trying to get in good again, but I had moved on and had no intentions of looking back. However, the invitation was so appealing to me. I no longer felt he was imposing on my life, but rather asking me to accompany him along with some friends on an excursion.

Although I was carrying Evan's baby, I was still young and always game for fun. Therefore, I was on board to go. What Byron didn't know about my pregnancy wouldn't hurt him. And besides, I made it crystal clear that if I were to go, it would be only as buddies; no homie-lover, nothing.

Byron assured me there would be other people joining us, and this little outing would strictly be on the basis of friendship and amusement. And on that note, I was down to roll. However, there was a small reason for hesitance loitering about, and his name was Evan.

Back Track

Chapter Sixty-Eight

After hanging up the phone with Byron, my next objective was figuring out how to explain my likely absence to Evan. I wanted to be completely honest about it. Telling lies hammered my conscience, and that disrupted my peace. I much preferred to always state the truth or at least parts of it.

However, I didn't want Evan to think the worst about the situation either, which anybody could easily do. I wanted him to know that he could trust me no matter what, but the question remained—would he? I went over and over in my head how I was going to present my little weekend getaway to him, and do so without a weighing conscious.

A couple of days went by, and Evan was at my duplex as usual, sitting on the living room couch, watching TV. I thought this would be a good time to let him know about my plans, so I did. I was walking down the hallway and I casually said to him, "Hey, a few of my friends are going to Dallas for the weekend, and I was invited to go."

Evan looked stumped for a minute. He responded, "Friends? ... I've never heard you mention anything about your friends until now, and out of the blue you want to leave for the weekend?"

I paused where I stood, and just blinked. Ironically, that was all I could do at that moment. Evan was right. I never talked about my girlfriends to him. Mainly because I didn't have any; I had guy friends mostly, but I had not been actively talking to them either. I stood there trying to come up with a quick explanation, so I wouldn't appear so guilty and avoid straying too far from the truth, but I couldn't.

"Well, yeah," I responded. And then I told an outright lie. "It's my homegirl's birthday; she wanted to get away for the weekend with some of her other friends."

"Oh, ok," Evan replied as he nodded his head, a puzzled look still on his face. Then he asked, "Will there be any guys there?"

"No, it's an all-girl's trip," I replied. By then my conscience was starting to set in. If I didn't look guilty already standing there, it sure as hell felt like it.

Although the getaway was totally innocent, I wanted to at least go with a clear conscience, which in turn meant fessing up. I withstood the desire for a few hours, but then I broke down. We were in the bedroom when I confessed. I sighed deeply and said, "Evan, you were right. It's not my homegirl, but my homeboy who is good friends with the family (*wink*). The friend's sister, her friend, and his best friend are going, and I will be just another friend tagging along. We will be as a group in the hotel room, but to be upfront with you now—yes, there will be guys around too."

Evan looked at me and simply said, "That's not my baby."

Baffled and shocked, I took a step back and shook my head in astonishment. Of all of things to say, what I totally didn't expect was for him to say that. "What?" I responded. "When do I have the time to cheat? And just because I want to hang out with a group of friends doesn't mean I'm fucking 'em!"

I became livid. How could he think that of all things? And there I was, trying to be open and honest. I did want to go out of town and explore, but not if it meant wrecking my relationship, so I folded.

"Look," I said to Evan. "I haven't been with anybody other than you. This weekend trip is a short getaway with friends, but if you feel indifferent about me going, then I won't go."

Evan looked at me and said, "No, go; have a good time."

I said "Evan, are you sure?"

He replied, "Yes."

And out of relief, I gave him a big hug and a kiss on the cheek. I could now set my sights on going out of state and doing so guilt-free. Although Evan was playing it cool on the surface, I could tell he wasn't 100 percent convinced that he could trust me. However, all I wanted him to do was rest assure that he could.

The weekend of the trip had finally arrived. I was ready and Texas bound. My overnight bag was packed with three outfits: one for walking, another for the club scene, and the last one for the game. Each set had its own pair of matching shoes, of course. I didn't know who I was going to run into down there, but I was prepared to be extra cute and on fleek for whatever. I had no belly yet, so my attire would fit just right, especially with my naturally enhanced, round and plump rump. Now that ass, to my amazement, looking in that mirror, had seemingly gotten bigger before anything else with this pregnancy. Nonetheless, it was all good and I was ecstatic about my first trip to an NFL game.

Byron and his crew had pulled up to the house and honked. I grabbed my weekend bag and was out the door.

Nothing Ventured

CHAPTER SIXTY-NINE

The drive to Texas was cool. Along the way, we made a stop or two for knickknacks and gas. When I travel, it is a must that I have some Laffy Taffies on board, so when we halted, I made a dash to restock my stash. There was small talk and joking around, of course, on the road. I made sure to sit in the back, so no one got any bright ideas. Byron drove and his best friend, Rick, was in the front passenger seat. His sister trailed along in her car with her friends. I dozed off a time or two, but nothing extra transpired, so overall, the drive down to Texas was chill.

We got to our hotel room, and it was decent. We each had our own sleeping areas. Byron had a room to himself; Rick took the sofa bed in the living area, and I took up space on a sofa lounge daybed across from the kitchenette in the foyer. There was one bathroom that we all had to share, but overall, I had no complaints. As far as I knew, everything was all right with our mini-suite and to make it even better, I didn't have to spend a dime.

The next day we all went to the Texas state fair, and that was cool too. I don't know what I was expecting; I suppose something bigger, better and more of an array of exotic foods than what the Tulsa State Fair offered, but it wasn't. I mean, it was for sure bigger, but not better, and the food was more of the same. Everything I ate was there no different than the food at the Fair in my hometown. And for that reason, I have to say, I was a bit disappointed.

We walked around and around the fairgrounds. Nothing caught my attention or made me feel like I had to have it. There was nothing thrilling or exciting going on, until we heard someone fire a shot. It sounded like a gun. The next thing we knew, a herd of people were running in our direction, a multitude of frantic and fearful people heading fast toward us. They saturated the entire walkway. I saw some folks fall and get trampled, and the chaos only seemed to be escalating. And the distance between us and them was diminishing quickly.

Byron and Rick looked at each other, with bug-eyes, and then turned to me. Nobody said a word, but we all knew that it was every man for himself. The guys split, ran off somewhere. I simply took a few steps away from the crowd, dipped behind one of the concession-stands and watched as the mob scurried by. People were screaming and really shaken up, but no one stood out to me as being the perpetrator from what I could see. Plus, no other shots were fired. Still, I stayed tucked away until the coast was clear.

Once all the commotion dissipated, we all gradually linked back up and left. The night was pretty boring until that rush of excitement came bursting through. Ironically, it sort of made my night, but I was thankful no one got seriously hurt.

On our last weekend day in Texas, we all headed to the Dallas Cowboys game. I had my makeup on point, my usual natural, cheeky- blush look with a glow. My outfit

336

was sporty, yet sexy; some places were snug and other parts were loose, and it all tied in nicely with my sneakers, which were stylish too, I might add.

I was ecstatic, super stoked, about this outing. In my head, I imagined I would run into all sorts of famous people or an NFL player or two. But nope, I got into that stadium and didn't see a one. Our seats were so far up in the stands, if my eyes did lay on anybody, I wouldn't be able to distinguish who it was. There was a decent crowd at the game, but there were still a lot of empty seats around us. I guess it was an off-peak season. We ended up clowning around, joking with each other and watching the game periodically on the overhead big screen monitor. And I do not recall who won or who the Cowboys were even playing, for that matter.

Overall, the trip was not what I expected it to be. In hindsight, I played it up much bigger in my head than what it actually was. There were no exotic foods, like something I've never eaten before. We did stop at a Popeye's chicken on the way back home, and that was before the franchise made its way to our hometown, but even that was just okay; the boys tore it up, though. And of course, I didn't run into anybody famous who could have soared my life to new heights. Nope. I left Big Texas with just one thing more than I came there with—an experience, one that was mediocre at best.

The ride home seemed a lot faster than when I was leaving. As soon as I arrived at my house, the first person I had on my mind to call was Evan. The whole time I was away, I kept in contact with him, hoping it would give him some reassurance. When I gave him a ring, there was no answer. But I didn't think anything of it. I simply left him a voice-mail letting him know I was back and figured he would call whenever he got the chance. However, after four hours passing, then six hours, rolling into the whole night, with no word from Evan, I began to get concerned.

The next day, I tried calling Evan again, and still no answer. I got irritated then, and worried. I thought we had everything all settled when I left for that weekend. We even spoke on several occasions when I was there in Texas. Yet now that I was back, he wanted to ignore me. That didn't make any sense to me. And since I was carrying Evan's child, it was a serious concern that he was dipping out on me under the assumption that this wasn't his baby.

For three days I wondered, which mistake was bigger than the other. Was it going on that weekend getaway, or telling Evan the truth? Perhaps if I had lied, his doubts about this being his baby would not have transpired. We could have been planning doctor's appointments together, as opposed to me proving to him that indeed it was his seed I was carrying. Regardless, it was too late to be crying over spilled milk.

With my present situation, I felt troubled heavily. By no means did I want to be a single parent of two kids with different fathers. I began to realize how drastically my life and DeLon's life would change. Here I was getting by with one, and now there would be two. I was sure that once Evan saw his child, he would know without a doubt that it was his. However, it was getting to that point that became a growing concern.

Carrying a child takes a woman's body through so many changes, emotionally as well as physically. And in my heart, I did not want to go through that emotional distress again alone with no mental support or any type of comfort. That was my biggest fear, and for that very reason alone, I vowed to not bear another child until I was married. It was bad enough that I was pregnant again before marriage, but now, the father would most likely not be around to be supportive of my prenatal needs. The worries of it all weighed me down.

Later on in the week, I made an appointment to see one of those HOPE doctors to find out how far along I was. It was a male doctor, a nice guy with blond hair and blue eyes. He did an ultrasound on me at the visit.

"There it is," the doctor said, as he moved the wand left and right across my belly. He seemed more excited about it than I was. I could barely lift a corner of a smile. It was too early to tell if the fetus was male or female. The doctor printed out a copy of the captured image and vertically across it in tiny print, it read, "nine weeks."

As soon as I left, I headed directly over to Evan's mom's apartment to hand the ultrasound right to him. I wanted him to do the math and count back the weeks of us being together. If my word wasn't good enough, now he had certifiable proof. However, when I got there, no one was home. My plan was foiled, so I left that printed copy of the baby's ultrasound right on their mailbox where he or his mom could see it. I don't know what I expected to accomplish by doing that. In the back of my head, the damage had already been done between us. But at least he would know that my word was true. Then, I got back into my ride and rode away.

At about ten weeks along in my pregnancy, no one even suspected that I was carrying. I suppose there was no reason to, just yet. Besides getting a bad head cold at the beginning of it, I had no other symptoms. I might have filled out a bit, but that was nothing too obvious. I say that confidently, because with all the people I saw on a regular basis—co-workers, associates, family—none had a clue that I was expecting. And I wasn't about to say a word.

One day at lunch, I decided to walk over to the Gilcrease shopping complex to grab a bite to eat. Two of the many businesses there were a convenience store and Mazzio's pizzeria; I visited both frequently. It was windy that day. Walking along the pavement with a jacket on, I was in my own world, contemplating my next move.

Then, the next thing I knew, out of nowhere here comes this person. Rendell of all people grabbed my arms, turned me anxiously toward him and said, "You're pregnant, aren't you!"

In disbelief, because it took me a minute to respond for a number of reasons. One being, he scared the bejeezus out of me. And two, how in the world did he know? I hadn't seen or heard from him in several months. It had been two and a half years since the breakup. And there he was, popping up out of the blue like that and instantly knowing that I was pregnant? I was astounded.

Quickly gathering myself after the shock, I closed my jacket with my arms folded and said sternly, "No, I am *not* pregnant." Then I snatched myself from under his grasp and hastily walked away.

Honestly, I didn't know how to address Rendell confronting me like that. When he approached me, the feeling I felt, after the bombshell, was shame. I did not want him to look down on me, and I didn't want him to know about my pregnancy. Somehow, my love still remained for him, because he still managed to touch an area that lay deep in my heart every time, I laid eyes on him.

Walking back to work from lunch, my mind had a new set of concerns on top of the old ones. It was filled with sighs and even more regret. What would be the odds? It had to be Rendell, of all people, to find the needle in the haystack; he knew straight out that I was pregnant. Now more than ever, I was determined to keep my secret hidden. And Rendell could not ever find out that his instinct was right.

That following weekend, I got more responses than I anticipated from the baby's ultrasound image. Evan finally reached out to me, and so did his father. When Evan called, he started out with some small talk, but I got straight to the point. I told Evan that I wanted an abortion. He paused for a bit, but seemed to be on board with the idea. He did make a point to mention that he wasn't paying for it, and I was quite all right with that. I quickly responded that I didn't need his money. And that was the end of that conversation.

The next day, Evan's dad came by to visit—alone, without his son. He pleaded for me to not abort the child, but my mind was already made up. Perhaps I would have had a change of heart if Evan was there too, asking me not to go through with it. However, he wasn't. It was just his dad, and the moral support I required to get through those nine months meant someone had to be there by my side. Apart from that, I was over Evan and his negative mannerisms. I wanted no ties to him. So, regardless of them reaching out to me, I just wanted this whole ordeal behind me and to return to my normal life with just my son and me.

That whole experience really took a lot from me. I love and adore children, but I required a genuine partner to bring another one into this world. After DeLon was born, I decided that every child I carried would be born in a harmonious and secure environment. Not with me harboring thoughts of instability, shame or overwhelming amounts of stress, as was the case with my first pregnancy. I wanted to have the utmost love and affection from a mate who admired every part of me and cherished the gift coming through me for us.

However, like before, that was not my reality. As much as I knew it was frowned upon and a sin to abort a child, for the sake of my own mental clarity, I chose to go through with the abortion a week later. In hindsight, though, I wish I would've placed all my concerns in God's hands. I'm sure I still would've been single with two kids. Nevertheless, I would have had double the love, and DeLon would have had a little person to look up to him, naturally making him feel his worth.

After the procedure was over, I felt a huge sense of relief throughout my body. *Finally*, I thought, *I can get myself back on track.* Later on, I happened to cross paths with a guy I knew in passing. He said he had a car for sale, but it wasn't running—a blue 97' Mazda 626. The guy said that he knew what was wrong with it. I could purchase the vehicle as-is, and get it fixed myself to save money on it. And that's exactly what I did. I bought that little Mazda for $600 and probably paid about $400 to have it fixed. After that, that car ran good with no problems.

Now with transportation, I was back in the driver's seat literally. I hurried up and got my son from over his grand-mother's house, and brought him home where he belonged, with me. I felt joy having my son back in my circumfer-ence. Once again, my peace was restored and because I was no longer involved with Evan and had no desire to befriend any more guy friends for the moment, my peace was still.

Recovery

CHAPTER SEVENTY

While I was still secretly healing from the abortion, my cousin Nella suggested that I run in the 2000 Miss Black Tulsa pageant. The deadline to enter was just weeks away in late January. Nella's boyfriend's cousin, Kory, had run a year or two prior and was one on the three finalists. I suppose Nella was curious to see how far I would get in the pageant.

In retrospect, I think for some reason amongst Nella and her boyfriend, there was this underlying competition between me and Kory. And with this pageant, they could see who would get the furthest in it. At that time, though, I was totally clueless of my cousin's intentions. But looking back, I can see how the subtle comparisons may have started. Kory was just a year or two older than me. We both went to McLain High School. We both were teenage moms, and we both were very pretty. And with me entering this competition, now we both would run for Miss Black Tulsa.

All things considered, I accepted the challenge and agreed to enter the pageant. For in my mind, it would be an opportunity to overcome my fears of performing in front of an audience. And it would allow Rendell the chance to see me in a different light, one that was glamorous and showcased my talents.

Yes, I still hoped that I would be able to recapture his

admiration and respect, and possibly regain the love lost. So, come January 2000, I ran for Miss Black Tulsa. I was twenty-two at the time.

The Preparation

CHAPTER SEVENTY-ONE

Part of being a contestant in the pageant was that you had to raise funds for it. We went about that by getting people to pay for advertisements in the Miss Black Tulsa catalog. Now, some girls went all out of their way; they were having folks buy full 8 x 10 pages and multiple ads that cost a $150 a whop.

As for me, I would ask the professionals I knew to do half a page for $75 or even a business card ad for $25, which was fine with me. If I recall correctly, in order for your spot to be finalized in the pageant, you had to raise a certain amount of money. I asked all the doctors I worked with to put in an ad and even got Rendell to pay for a business card print. By that time, he had his own barber shop up and running, which he had named Black Art. He supported the agenda by paying for a business card printed advertisement in the MBT catalog.

When I was at Rendell's shop, I tried my hardest to get him to buy a ticket to the event. I really wanted him to see me perform. I stood there and talked with him as he cut his clients' hair, trying to convince him to come. Rendell rambled on about how the lady running the pageant was pimping all of us girls. Nonetheless, what did that have to do with him coming to the pageant and showing some support? Nothing. I wanted Rendell to show up so he could hear the song that I chose to sing and would dedicate to him, but he outright refused to buy a ticket.

I did not disclose any of my plans to Rendell. I wanted him to find out as I was about to perform; it would've been a pleasant surprise. I gave every reason for him to go except for the very heartfelt reason I wanted him there. Unfortunately, I could not talk him into attending the event. He did not budge on his decision.

Disappointed by this, I still began practicing for the event and steadily sought more ads for the Miss Black Tulsa catalog. I bought a tape with just the music and no vocals, and I rehearsed singing that song for hours. I edited it down to three minutes, because that was the required time limit for the talent competition. Therefore, it would be a quick performance. Still, when I wasn't occupied with work, being a mom or going around various businesses promoting the pageant and selling ads, I was at home dedicating countless hours toward perfecting my craft.

Ads UP

CHAPTER SEVENTY-TWO

During the weekdays right after work, I would be out seeking funds. A friend of a friend, Terry, introduced me to an optometrist named Tim. Terry and Tim were good acquaintances. Terry was the co-owner of an established and well-known funeral parlor located in North Tulsa. He bought an ad for the MBT catalog and introduced me to Tim, so that he could show support and place an ad too.

Tim was a recent graduate and had recently partnered up with another optometrist to start an eye care practice. Ironically, that practice was in the same building as Dr. Thorne's office, right across the hall in suite 1.

Getting an ad from Tim seemed to be a long and drawn-out process. It wasn't a difficult task to give money and receive a receipt for a printed business card in the MBT book. However, with Tim, he would always want to meet up somewhere. Then when we'd meet, he'd need more information or additional time, and he'd want to schedule another meeting.

I was beginning to get annoyed and wondered if he had any money to give. I mean, it wasn't like I was asking him to sign his life away. It was a freaking ad in an advertorial magazine. After Tim got all my contact info and met with me at numerous locations, he finally paid for the ad—a whopping $25 (after all of that) in addition to an entry ticket.

Then he had the audacity to try and holler at a sister. I should've known.

Pursuit

CHAPTER SEVENTY-THREE

I kindly took the cash, gave him a smile and told him that I was not interested. Now usually, guys would accept that and keep it moving, but not Tim. He was very persistent. Tim was this very shorty-short guy. He had a round face with big eyes, and a medium brown skin tone. He had wavy, dark, thick hair that he kept low and edged to perfection. He wasn't an ugly person per say, but he wasn't an attractive one either, at least not to me. And to make things even more awkward, I towered over him by six inches without heels. Therefore, I guess, Tim might have stood about 5'1" or 5' 2". Surprisingly though, the height differential didn't make the slightest difference to him.

When dealing with Tim, I noticed that he liked to play on my kindness. He would make certain comments to let me know he was interested in dating, but I usually would smile and tell him in different ways that I was not interested. He would often say things like, "Aw, you just don't like me because I'm short."

Which was absolutely true, but I wanted to spare his feelings and the embarrassment. Therefore, I would just say, "No, I'm just not ready to date right now."

And that was also true. But Tim liked what he saw and would not give up easily. He would constantly attempt to make me feel bad for not accepting his advances.

Leading up to the pageant, Tim kept in touch. He would call and act interested about my daily agendas regarding the big event. I worked across the hall from him, so Tim would stop me on the way out for small conversations. I still was adamant about the way I felt and nice enough to give him the time, but only for so long.

On one of our outings with the rest of the pageant girls and mentors, we came across this young lady named Star. She, too, was a pageant winner, but years back. Star would sing at local events and enter other talent shows. Watching her perform was breathtaking; she appeared confident and her vocal cords were strong. Star was cute and spunky, but most importantly, she was short; like 4'8" maybe.

When my eyes landed upon her, instantly I thought of Tim. Star would be the perfect match for him. Through my eyes, they had so much in common. Tim and Star both seemed confident and successful. They both were extra short, and Star was even shorter than Tim. I thought the two of them would make an ideal couple and if the potential hookup was a success, I could get Tim off my bumper once and for all.

That following week at pageant practice, as soon as I ran into the pageant director, Ms. Janetta, I started inquiring about Star. I went on to say that I had a potential mate for her, but Ms. Janetta just skeptically looked at me as if to say, *What are you trying to do?* I asked her if Star would be around. Ms. Janetta just looked away and pretended like I never asked a thing.

For reasons unknown to me, Ms. Janetta would do rude

and unkind things like that to me, but I would just overlook it. It was common for people, primarily females, to not like me for any apparent reason. Therefore, I kept a distance with Ms. Janetta, and needless to say, I didn't inquire about Star to her anymore.

However, I did keep a lookout for Star, if by chance she happened to come around.

Pre-Pageant Day

CHAPTER SEVENTY-FOUR

That morning before the pageant would be our last drill practice. After about an hour or two of going over our dance steps, moves and stage presence, Ms. Janetta requested for all of us to line up. She told us each to choose one slip of folded paper out of a hand-sized brown bag, and we were further instructed to not open or unfold our slip until told otherwise. The rim of the bag was tucked under twice and it had creases all through it, which showed it had been used multiple times. It was not torn though, and the bag was deep enough to prevent us from seeing inside as we reached in for that small sheet of paper in blindness. Therefore, it served its purpose.

That little brown used paper bag kept us all in suspense as it went down the line and paused while each pageant girl made her pick. When it finally got around to me, I stuck my hand inside and grabbed my folded piece of paper. The girl after me was the absolute last to pull, and she reached in and chose the only folded paper left. After everyone in line had made their selection, the director then gave us the OK to look. Written on the paper was a number that would be the order in which we would go on stage to perform.

Hearing that from Ms. Janetta made my stomach turn, because that little sheet of paper in my hand had the number 2 written on it. The last girl to pick had the number 1 written on her paper. This meant she would be the first to go up in front of all those people come pageant day, and I would follow right after. The notion alone made me nauseated.

I tried to gather my wits in that short-lived moment of fright by giving myself a little pep talk. *Ok, Olivia, this is it. You can't back out now*, I thought to myself. The whole purpose of entering this competition was to get over this fearfulness of public experiences. Stirring up internal courage, I coerced myself.

The time is now, Olivia, for you to show what you have in store and shine like the star you are. Do not let this fear and shyness keep you still.

I went round and round with myself, contemplating. Then I said out loud to myself, "Get over this fear!"

This was the main reason why I decided to even enter the pageant—to prove to myself that I can do something like this. Having the heart to display my talents in front of an audience in addition to dedicating a song to Rendell, if he were present to hear it, was the goal at hand.

Showtime

CHAPTER SEVENTY-FIVE

That next morning, the process of pageant preparation had already begun in my head. First, I was going to rise early that morning and hit the gym for a good forty-minute workout. Then afterwards, I'd sit in the dry sauna for about thirty minutes and let the steam hydrate my skin and my voice box.

After the sauna session, that steam would have my vocals on point. My lyrics would flow out with such clarity and fluidity, like notes floating from the magic carpet of Aladdin. One just might even say I sounded like Whitney. Incorporating the workout and dry sauna into my pageant preparation regimen would certainly take my singing abilities to another level, eliminating the competition.

Post sweat fest. The plan was also to go home, grab my outfits and accessories, and head over to the Greenwood Cultural Center where the event would take place.

However, all that is what I initially thought to do. Instead, I ended up skipping the gym altogether and took that morning to shop for last-minute apparel. Then I went to the Cultural Center to practice my stage moves.

I picked up some clear pumps with a silver heel strap that fit my size nine-and a-half feet perfectly. They looked beautiful, simple yet elegant, and as an added bonus were comfy too. The shoes went with all my pageant attire seamlessly. However, weeks prior I had already purchased and had my mind set on wearing a set of bedazzled pumps, these extra fancy-looking heels that were three times the cost of the simple, classy pump that I recently purchased.

The only downside of the fancier shoe was that they were strapless heels. I typically never bought heels with strapless backs for one reason—safety. Of course, I would be the one to sprain an ankle or something. That day, I went against my better judgment and wore the fancier, yet risky strapless-back heels. They were so cute and made my sequenced white gown even more glamorous.

Later that day on Saturday, March 4th at six p.m. to be precise, it would be pageant time. My heart was beating out of my chest, but I looked stunning. I had gotten some micro-braided hair extensions put in previously, that looked like my very own root-grown hair from a distance. At the beginning of the event, we pageant girls had a group dance routine that allowed each of us to introduce ourselves to the crowd and judges, which wasn't so bad.

After the dance assemble was the swimsuit competition. Initially, I had a beautiful white and black bathing suit that was elegant-looking and fit me perfectly. Since the suit was two solid colors with a horizontal division underneath the breast line, I thought it could be suitable for the competition. However, Ms. Janetta wanted all swimming suits to be one solid color. When I showed her my swimsuit to get her approval, she said it was unacceptable, so at the last minute I grabbed a solid-colored swimsuit earlier that day. Come competition time, that was the suit I used.

Immediately after leaving the stage, I ran to the dressing area to put on the plain-looking swimsuit. The bathing suit was so underwhelming that I don't even recall the color precisely. I know that it was a dark color, perhaps navy. Behind the scenes, there were some beauticians who volunteered to style our hair. One I knew personally, because she was related to my son on his paternal side; her name was Michelle. Michelle propped my hair up and gave it that extra lift it needed for that dramatic effect expected in a pageant. The hairstyle even made my swimsuit look batter.

As soon as she was done, I put on my clear pumps and ran to the stage to be second to go up. I was so nervous, chest beating through my eardrums. But everything was so fast-paced; there was no time for second guesses or doubts.

The talent competition followed after the swimsuit portion. I rushed back to the dressing room to throw off the swimsuit and put on my elegant dress and shoes. Again, my first thought to just put on the simple pumps. The dress was long enough to where people wouldn't even notice my shoes, but again I chose the fancier, strapless shoe. I was fully dressed, touching up my makeup, and Michelle came to spruce up my hair once more. Then, off I went to be second in line for the talent part.

One of the pageant girls, Jenjit, who was third to perform, gave me a compliment on my evening gown. She said that I looked pretty and asked what song I was singing.

I told her, "Whitney Houston's song, 'I Have Nothing'."

Jenjit replied, "Ok, I can see that. Your attire is fitting."

And I told her, "Thank you," as I was about to go up and perform.

Whitney ruled the platform wherever she performed, and she always represented elegance. Therefore, when I chose to sing her song, I had to embody what Whitney meant to me. The announcer called my name, and it was my time to shine. When I walked up, the overhead lights were so bright, I could not even see anybody in the audience or directly in front of me. That was a good thing, because I couldn't see the hundreds of people staring up at me. Therefore, I stood there calmly in front of the mic, waiting for my song to play. And when it did, I let my vocals loose.

My lyrics weren't as crisp and clean as they could have been if I'd taken the steam session; however, I still sounded amazing. After my performance, I turned around and saw one of the other pageant girls who also chose singing as her talent staring at me with an expression of shock and intimidation. I began to walk toward the back of the stage when the back heel of my right shoe got snagged in the carpet. I tried to walk forward, but that shoe was stuck.

Instantly, I contemplated how I could get out of this situation. I could try to finagle the shoe out from the carpet by leaning all my support on the other leg, because there was nothing else to aid in supporting my balance around me. If I decided to do that, I would be taking a huge risk of falling on stage in front of all those people, including the judges, and I doubted very heavily that it would be a pretty fall. Also, in the process of wiggling the shoe out from the carpet by wiggling my ankle, I could risk the shoe flying off somewhere, and then I would have to walk off the stage with one shoe on and the other off. And that wouldn't be a good look either, considering that I was wearing four-inch strapless heels.

To avoid all that, I simply said, "F– it" and bent over, straight-legged to unsnag that shoe. Then I straightened up and walked off the stage with both shoes on my feet.

Afterwards, the 1999 Miss Black Tulsa winner, Marquetta Logan, walked over to inform me what I should have done instead. Apparently bending over like that, I mooned the judges. Marquetta said that I should have just stepped out of both the shoes, left them behind and walked off the stage barefoot. And I could have done that, but I have never been one to walk barefoot anywhere except in the house, so naturally that wasn't in my mind to do at that crisis moment.

However, as she was telling me that, I did recall hearing gasps behind me. They were shaming me, as if they saw my panties or a bare ass or something, and I know that didn't happen. So, ok, I mooned the judges. I was just glad to have gotten off that stage without falling, because if that would have happened, I know I would have been clowned for years along with not winning the competition.

I was ticked off at myself though, for choosing to wear those strapless heels. I should have known, if something were to go wrong, it would and it did—Murphy's Law. I was so stuck on the aesthetics of that shoe, despite it being a strapless shoe, that I didn't even consider the heel getting stuck in that raggedy ass stage carpet. If I had been in those simple pumps with the supported heel straps, I could have muscled my way out of that stupid carpet snag. I was perturbed with myself, because I knew better.

Following the talent competition was the part where the judges would choose their top five finalists. All sixteen pageant contestants, myself included, stood up on stage in line anticipating. Each of us, hoping that our name would be called to be one of the five contenders remaining. And guess what, folks? My name was not called to be one of them After the fifth person was called, they started the one-on-one stage interview with the judges. As each one of the top five answered their questions, I pretended that I, too, was being asked, and I answered their questions better than most of the selected top five.

It did suck, not even placing in the pageant with all that money and time spent; however, I was not bitter. I was a working young mother, so I wouldn't have had the additional time or support to handle the responsibilities that of what the Miss Black Tulsa crown held, even if I did win. And besides, I accomplished what I needed to; I overcame my fear of singing in public. Therefore, I stood there on that stage with the other losers and looked on, but unlike them, I kept a smile on my face until the very end.

After the pageant was over, it was a big sigh of relief. I went back to the dressing room to find that all but a few of my personal belongings were gone. Both swimming suits seemed to have disappeared. My shoes were untouched, but the garments were missing.

The Feedback

CHAPTER SEVENTY-SIX

The next day or shortly after, I got word of what the family members and friends who attended the event had to say. I got some good comments, but I also heard some sarcastic ones too. My neighbor-friend said that I looked absolutely beautiful, which was a consensus across the board. An auntie said the swimsuit I wore was entirely too small; it was all in my butt. My cousin Nella, said that I did better than she thought I would. Now, you tell me what you would've made of that statement?

After listening to everyone's critiques, I could decipher between two things. The ones who were there to show genuine support of me, apart from the ones who, perhaps lowkey expected to see me make a spectacle of myself and fail.

I also heard about what was happening in the audience during the performances. My home girl, Monique, and her friend Dawn were there to show support as well. Monique said DeLon saw her and her friend there and came over to sit with them, greeting her with his signature nickname he gave her, "Hey, Chocolate." Monique said DeLon was eating some French fries from McDonalds and teasing Dawn with them, waving them in her face. The next thing she knew, Dawn snatched the French fry out of DeLon's hand and put it right in her mouth, rubbing her belly as she swallowed the fry. Apparently, the expression on DeLon's face was priceless as Monique and Dawn both almost fell out their seats, weak from laughter at his reaction.

Tim was there, too, to show his support, I suppose. He sat with his friend Terry, who was at the event in support of his wife, Kim, who was the one of the two emcees of the show. Kim at that time was a young journalist who worked for OETA, Oklahoma Educational Television Authority.

I had known Kim for years prior to the pageant day. I was first introduced to her by my cousin Kim. The two Kims both attended high school together and were good friends. The friend Kim came over to my cousin's house to visit on a day that I was there. She drove up in this itty-bitty sports coupe that looked like it might have sat about three inches from the ground, maximum, and it barely was four feet long. I think the vehicle might have been dark grey in color.

The make and model of the car is unknown to me. At the time, I was about fourteen years of age and paying close attention to car models was not on my top ten to-do list. However, what I did notice about this vehicle was that it could have very well been the littlest sports car I recall ever seeing.

Prior to her arrival, my cousin Kim had mentioned that she was about to have some company and opened the living room door. I stood at the front door and peered out as Kim's friend Kim pulled up in that tiny car. She got out of it and then pushed the driver's seat forward to pull out not one, but two infant car seats. I couldn't believe it. My mouth dropped opened as I looked on in amazement. Kim's friend Kim had very recently had twins, a boy and a girl; and she brought them by to show them to my cousin Kim. And by the gleam in her eyes, I could tell she was so proud of her babies.

Now, eight years later our paths crossed again during this event. Kim had done a great job moderating the pageant. She was emceeing with a guy who kept getting tongue-tied and mispronouncing the contestant names. Without Kim by his side, the commentating portion could have been a train wreck. However, due to Kim's witty personality and professional skills, she was able to maintain a smooth transition between each competitive category.

Offstage, I didn't see much of Kim; however, I ran into her husband quite a bit. Terry and Tim stayed around after the pageant, I assumed waiting for Kim. They both mentioned that I looked beautiful and did a good job considering the stage mishap. Tim was still tickled about the mooning incident, as he commented about it and started to giggle. Terry kept his composure and just stood there and smiled as Tim talked on.

I explained to the two friends what had taken place on stage that they couldn't see. Avoiding a stage fall, I wasn't embarrassed the slightest bit about; no matter how the audience's standpoint looked. I knew the outcome could have been a whole lot worse trying to stay pretty. It had been a long day, so after a few chuckles I ended the convo with, "Good night, gentlemen." And we parted ways.

Work as Usual

CHAPTER SEVENTY-SEVEN

After the pageant, life went back to the typical work pattern. I gained no notoriety. The person whom the song was dedicated to wasn't there. I didn't win, much less place as a finalist, so prizes or tiaras of any sort were out. Nope, just as the day comes and goes, so did that pageant, with only an experience and a not so fond memory of a shoe coming off in front a crowd of people to set me apart. Oh, yeah and the unintended mooning incident.

When I arrived at work the following morning, my co-workers all asked how I did in the pageant. With a little hesitation, I told them what went down on stage. And they all gave me that ole generic saying: "Aw, better luck next time." But in the back of my head, I was thinking, *there isn't going to be a next time.* That was it.

With Tim's optometry office being right across the hall from the dental practice where I worked, it was convenient for him to pop his little head in to say hello. He did so quite frequently. Tim would come in the dental office and smile all big. He'd walk up to the reception desk that stood about four feet high to greet me, sitting behind it, all I could see was his big round head, bulbous eyes and dark-pinkish, in-flamed-looking gums. He apparently did not floss and had severe gingivitis; Tim's breath even had an odor. Being in the dental field, the sight was off-putting. However, with the way Tim was grinning all in my face with gums that looked like, if you poked 'em, they'd be gushing with blood, the man was unaware of his dental needs obviously.

After so many of Tim's walk-in greetings, I finally suggested for him to make a dental appointment. I gave him my professional spiel about getting routine professional cleanings twice a year and how it aids in preventing severe gum disease, which eventually leads to loosened teeth. Tim understood the concept, because he made an appointment for the next day. I was glad too, because I was tired of looking at his swollen, plaque-lined gums staring back at me, as he consistently attempted to gain my attention.

The next day, Tim was on time for his appointment. Shelly, the hygienist, gave Tim the best teeth cleaning of his life. Shelly was good. She would get underneath those gums and scrape all the crap from underneath them. She had extra time to spend with Tim too, because her next patient had to reschedule. When Shelly finished up with Tim, she wanted to see him back in a month to check the healing progression. Tim walked up to the check-out desk, gums looking like they got worked over and said he had never had his teeth cleaned like that before. He had this look on his face like he had just been manhandled, on a light scale, but in a good way and scheduled his follow-up hygiene appointment.

At Dr. Thorne's dental office, I worked on the business side. I filed insurance claims, rebutted denied dental claims, collected monies, and scheduled appointments. While I did not mind being a business assistant, my heart was steered more toward the clinical side of dentistry. I absolutely enjoyed serving people and giving them a little pampering in the process. Working at the front desk, shoveling papers, getting into people's wallet—it lacked the satisfaction that I craved.

With the location of the dental office, while doing my job, I could observe through the glass doors who came in or out of the building between both offices. The main person I saw more than expected was Terry. I could tell he and Tim were very good friends. Sometimes they'd go off to lunch together and oftentimes, Terry would just be up at Tim's job hanging out.

When I wasn't with patients, I was able to go out and speak to Terry. He was very friendly and approachable, so we'd chop it up a bit from time to time. I'd say hello or ask him what he'd been up to. The topic though, nine times out of ten, was usually him talking about what he had just bought his wife, Kim, or trying to decide what to buy Kim next.

There was a jewelry guy who traveled around to sell and deliver gold jewelry in North Tulsa. From the outside looking in, it seemed like Terry was his number-one customer. Terry was always hitting him up for something gold and dangly for his wife. He would occasionally meet up with the jewelry guy at Tim's office. The times I'd be on break or free for the day, I'd check out J-man's inventory too. However; I didn't have the extra cash for anything that wasn't keeping the lights on or the water running. Therefore, I'd just look, but Terry would sometimes buy one or more gold pieces whenever the jewelry man came around.

You know, after so long of tolerating certain people and

the utter annoyance that follows their existence, at some point the intolerability minimizes. Like, the more they come around, the less bothered you are by them. I don't know if it's because of our neurotransmitters that signal irritation become coarsened, or eventually those annoying people just mentally break us down. Whatever the case may be, when Tim popped his big head into our office or wanted to show his face, oddly enough, seeing him more and more didn't agitate me as much.

I was trying to figure out what brought on this perception change. He still had a six-inch height deficit compared to me. He still had that wimpy looking smile, but with much healthier looking gums. I must admit, that did ease the eye tension a bit. Plus, it helped that I wasn't always hit with the ole one-two when it came to his breath; you know, that kind that dazes you a bit and make you want to take a step back. Yeah, that part.

So, anyway, let me refocus. What was different about him? Nothing. He was still short. But maybe I was changing my mind about him, either that or Tim had finally worn me down.

Change of Opinion

CHAPTER SEVENTY-EIGHT

Four months and some change later after pageant day, I hadn't heard much at all from Rendell. I would take my son up to his barber shop to have his hair cut from time to time, but other than that, Rendell was distant. I'm sure he was just out living his life, which sadly was separate from mine. He did have a shop to run and maintain. Plus, Rendell was young, single and cute, so he had enough in his surroundings to occupy his time with; I'm sure.

Tim had still been pestering me and making me feel guilty for not wanting him. For the entire time I'd known him, he had been steadily trying to get me to go on a date with him. He bugged me so much about it that there were some days I would hate to see him coming. Why couldn't this dude just take, no for an answer?

Then one Saturday evening in late April, I sat myself down to have a heart-to-mind deliberation. I was sitting in my living room, resting in my extra cushiony, green striped chair. The head rest was so soft and plush that it cradled my head as I leaned back. I inhaled deeply and then completely exhaled, and at that moment, I decided to come off my high horse and really consider what Tim had to offer.

I put together a checklist for myself. I was like, "Olivia, are you being unreasonable?" Despite the height conflict, which was a noticeable issue, Tim's intentions seemed to be genuine. He was very persistent; plus, he was a doctor. However, he was a recent graduate with doctorate level school loans to repay as well, I am sure. Still, my son could have another professional to look up to, besides his mommy. With all the advantages of dating Tim, the question I asked myself was: "Am I being too vain to risk a possible good thing, simply because this guy is way shorter than me?" After about forty minutes of serious, deep thought, I decided to go on that date with Tim.

Our first outing together was cool; we did the typical dating stuff. Tim picked me up from the duplex. We went out to eat, and might have seen a movie; that part is a blur. However, I do recall quite vividly that over dinner, we had a really good conversation. I was totally comfortable with the verbal exchange taking place during our date.

Tim didn't come off like an arrogant a–hole, which usually steered me away from the young, single professionals that I knew. Being in the dental field, I had come across a few eligible men with doctorates, and the ones I chose to share my time with typically ran me off with their atypical arrogant behavior. Heck, Evan's arrogance was enough for me, and he hadn't even gotten accepted into law school yet. However, with Tim the energy was different. Sitting at a table with him, having face-to-face, comfortable adult conversation was very inviting to me.

After our initial and very casual date, a string of other dates followed. Being out in public with Tim, walking side by side with him was indeed awkward for me in the beginning. However, the more time Tim and I spent together, the less his height deficit bothered me. I found a fondness for

Tim, which was a surprise to me, because I never thought I would. However, eventually those many dates led to a romantic beginning.

Tim and I would find a way to converse with each other every day. If we were not chatting on the phone, we would see each other in passing at work. If we weren't at work or talking on the phone, we'd be on a date talking about everything. No matter what the occasion, the social interaction between Tim and me stayed on fleek.

After two months of Tim and his partner's optometry office being open, Tim mentioned that he was looking for another receptionist. The one they had currently wasn't working out. His explanation for deciding to replace her was that she kept asking for raises, but did very little work. Therefore, Tim thought that it would be better for the office to find another receptionist.

Tim asked me if I knew anybody who would like a front office job. Initially, I drew a blank at the question, but then Ms. Janetta came to the forefront. If you recall, Ms. Janetta was the director over at the Miss Black Tulsa pageant. And despite her shady behavior toward me during the pageant, I looked past all that and still put in a good word for her. Tim must not have had any other candidates, or perhaps Ms. Janetta was the most qualified. Either way, he called her up and she got hired for the office position soon after.

With all the dates Tim and I were going on, feelings seemed to be developing on both our ends. The notion of becoming a doctor's wife had become a serious thought. It never was a goal of mine to be a spouse of doctor. In fact,

ANGELS DON'T WARN FOR NOTHIN'

I wanted to be a doctor myself, a dentist. And with a supportive professional mate, it would certainly make the road to my high achievements a lot less challenging. Having a doctor as a hubby would also, give my child high expectations to reach for. Yes, I could foresee it now, the benefits of being the wife of a doctor had finally resonated with me. The idea of it all attracted me even more, and wouldn't you know it? I actually got a little snooty.

On one of my many visits to Tim's office, I was surprised to see a face that was unfamiliar to me, yet very familiar to Tim. I was standing at the reception desk talking to Ms. Janetta, when I turned around to see this tall, super lean, light-skinned lady with braces walking in beside Tim, wearing police attire. This lady cop was taller than me by at least three inches and made Tim look like a micro-shrimp.

Surprised, I stopped in my tracks. Tim, whose body posture was relaxed, introduced the lady cop as his childhood friend, Regina. I greeted her with a smile and shook her hand. Then I told them I had to get back next door before dashing out. Although that was my first time ever seeing or hearing about Tim's close childhood friend, it appeared that they were just that—friends—so I had nothing to be alarmed about.

Weeks later in the early part of June, I got word that DeLon's dad, Eric, would soon be released from prison. I arrived home after work, did the usual routine of checking the mailbox, and discovered a letter from Eric. In it, he mentioned that he would be coming home in the near future and wanted to restart a relationship with me. He also wrote about being excited to see his son. The last time Eric saw

374

his son, DeLon was nine months old. Now here it was, six years later, and our child would be graduating from kindergarten within days. According to Eric's letter, he would be released back into the free world right around that same time.

I had mixed emotions about the letter. Although I was glad Eric would be free from incarceration, I didn't want him stirring up trouble in my social life. I also did not want to be in relationship with Eric and thought I made that clear in previous correspondences.

However, that had nothing to do with Eric forming a father-son relationship with our child. But, knowing him and his crazy ways, just the idea of Eric being free again did make me a bit nervous.

Craze E Ways

CHAPTER SEVENTY-NINE

I had good reason to feel the way I did about Eric. I know everyone has their demons, but I never saw his until after I got pregnant. The things I underwent when carrying that man's child—it was unnecessary, extremely stressful, and in some cases dangerous.

Upon the knowledge of Eric getting out of prison, I had mixed emotions that were followed by bad memories. It seemed there was never any normalcy within our relationship; I dealt with harder issues than just his cheating.

One of Eric's crazier moments happened when I was at home. He and I were talking on the telephone. It was late, perhaps after midnight, and he said that he'd been drinking. I was in my bedroom as usual, stretched across the bed while on the phone. My mother and siblings were in the house, asleep more than likely. As usual, Eric got upset about something and threatened to come over to the house and cause a disturbance. Of course, I didn't need that with all the other family drama I had going on, so I begged him to not come over.

But did he listen?

I hung up the phone and went to the kitchen for something to drink, then went back to my bedroom. Now, Eric didn't live very far from me, I had walked over to his place a time or two, so it might have been about a 35-minute walk. However, as soon as I came from the kitchen to my room and closed the bedroom door, this fool was knocking at my window, and my heart sunk.

I am unsure of how he got over to my place that quickly. I wondered if he rode his bike or caught a ride, because he came over to my house within ten minutes. I didn't even have time to cut off the lights and at least pretend I didn't hear this fool knocking at my window.

Stunned and apprehensive all at the same time, I hesitantly peeked through the blinds. There Eric stood, looking evil, like a light-skinned Lucifer with his dark, beady eyes. Right then and there, I knew he came to cause havoc, and for what, I had no clue. I looked at him looking at me, and I didn't say a word. Finally, he broke the silence and told me to come outside. Lord knows I did not want to, but I didn't want to take the chance of him disturbing the slumber of the others who were in the house. Nervous to the core, I closed the blinds and met him in the backyard.

It was still summertime, so the outdoor temperature at night was perfect for me, about 77 degrees. I had on a t-shirt and shorts with a light knee-length robe when I went outside to meet him. Again, I didn't understand what his problem was with me. It seemed like he would be unhappy with his life, but trip with me about it.

Being a light-skinned young man in the hood of North Tulsa, living middle-class was hard on Eric. Eric had both parents at home, who gave him anything he wanted and that was a stress, I guess. As I mentioned earlier, Eric's nice clothes and multiple sets of gangster Nikes made him a target for those who lacked what he had.

Having easily attainable items would cause Eric to be a victim of his circumstance. He would get into fights, and often in the process somebody would steal his newly worn shoes or whatever else they wanted of his. Usually, it would be multiple boys involved in the altercation with him. Sometimes he would fight and get beat up; other times, he would just run. However, whatever his issues were, it still had nothing to do with me, yet I was one he decided to take his frustrations out on.

I stood on the patio and said something like, "Nice night." I really felt uncomfortable, because he had been drinking, so there was no telling what he was thinking or what he would do. Eric was too much in an evil mood, because he didn't even bother commenting on the weather. He just went right into attack mode verbally. Eric said something shitty to me, to get the vibe how he wanted it—negative.

I can't recall what was said between us; however, I do remember Eric pulling out a gun and threatening to shoot me. I was so scared. I never even saw a gun in person, and here this fool had one up to my head while I was carrying his child. Instantly, I started crying quietly because I didn't want my mom to hear. But, how could he do this, of all things?

I begged for him to put the gun down. I begged for him to leave. I begged for whatever I could to get him away from me. Eric was holding that gun and saying he was going to blow my brains out. I was so frightened; I remember thinking, *Lord, how did I get myself into this mess?* It was crazy.

Then in the middle of it all, a dog casually comes toward us from out of the bushes. It was the poodle that an aunt had given to my mom, because she could no longer house it. The pet came walking over to me. Eric saw that dog and turned the gun on it. He threatened to shoot the poor dog. The poodle was obviously an inside dog, but my mother never took care of anything. At our house, that poodle was an outside dog and its hair had grown all out of control and began to dread up. That poodle had his head down, sniffing at something on the ground, oblivious to the actions of this troubled man with a gun pointed at it.

Then Eric fired the gun. Thank God for all that dog hair that had grown on the animal, because the bullet went through it and into the ground. The dog, suddenly scared by the loud noise, ran off.

I was scared out of my mind too. I held my hand over my mouth, so no one could hear me scream and cry. Then Eric, as if he didn't know he had bullets in the gun and was frightened himself, took a few steps back in disbelief. Then he turned around and jumped over the fence, running off.

Still shaken up, I had to stay outside for a minute to gather my composure before I went back in the house. After that insanely stressful incident, I got morning sickness again for the second time during my pregnancy.

Those two highly mental and emotional encounters were the worst I've ever experienced with Eric or anyone else, for that matter. Eric would threaten and scare. He would raise his hand to me, but he never struck me. However, at age sixteen, with all the other life stressors I faced being young and pregnant, that was enough drama to last me a lifetime.

Bygone

CHAPTER EIGHTY

Now, five years later, Eric was about to be released from prison and I wasn't sure how to feel. Of course, I didn't want him locked up forever, but at the same time, I didn't want him or his crazy ways disturbing my peace either. I do understand that people change, but nothing can turn back the hands of time and the memories, bad or good, will always remain.

Eric had been writing me during his time of being locked up. He wrote about how he wanted us to be a family. I would write him right back, explaining that he should work on being a good father to his son, first and foremost. He and I, on the other hand, could be just friends. I wanted nothing more than for him to make his own way in life and be a good father to our child. However, that had to be accomplished without me.

My eyes were open to the kind of person Eric was. Through my experiences with him, I could see that he was a very weak-minded individual. Anyone but the right people could talk him into doing anything wild for a "quick come up." Sadly, Eric would choose to listen to his "friends" who were school dropouts, gang affiliates, and not those who actually cared about his well-being and future.

Eric's street hustle mentality and mental flaws were totally the opposite of me and what I stood for. I believed in educating oneself and earning the things you got in life, even if that meant starting from the ground up. Eric wanted to steal and rob. Also, as a strong believer in Christ, I understood the consequences of making good and bad decisions. Although Eric attended church with his mom often, from his actions and choices made, it was clear he did not fully grasp the message that the Bible taught.

I also comprehended that for us to be a thriving couple and be able to achieve a life together, Eric and I both had to be on the same wavelength. In which, we were not. Therefore, our purpose as a unit would be of no effect, causing hindrances instead of growth. Eric would likely be more of a burden than an asset within the relationship. In my close interactions with him, I realized that having a boyfriend with a cute face and a nice body was not going to cut it. I had to have someone in my life who had similar attributes as me. Those who are of strong-will and conscience-driven, unlike the characteristics of Eric.

It was difficult for me to even consider being back in a relationship with him. If there was a remote chance of Eric and me ever being a couple again, it would be years from now. I would have to see for myself his growth and maturity at a distance. I cared for Eric deeply, but I also cared for and loved myself. The things that I encountered with him, his verbal and mental abuse; the bad certainly outweighed the good. He took way more than he gave, unfortunately for him.

I thought to self. How could I be everything that I need to be in this life, if the one I love is going against me? One who is constantly being beat down with insults and having their energy detracted, as opposed to having charged energy invested in them, cannot prosper. And although Eric did father a child with me, I wasn't about to take the chance and put myself back in such insanely, unfavorable situations as the ones that man orchestrated. No ma'am, Pam.

At Last

CHAPTER EIGHTY-ONE

The day had finally come that Eric was released from incarceration. It was four days before DeLon's first-grade promotion ceremony; he was six years old at that time. Eric had gotten out in time enough to at least witness one staple in our son's life.

Eric had been locked up since DeLon was nine months old, so they were practically strangers to each other. When I got the call that Eric was home, I was nervous for both of them. I took DeLon over to his grandmother's house, not knowing what to expect. As we pulled up, DeLon and I noticed that Eric was standing in the doorway. We got out of the car and made our way towards the house.

Eric, seeing us, opened the security door and invited us in. He looked at me with a reminiscent grin, then looked down at his son and said, "Ole DeLon, I heard a lot about you. I am your dad, and it's good to finally meet you."

DeLon was a little shy at first. He didn't have much to say, but he did smile a lot, showing his cute little snaggle-teeth. Eric would ask DeLon questions, and DeLon would answer with either yes or no by nodding his head, but still with a sweet smile.

We all were sitting at the dining room table, and I was observing the two get to know each other. DeLon started talking more as he began to feel more comfortable with Eric. Eric was talking loudly and causing my head to hurt, but that didn't seem to bother DeLon. Eric had grown his hair out and had it in six ponytails, three on each side of his head, and they hung about six inches long. His chin hair was long too, and he had three red rubber bands around it, looking just like an Ese. Although I was a bit embarrassed by Eric's appearance, DeLon didn't seem to mind at all. It looked like he was just happy to know he actually had a dad.

Observing those two together made me happy, but I still had my reservations. I really made a valid effort to let by-gones be bygone regarding my differences with Eric. It was more important for me to see him truly build a relationship with his son. DeLon needed a father around, and he had been asking about his since he was two. With Eric being locked away for all those years, he missed out on a lot of maturing for himself and the opportunity to watch his son grow.

Because Eric was talking so loudly, I wanted to say, "Eric, you are not behind bars anymore." But I held back. I knew that he just needed time to get acclimated to having his freedom and being amongst the working society again. Although I was well aware that Eric was clueless on how to be a dad, I still had high hopes for him. I wanted to see him positively develop into that role.

Topsy-Turvy

CHAPTER EIGHTY-TWO

Everything seemed to be going fine between the two until Mrs. E, Eric's mom, came home. DeLon saw her come through the door, and he dashed over to her to give her a hug. Eric watched but didn't say much.

Mrs. E's attention was all on DeLon. She asked, "Are you hungry? Do you want something to eat?"

DeLon said, "Yes! I want some Church's Chicken tender strips." It didn't matter where DeLon was, Mrs. E would always go get him whatever he wanted to eat, and this time was no exception. Mrs. E wasn't even in the house good, when she turned right back around to go get some Church's Chicken for DeLon.

Once she left out, we were back alone with Eric and things did a flip-flop. I don't know what happened in that short span of time that triggered that backwards-ass reaction from Eric, but he started picking on DeLon. Like, for real bullying him. Eric started calling DeLon a momma's boy and got rude with it. DeLon's feeling got hurt and he started crying.

Inside, my stomach turned. I was anxious, disappointed and upset all the same time. I thought, *Oh, no, here we go.* My mommy-protection mode kicked in, and I reached to comfort my son, but Eric had quicker reflexes and grabbed

DeLon away from me.

Eric took DeLon in the bathroom with him, then shut and locked the door behind them. I was on the other side, panicking internally, but trying hard to keep my composure. I said with a firm voice, "Eric, open this door!" while I beat on it continuously. I could hear my baby steadily crying in the bathroom. I repeated myself again, only this time with an increased intensity that was close to yelling. I told him, "Eric, if you don't open this door, I swear I will kick it in!"

Finally, after about five minutes, the door opened and my son came out sobbing. I was frightened, because I feared that something like this could happen. I did not want my son to observe any sort of violence, but in his defense, that whole house would have been tore up, because it would have been a full-on war. However, thank God I did not have to go there. My appetite was gone, and I'm sure DeLon's was too. I took my child's hand and darted out the front door.

Eric followed us out the door and kept repeating in a loud voice, "I wasn't going to hurt the little nigga." At that point, it didn't matter what he said; I was just ready to get the heck out of there. I got in the car and put DeLon next to me in the front seat. Eric walked around to the passenger door where DeLon was. Our son was sobbing, and I was so focused on DeLon that I didn't even notice Eric walk around to his side. I had my hand on the gear, about to pull it in reverse when suddenly Eric opened the passenger door. He reached in and pulled DeLon out of the car.

I sat there with the steering wheel in hand, thinking, *Ok, Lord, am I going to have to knock this fool out?* I quickly scanned the yard for any hard objects that would fit in my hand.

DeLon started crying all over again. Eric picked up our son and hung him upside-down over the city trash can. My heart dropped because I didn't understand Eric's behavior, but that was nothing new. He couldn't help himself, I guess. I got out of the car and demanded that Eric put my son down as I watched my baby sway back and forth over the canister with fear in his eyes. All I wanted to do was grab my son and be gone.

"Eric!" I yelled. "How could you do this to your son?"

I guess he got to thinking about it, because shortly after that, he put DeLon down and claimed that he was just playing. I gave him a glare so sharp that if it was lightning, it would have struck him down. I said, "Fool, nobody's laughing!"

Then I got my son and put him back in the car, but this time I locked the doors. I put the car in reverse and pulled out of the driveway so fast that if Eric would had been behind me, he would have gotten ran smooth over. When we got far enough away, I pulled over to hug and comfort my son.

"Are you okay?" I asked.

With tears on his little cheeks and eyes watery, he nodded his head yes. I felt horrible; my baby was damn near traumatized by his own father. Sadly, there was nothing I could say more to make the situation better. I was at a loss for words. I feared that something bizarre like this would occur, and here it had on their initial meeting.

Turn of Events

CHAPTER EIGHTY-THREE

The next day I woke up troubled, still confused and upset about what had taken place between my son and his dad. Thoughts of how to rectify the situation or eliminate the problem raced through my head. In what manner was I going to protect my child? I thought about disallowing Eric to see our son, but that would also mean to forbid DeLon from seeing his grandmother. After all, Eric was staying with her for the time being, which elevated the task immensely, and I could not do that.

I thought about just moving away to a different location out of state. However, that would mean I wouldn't be able to see my own family as conveniently as I currently did. But, in retrospect that might not have been a bad notion. In any case, I was bogged down with the concern about how I was going to secure the safety of my child against this loony personality he called dad.

Later that day, my mind was put somewhat at ease. It was mid-morning Saturday, and I was doing household chores. Still in a daze regarding yesterday's events, I vacuumed the floors and straightened up the house with a hardened expression on my face. I could tell it was tight too, because occasionally I could feel the tension in my forehead. Conscious of what I was doing, I'd straighten up my face and exhale relaxingly. That alone gave me some mental relief.

Although I did not say a prayer, the angelic gods must have been feeling my energy. In the midst of doing housework, I got a phone call. The caller ID indicated it was from Mrs. E's residence. I picked up the phone, hoping it was DeLon's grandmother.

But as I answered, I heard, "Hello, Olivia." It was Eric.

I went quiet, because what I really wanted to do was hang up in this idiot's face. However, I decided to keep the receiver up to my ear and just listen to what he had to say.

After a minute of no response from me, Eric went on to apologize about what took place the other day. He revealed that being locked up all those years, it was like time had stopped for him. Then after five years of being in the pen, he goes home thinking that everything would still be the same; and it wasn't. He was no longer the baby boy of the house who received all the attention; it was now DeLon. Eric went on to say that he felt like DeLon had taken his place and he no longer mattered, which caused him to react so negatively toward his own son. He understood that his actions toward our son were wrong and unfounded. And for that, he wanted our forgiveness.

As I listened, I could feel the stress totally ease from my body. The hefty feeling of annoyance that engrossed my mind now turned into compassion toward Eric. The words that came out his mouth were those I desperately needed to hear. And it was a pleasant surprise to know that Eric was mature enough to zone in on the cause behind his negative output, especially so soon, because I was sorely concerned about all other future interactions with him. That mental state of emergency, "mommy fight to protect" mode had kicked in and overtaken me since Eric's disastrous first meeting with DeLon. Now, I was relieved and thankful that I didn't have to take action.

I now could rationalize his perspective of the situation. And although his past actions were not entirely excusable, it gave me some sense of relief that Eric was humble and sane enough to acknowledge his wrongdoing. That phone call was a welcome attempt to make amends, and at the end of our conversation, I hung up the phone with a grin.

After getting over that initial setback between DeLon and his dad, things seemed to happen on a more positive note. Eric talked with DeLon too, and apologized for his actions. Shortly after that, Eric got a job at Walmart and bought DeLon his first dirt bike as an appreciation gift.

DeLon got promoted to the first grade, and this time at his advancement ceremony, I wasn't the only person there cheering him on. In attendance were also his dad, paternal grandmother and DeLon's Auntie Tam. This was one of the few and far in-between times we would come together in celebration of Delon's achievements. With all the smiles and good vibes going around, I could tell that DeLon was glad to finally have his father become a part of something in his life. And on that same token, Eric appeared proud to have taken part in something great that he helped create—our son.

On the outside looking in, Eric was doing well for himself in the beginning. He worked at Walmart for a few months, saved money, and was able to buy the things he wanted. Shortly after that, Eric got that ole car his mom refused to let me drive, the one that was sitting in her yard, up and running. Eric even bought the white Dynasty some fancy shoes—a set of strait-laced chrome rims. I saw that he was very proud of that too.

Eric promised himself that he wouldn't hang out with that same old troublesome crew like he did before getting locked up. He kept to his word, at least for a short while. For Eric was too occupied with earning money and getting reacquainted with his family, so there was no time for nonsense like being gang affiliated.

However, things changed. Just as Eric was getting himself together by adjusting and growing with this new outside world, he met a girl named Julia.

Julia was a stripper who had two kids and lived in some income-based apartments called Mohawk Manor. Julia looked biracial, like she was mixed with black and white, but could pass for Puerto Rican and her kids did too, though they were light-skinned with straight, light-colored hair. Eric himself looked mixed with his fair skin and dark features. If there was a paternity test and it was correct, Eric's father was black; some would still doubt though.

Julia took to Eric and perhaps Eric took to Julia, but more so for the sake of her kids. Julia had a little boy and girl who were about two to four years of age. Eric used to tell me how he felt sorry for Julia's kids, because she would mistreat and neglect them. And the more time spent with Julia, the more Eric felt obligated to look after her children.

One day, while I was on the job, Eric called me in the

middle of the day. I asked him why he wasn't at work. Eric told me that he had quit. Julia told him that she would make enough money for the both of them stripping and that he didn't need to work. Julia promised him that she would give him all the cash she earned every night. Apparently, that was all the convincing Eric needed. During that conversation, I mentioned to him that it's best to be in control of your own earned money, but Eric liked making sure her kids were all right during the night. Plus, Julia was bringing him back wads of cash in the beginning.

After a couple of months, Eric had practically moved in with Julia. He spent a great deal of time at her apartment and consistently had her kids. A few times, I would see Julia's kids over at Mrs. E's house; Eric and his mom would be watching them for her. It was like Mrs. E, in an instant, had another set of grandkids, which felt odd to me initially.

Eric was so occupied with his new girlfriend and her kids that he saw them way more than he did his own and only biological child. He would tell me how some of his female friends gave him grief about it too. I suppose he wanted some sort of reassurance from me that he was doing the right thing, but I just told him to keep doing what he felt like doing. He was out of my hair and not stirring up any trouble in my dating life with Tim, so I was cool.

Eric would call and confide in me quite a bit, surprisingly. He would vent about Julia and his mom. His mom was going out now and hanging with folks her daughter's age, in their late twenties and early thirties. It was like outside of work and her marriage, she had a whole other life and name. Julia got lazy and didn't want to be gone all hours of the night making money for "them both," and the money became scarce. He would observe some things about her that he didn't agree with and then call me up to get the frustration off his chest.

Julia and Eric started having problems within their relationship, which drew him away. She started showing her ass, getting drunk and even being violent in some cases. Eric did not like that. It started to create distance between them.

Now, with all the idle time Eric had on his hands, he began to revert to his old ways. Due to being unemployed and now unoccupied with Julia's kids, he started hanging back with the crew that he said he wouldn't see anymore. He went back on his promise. With that came the gang signs, and more of the red attire—shoelaces, hats, and so on. Half of his clique didn't have jobs, sold drugs, and didn't have any inspiration outside of black women. And there Eric was, despite all his accomplished growth in that short span of being released from prison. He fell right back in with them.

One of those misguided people in that clique was this dude named Pumpkin. I didn't know much about Pumpkin besides that he claimed Blood, was good pals with Eric, and he dated a friend of mine named Candace. Candace was beautiful and must not have known her worth, because she settled for a dog like Pumpkin. And Pumpkin was no looker either. He might have been winning below deck, but above was a lost cause, so to speak. Candace had two kids with Pumpkin, and she had been with him for a long time. She was a teenage mother like me, only her story was not just about verbal abuse. Pumpkins used to lay hands on Candace, and it wasn't just a slap or two; they got into some dangerous altercations.

Through Eric, my impression of Pumpkin was not good. He was a school dropout, a young thug who was trying to make fast cash by any means, including selling drugs and thievery. Eric spoke a lot about Pumpkin, like he was making moves or doing big things, but I wasn't convinced. From the stories I heard from Candace, Pumpkin was just another insecure jerk who took from his baby mamas. Eric fell for all the boastful talk coming out of Pumpkin's mouth, but I knew it was nothing but hot, funky air.

Sadly, Eric and Pumpkin started hanging on a regular basis. One day they were riding around, both in the back seat sipping and smoking weed while some young kid drove them around. From what I understand, the car paused at a stoplight and some dudes just rolled up to them. Then, one got out of the car and started dumping on Pumpkin. Eric was sitting right next to Pumpkin when he saw the bullets enter his friend's body. The sounds of the loud firearm rung in Eric's ear, he told me. The smell of gun smoke circulating throughout the backseat singed his nose. Blood splattered everywhere, even getting on Eric.

Eric was scared shitless. With all the drive-by shootings he was involved in as a youth, Eric had either been the shooter or riding with the shooter. However, the targets were always at a far distance. There were many cases where he himself would be shot at, but again from afar. Never had he had an up-close and personal encounter with a near-death experience such as this. This time, though, Eric saw firsthand, within inches of his own body, the devastation bullets cause when they rip through flesh. He was petrified and rightfully so.

Sitting in the backseat with Pumpkin when he got shot put Eric in a compromised situation. He said seeing it at close range like that, he didn't know what to do. He was paralyzed with fear. In an instant, Eric too could have been shot or even killed. Luckily, the gunner was just aiming at Pumpkin that time. However, seeing firsthand the aftermath of it all, Eric had a sudden fear for his life.

Eric knew that to feel safe again, he had to get away, leave the state. In prison, he'd become pen pals with a girl from Little Rock, Arkansas. Over the years, they developed a close friendship of some sort. When all this went down regarding the shooting, Eric contacted his pen pal from out of town and bounced.

Departure

CHAPTER EIGHTY-FOUR

Eric was on the highway heading east, leaving the state, when he called me. I answered the phone, but I could hardly understand him. There was so much static and distortion on our call; I could only understand every two or three words that he spoke, and his voice faded out a lot. However, what I could hear clearly was the fear in his voice and the engine accelerating in the background. He had his foot to the metal, laid heavily on the gas. From what I gathered, he was leaving T-Town and was not looking back.

Hanging up the phone, I became somewhat sad. Eric and I were beginning to be chums. And despite our differences and rocky past, he was still the father of my child and my first love. I wanted to at least have the privilege to observe at a distance the kind of man he would evolve into. And who knew if, by chance, that as I witnessed his growth, along with us both being available, it might have caused me to view Eric in a romantic way again.

Yet, I also knew the likeliness of Eric and me regaining a mutual attraction had little to no chance of being a reality. It probably would have come around when we grew old, in our sixties, and just wanted companionship. Therefore, I wasn't totally opposed to Eric fleeing hundreds of miles away. However, I would be deprived of seeing his mental and physical growth firsthand, and so would our son.

DeLon would lose the advantage of not having his father nearby.

Weeks went by, and although I had not talked to Eric directly, I heard through his mother that he was doing okay. She said that the father of the girl Eric went to stay with had a church. Eric joined their congregation and even played the drums in the choir. Therefore, according to Mrs. E, Eric was doing all right.

Mrs. E discussed many things in that one conversation, for she was a big talker. However, an hour so later at the end of our talk, I got the idea that she was relieved that her son went away. For one thing, he was safe and with positive people to help him along the way. And two, he was no longer around to nose all up in her business. Now that Eric had set off to start a new life elsewhere, everyone could go about their daily lives and not be concerned with him interfering in their personal affairs.

"Houston, We Have a Problem"

CHAPTER EIGHTY-FIVE

In the meantime, Tim and I continued to date. Our routine conversations no longer consisted of me griping about Eric, since he had left. Prior to that, I would talk to Tim in lengthy detail about the things Eric would do, such as how he would curse around DeLon with no restraint. Tim would just laugh and say, "It's okay, DeLon should be exposed to stuff like that." When Eric was around, all I did was complain about him. However, now that he was out of sight, I was able to see that all of my complaining was over frivolous things really and I was being too critical of him.

Months into our relationship, I was expecting to see Tim on my lunch break, when we'd routinely hang out. However, when I crossed the hall over to his office for small talk on this one particular day, Tim was not there. The receptionist, Janetta, was sitting at the receptionist desk filing her nails. I asked Janetta where Tim was, and she said that he didn't come in to work. It struck me as odd, because I had talked to him the night before and Tim didn't mention anything about missing work the next day. But I casually blew it off and chatted with Ms. Janetta for a little bit before leaving to grab a bite to eat.

After work I checked my cell phone. I had two missed

calls from Tim, and there were voice messages. Without checking the voicemail, I immediately returned Tim's call, but it went straight to his voicemail. I called again to only get the same outcome—voicemail. I thought this to be strange as well.

I had begun to get concerned, hoping that nothing bad had happened. So, I checked the voicemail. Tim had left a message saying that he had a class reunion meeting. He was on the board and would probably be unavailable until six or seven o'clock that night. By the time I checked my messages, it was quarter 'til seven. Therefore, I hung up the phone and went about my evening, still waiting to hear from Tim.

After picking up DeLon, grabbing some dinner and going home to eat, it was a quarter past eight and still no word from Tim. I was puzzled because this was unlike him; normally we would have had some sort of verbal conversation by now, so I initiated contact once more. I called him. The phone rang a few times, then it went to Tim's voicemail again. Without leaving a message, I hung up the phone with a raised eyebrow, because things were not adding up.

Shortly after, Tim returned my call. The first thing I heard were echoing sounds in the background. By the sound of it, it was a very spacious room where Tim was. The noise was choppy, competing with Tim's voice. He sounded winded, as if he had just run up a flight of stairs, which made it even more difficult to understand him.

"Hey, Babe, how's it going?" he asked quickly.

I was so focused on listening to what I thought could be going on in the background that I was missing the bulk of what Tim was saying. He had to repeat himself a few times, before I could understand him enough to give him a proper answer.

Irritated, I ignored Tim's question altogether and asked him firmly, "Where are you?"

Tim, unbothered by the sharpness of my tone, responded casually and said that he was still at his class reunion meeting. Tim went on to say that the encounter lasted longer than expected and afterwards, he and a few others were going out for drinks. By the end of the conversation, he had caught his breath and collected himself. Now composed, Tim said that he would see me tomorrow. This temporarily eased my doubts, because whatever Tim had going on, he still was able to reach out; and that made me feel a little better about his sudden workday absence. I told him to have a good night; then we hung up.

That next morning, I went in to work as usual. I was majorly occupied for most of the morning, upholding my office duties and successfully appearing undistracted by the weighing concerns of Tim's whereabouts. Things were moving so quickly; I just wanted to stay in the zone and not be disrupted. The recent time-gaps between me and Tim caused me to feel guarded, which I did not like; and today I needed for him to take the initiative for a pop-up visit. I was not in the mood to go across the way, displaying a smiling, pretty face. Uh-uh, not that day.

Although Tim was talking like everything was cool, his actions were telling a different story. Due to that uneasiness, I was really hoping that he would drop in on his break to say hello and ease the tension that was building. However, to my disappointment, he didn't come by at all, and that was unusual for him at that stage of our relationship.

After clocking out, I decided to stop in at Tim's office before leaving for the day. I walked in just as Ms. Janetta was hanging up the phone. I asked if Tim was in the back seeing patients, and Ms. Janetta said, "No, Tim didn't come in at all today again."

Stunned, I asked, "Why not?"

Without hesitation, Ms. Jeanetta replied, "Tim got married yesterday."

"What?!" I struggled to keep my composure.

"Yeah," Ms. Janetta casually went on to say, "Tim called in this morning and told us. Nobody knew anything, not even his business partner, Gus."

I stood there, looking off into space, flabbergasted. By the time all of what I had heard sunk in, I was already feeling my anger stirring. My blood was boiling, and I felt all the way misused. I thought to myself, *That little, short fuck played me!*

Ms. Janetta saw this grimace expression form on my face. Oblivious to my interactions with Tim, she could not understand why I was bothered by Tim's sudden marital news. Becoming concerned, she asked, "What's wrong?"

Her questioning brought my mind back to where I stood, which was in front of her desk. However, before I could answer I had to first gather my emotions and thoughts, and bring them back down to a presentable state. I tried to respond in a timely manner, but my teeth were clenched tight, making the reply a little slower to come out. Finally, I turned to her and calmly said, "Tim and I were dating."

Astonished, Ms. Janetta now looked at me with a puzzled expression. To make sure she heard correctly what I said, she repeated, "Dating? But I thought you didn't like Tim. You were trying to hook him up with Star."

I nodded my head then stated. "Yeah, at first that was the case, but then after almost six months of declining Tim's advancements, I eventually gave in. Tim and I have been dating for, like, three months now." Hearing my version of events, Ms. Janetta sat there speechless and just shook her head.

The thought of how hard I was played went round and round in my head. After all that fucking time of him bugging the shit out of me about giving him a chance, playing on my kindness and making me feel so badly for not liking him because of his height. And that short twerp had a woman this whole time? The notion of it all—his lies, the cheating, this secretive wedding—it all made me nauseated, and I was so done, you could stick a fork in me.

I asked Ms. Janetta, "Who did Tim marry?"

Ms. Janetta responded, "His police lady friend."

"The police lady?" I repeated. That tall, lanky chick? Tim had introduced me to her as his childhood friend. That woman towered over me, and yet she had married Tim's 5'3"-sized self. The whole top portion of her body was taller than him.

I was hoaxed. This fool called me on his wedding day. He held multiple conversations with me and chatted about the things he was involved in with this "class reunion." He spoke about the meetings, his friends, and such—all lies told to me on the very day he vowed himself to another woman. There were no class reunion meetings taking up all his time; it was more like a wedding rehearsal and the actual wedding itself that consumed Tim's time, and rightfully so since he was the groom. Ole Timothy's reason for staying out late with his friends at a bar was actually him toasting it up to his newlywed wife and in-laws. Whom I had no clue about. He played me something serious; I was livid and wanted vengeance.

My first reaction was to cause damage. I pictured myself going to his apartment, kicking in the front door and just trashing the place, but then common sense kicked in. Tim's wife was a police officer, and if I were to show my ass like that—worst-case scenario, I could get shot and justifiably so. And if I acted upon my anger and went forward with successfully junking his apartment, I would have been a strong suspect in the matter, causing more unnecessary stress in my life. Tim would certainly know it was me, and now knowing the type of sneaky, snakish type person he was, I knew he would slander my name. I could foresee him making up all sorts of lies about me. Convincing people that I was this obsessed person who was stalking him. Tim was obviously good at telling lies to cover up his discrepancies, and he would be just that person to go about it in that manner with me.

If I did choose to give into those vengeful emotions that

overcame me, I would have tarnished my own reputation. In addition to putting my own freedom and livelihood at risk. And Tim simply was not worth that. Thankfully, I put my irrational thinking aside and took on a more rational approach.

Although common sense had kicked in, venomous anger still lurked all through me and I needed to release it. I had yet to confront Tim, but if I did so while carrying around all this strife, I would have surely gone to jail for aggravated assault. However, one night at home in my bathroom, I was able to channel that fury and free myself from it.

I was at home alone; all the lights were off in the house. DeLon was at his grandmother's place. I went into the bathroom, looked in the mirror and saw what I looked like filled with rage; and it was not a pretty sight. I cried, screamed and screamed some more until I had let go of all that strongly felt inner wrath. When I had done so, I could feel a dark energy leave me. I found myself on the bathroom floor wiping away tears. I picked myself up and took a breath of relief. Physically exhausted, I lay in the bed until I fell asleep, still with tears drying on my cheeks.

The next morning, I woke up at ease. I no longer felt that dark energy dulling my light. I no longer had bad thoughts of breaking Tim's bones for his trespasses against me. I had freed myself from that dark energy, and my mind was now positively set to push forward. I was not going to let Tim get the best of me. I wanted to show him that he was as irrelevant to my life as a hill of beans, and with this renewed mindset, I was able to take back my power. I had no intentions of letting that little twerp see that I was bothered by his grimy-ass ways. No matter what bullshit came out of Tim's flappy-lipped mouth, all I planned to do was smile right in his face and act unbothered.

And the following day, when Tim returned to work, that is exactly how things played out.

I was leaving for lunch when Tim spotted me in the foyer. He was hesitant at first, but proceeded to walk toward me. I saw him first, but acted as if I didn't and pretended to be surprised when he walked up, meeting me at the glass entryway.

"Oh, hey," I said with a smile on my face. Tim was looking at me, but his eyes were scrunched, as if he was confused at my cheeriness. I could tell he was not expecting that type of reaction from me. He slowly began to talk and started out with chitchat, asking how my day was, I responded dryly and looked at him with an emotionless facial expression. Tim's puzzled look remained on his face. He was still not sure if I knew or not about him covertly getting hitched.

I could tell that Tim wanted to say something of significance. However, he couldn't fix his mouth to mention it. He went on to talk about his class reunion meetings and how some alumni officers were noncompliant or what have you. I nodded my head, listening with bogus concern as the constant lies seethed out from his mouth. At that time, it would have been ethical of Tim to fess up to his low-down actions, but being upright was what Tim was not. Instead, he chose to continue on with his deception.

From there on, the sound of Tim's voice annoyed me. I

utterly felt disgusted with myself for even giving this low-down dirty dog a chance. In the middle of his blabbering, I suddenly looked at my watch in an attempt to rush him off with an excuse that I didn't have more time for lunch. This interrupted Tim in mid-conversation, and he looked surprised again. Normally, I would try to soak up all the time I had with him. However, with the sudden turn of events, I was determined to show Tim how detached I could be with his dishonesty and foul play. I was all smiles and chose not to display the revulsion I felt brewing on the inside just from hearing him speak.

It took a lot of energy to pull off those placid moves with Tim. However, the longer I gloated in his face, the easier it got, because I could see that it was getting to him. Tim might have suspected that I knew something. However, my cool-headed and self-composed behavior confused him, which made me smile even more. Nonetheless, smile or no smile, I wasn't going to acknowledge his marriage until Tim first came clean about it to me.

My actions spoke louder than what could have been said. Those pleasant pop-up visits I used to do over to his side of the building during my fifteen-minute breaks certainly came to a halt. Our routine nightly conversations absolutely ended. Tim would call me and act so concerned about my sudden change of affairs. Half the time when he did call, I wouldn't even pick up. And when I did answer, at the drop of a hat, I'd get off the phone for some random, off-the-wall reason.

Finally, after two weeks of getting the cold-hearted side of me, Tim got fed up. This rigid persona that I embraced, who had limited things to say to Tim but always smiled in his face, Tim got tired of. And one morning before we got busy with patients, Tim wobbled his big head over to me and said, "We need to talk."

The Acquisition – He Tried it

Chapter Eighty-Six

I was sitting at the reception desk when Tim walked over and demanded we talk. I was a bit taken aback, because this boldness was somewhat out of his character. However, his sudden action did excite that disgruntled spirit within me that still lurked about. *Oh*, I thought to myself, *what else will Tim have to say*?

Therefore, with a composed look and a slight grin, I looked up at him and said, "Ok, we can talk at my house. Meet me there at seven tonight."

Tim gave a big exhale and said, "Ok."

I told Tim seven p.m. to allow myself sufficient time to get situated. Getting off at four that day, I could have time to run an errand, pick up DeLon and grab something for dinner that night, plus be home in time enough to relax and get dolled up just a bit, to enkindle Tim's mind. I got a lot done in those three hours, so when Tim pushed the doorbell at 7:05 p.m., I was ready.

Before I opened the door, I gave myself one last look in the mirror. I had on my short, cotton fitted, grey shorts. They were nicely creased and showcased my thick thighs and cocoa-buttered up, long legs. I put on this subtle carda-mom fragrance—a dash behind the ears, shoulders and back of legs. It was fragrant just enough for that whiff of spice and bitter floral notes to gust by Tim every time I happened to pass him. My blouse was a long-sleeved, buttoned pink and blue plaid shirt that somewhat loosely hung and rested slightly on the curve of my lower back, nicely settling just above my buttocks- silhouetting my hourglass figure. And I had the top three buttons of the blouse casually undone. I put one final coat of clear lip gloss on my lips and puckered at the mirror. When I walked out of the room, everything was in its rightful place.

I opened the door to let Tim in. He looked at me for a long minute, then walked inside.

"Have a seat," I said. I stood by the door until he sat down. Then I closed the front door and walked past him to go check on DeLon, who was occupied with playing video games. Then I came back into the living room, walking past Tim again to sit down on the loveseat that was catty-corner from where he sat.

I sat with my shoulders back, legs crossed, looking cute but prepared for serious business. I leaned forward, rested my left elbow on the knee most prominent, looked into Tim's eyes with a stern face and slight smile, and asked him the question. *"What is it that you'd like to discuss, Tim?"*

Tim stalled a bit, looking somewhat displaced before answering the question. His focus was all over the room; his eyes peered at every corner of it, as if he was anticipating an attack of some sort. He looked down the hallway a few times, adjusting his pants legs every time he shifted his body weight. Observing Tim's behavior, it was now more obvious than before that he felt unsettled about something; and I was laughing on the inside.

The room was still quiet, with no response from Tim. I sat there patiently waiting to hear what he had to say. After this long stall, I was wondering if his throat was dry. I was becoming impatient the more I looked at that little shrimp sitting on my sofa, so I offered him a glass of water. He nodded his head, yes; in a want to-be-cool, but apparently fake way. I got up to fix Tim a glass of ice water. The whole time Tim's eyes were fixated on my every move, to and from the kitchen. I handed him the glass of water; he took a couple of sips and began to relax a bit.

I was losing my patience. My eyes cut over to the clock on the wall in my dining area. What the hell did he come over here for, to drool over something he couldn't have anymore? I mean, I know I was looking scrumptious as intended. However, Tim's strange behavior was beginning to weird me out. He'd been sitting in my living room for at least ten minutes without mumbling a word. I was on the verge of asking him to leave when finally, he broke his silence.

Tim looked me in the eyes and said, "Look, Olivia, I know things have been strained between us. I haven't been attentive as I normally am, but I do still want you."

I looked at him in amazement, because what nerve did this bastard have? Did he think that I was never going to find out the truth? Fed up, I finally let the cat out of the bag.

"Look Tim, I know you got married."

Tim's eyes got bigger than they normally were. "Huh?" he said.

"You heard me." I was telling it raw, like it was. I was tired of acting oblivious to what was going on in Tim's personal affairs; I was aware of the truth and now he knew it.

Taken aback by the sudden news, Tim got nervous. A light sweat formed on his forehead and he even stuttered a little. "H– how did you know?".

"Don't worry about all of that," I said sharply. "Did you think that I was never going to find out?"

After thinking about what I said, Tim let out a huge exhale, as if he had just freed up some weight from off his shoulders. Then he looked down at the floor in defeat.

I got up from the sofa and walked to the door, making the gesture that he should leave. I stood there with the doorknob in the palm of my hand, waiting for Tim to get up, so I could open the door for his departure. Looking at my motions and getting the hint, Tim slowly got up from the couch and met me at the door.

Tim stood there in front of me, seeing what was now untouchable to him. He looked me up and down, got an eyeful of this physique. He took in the sweet, aromatic cocoa butter scents that drifted from off my skin. Then, suddenly in a final attempt to keep me, Tim felt the need to play one last card.

Tim must have gotten inspired by a burst of asinine con-

416

fidence. Out of nowhere, he grabbed my right hand, and aggressively pulled me close to him. Then he looked up at me and said with all assertiveness, "Olivia, you ain't going nowhere; you are mine!" It was a demanding, last attempt to intimidate me into settling for the bullshit.

I snatched myself from out of his grasp and blatantly gave Tim a piece of my mind. "*Fool, you must be crazy if you ever thought I would still be with you, knowing you're married to someone else!*" Heck, it was no secret that I didn't even want Tim as a single man, but the sucker played on my kindness and squirmed his slimy ass into my heart. I was pissed, and now Tim could clearly see that.

After Tim saw that he was on the border of things getting strongly out of hand, by the sight of my clenching fists, he backed off. Then he asked me, "What are you going to do, tell my wife?" with a smirk on his face.

I responded, "No, I'm not going to be the one to disturb her façade of a perfect marriage."

Then he asked, "Are you going to get revenge?"

I looked at him and chuckled. If he only knew. Then I said, "The best revenge is being the best me I can be."

Apparently, that tickled Tim, because he snickered at my comment. However, I was as serious as a heart attack and slammed the door shut after he walked his little, miniature ass through it and out of my sight. And that was the last time I gave Tim anymore of my attention.

Dreams

Chapter Eighty-Seven

Dreams are a mysterious phenomenon. They can be bizarre and illogical, yet act as a messaging board from the spiritual realm to you. Dreams can be lucid and resemble fragments of reality; full of emotion, color and taste; ignited by the past or present experiences. Dreams can also serve as preparation for the future. Within our dreams, we can view a mirrored version of our unconscious state, enabling us to mentally analyze things that we are not consciously aware of. Dreams can also serve as inspiration to the mind from your spirit, awakening the passions that lie dormant in your heart. When the mind dreams, it can act as a doorway for the unconscious state to connect to the universal consciousness; all while rejuvenating bodily cells stimulated by what we know as R.E.M sleep. Dreams have been at the core of mankind's progression and studied to great lengths, since biblical or ancient years. Scientists today are still trying to unravel the enigma of how brain wave patterns, while in deep sleep, cause the mind to wonder and dream.

Everyone dreams at some point or another. The word *dream* is defined as: *a fantasy, hallucination, nightmare or a vision*. I have had plenty of dreams in this life. Some of my dreams have been fantasies of hidden feelings. And as a youth, I've had my share of nightmares too, especially with my love/hate fascination with the fictional character Freddy Krueger played by Robert Englund back in the day. Howev-

ANGELS DON'T WARN FOR NOTHIN'

er, the majority of my dreams or visions have also had some sort of spiritual significance.

My ninth-grade year, I had countless dreams about the end of the world. I remained on this earth surviving the world post-Rapture. In those dreams, I was running and hiding from satan and all those who wore the mark of the beast. Satan walked freely on the earth after that, and if you didn't choose the mark, you violently died. I was dodging the enemy left and right. In the dream, if satan and its followers had caught me, by God's grace and power, I would escape always.

In one dream, I was actually in the center of an active tornado that lifted me high above the ground. I was above the trees, the houses, far up in the sky. I recall being upright and in a broad funnel of rotating winds, unharmed, yet still yelling for God to save me. I recall that dream being so intense, it felt so realistic, and like all the other dreams I'd wake up in awe, questioning how these dreams were forming and why I was having them in my early teen years.

On the morning of my twenty-first birthday, I had a very bizarre dream. I dreamed that I was a contestant on the popular game show, *Jeopardy*. However, the host was not Alex Trebek. Although it presented itself in Alex Trebek fashion, with the suit and tie; the game show host was satan. It had its full black, polished horns hooked outward and its big broad head with horse-like nostrils; a close imagery of it would be the devil in the Tom Cruise movie, *Legend*. On the gameshow, *Jeopardy*, it was I, along with two other contestants playing. We were answering the questions in the categories that we selected. The devil would read the

420

category out loud, and oddly enough none of us contestants felt frightened, and answered the questions in normal *Jeopardy* form. Strangely, we were focused on playing the game, despite the game show host being, the devil himself.

My other competitors were doing well. They were getting the majority of their questions right, but as for me, I wasn't having that same luck. Every one of my responses, the devil said was incorrect, even when I knew for certain my answers were indeed correct. I'd pick a category and satan would ask the question. I'd answer, then hear the buzzer.

"Wrong again," he would say with a deceptive smile. Question after question, I would answer with all assertiveness, but satan as the gameshow host would count it wrong every single time.

I woke up from that dream, weirded out. What did it mean? I couldn't ponder on it for too long though, because it was a workday and I had to rush and get ready. However, that morning I had the best bowel movement that I'd had all year long, and that alone was a gift within itself. I went into work that day a year older and feeling light as a feather.

Although that *Jeopardy* dream was a for-real trip, it wasn't too difficult for me to interpret. The biggest curiosity for me concerning that dream was, why did I have the best poop in a long time right afterwards? Delving more into dreams, along with taking biology classes, I later learned that when the human goes into deep sleep, not only does it permit dreaming; but it also rejuvenates the body on a cellular level. During that stage of rest, the brain activity increases, causing a greater influx of light energy into the cells and tissues, so that toxins can be removed. And that explained why I had the best poop of the year, on the morning of my twenty-first birthday following that very bizarre dream.

Another dream, I had stood out further than all of the others. This one was unlike any of the other dreams I had ever experienced, more so because it lingered on my conscience for hours after I awoke. On this particular night, I went to bed like any other time during the work week. De-Lon was sound asleep in his room, and I hopped in the bed and dozed straight to sleep.

In this dream, I was at a funeral. Eric's funeral. His service was being held at a red-brick church on a hill, and it was full of people. Amongst all those attending Eric's going away service was Eric's spirit itself.

I could hear his voice just as clearly, and feel his emotions plainly, as well as I could see him. Watching from afar, I saw him walk amongst us and observe us in his spiritual form. He was surprised at all of us who attended his going away services; all those people were there just for him and the church was packed. He didn't think he was loved by so many people. Eric felt cherished and excited all at the same time, viewing all of these folks at his funeral.

I saw myself there too. I was up in the first pew with my son sitting on my lap. My head was down, and I was grieving. My hair fell forward, blocking me from seeing my face. However, I did see that my hair was shoulder-length, straight but bumped underneath on the ends, and it was dark brown in color like my own natural hair. It appeared that I had the perfect bob haircut, which ironically was the most adored hairstyle that I could never naturally achieve, due to my hair growth pattern. I watched on: head bowed down to my knees as both of my hands were held up to my face, partially hiding my grief and wiping away the tears; I had saturated mounds of tissue. My hair bounced and flowed with every bodily movement made as I wept uncontrollably.

After that, I recall sitting in a black limousine with Julia, Eric's then-girlfriend. Oddly enough, it was just the two of us, and there was a big gap between us. I was on the left end of the limousine and Julia was the last to get in, so she was on the side opposite of me, and it was very quiet; nobody said a word.

Still viewing at a distance, I saw myself just looking out the window. We were being taken to Eric's burial site and during the ride there, I saw Eric sitting in between Julia and me. He looked at me, smiled, and said, "Ole Olivia, I knew you still loved me." He was smiling as he looked at me as I rode along in the limo. Occasionally, he would turn for a short time to look at Julia, but then he'd turn his attention right back to me and gaze on as I peered out the window.

We finally arrived at the memorial park; it was roughly forty miles away from town. We all got out of the limousines. There may have been two limo cars; I don't recall a third one. Nevertheless, we all walked to the burial site and watched as Eric's body was lowered down into its final resting place. Once the casket was underground and covered by dirt, we each took a rose or two, then departed back to the vehicles to go back home.

This is where and when Eric became immensely saddened. Although he got to walk along with us on his final journey to his resting place, he could go no further than, but a short distance away from his body, or so that is how it appeared. Eric could not come with us. At that moment, he realized he would forever be separated from the living, and we could never see him again physically. I saw Eric stay behind and look on with sadness as all of his loved ones, one by one got into the limousines and rode away from his burial site.

Then I woke up from the dream. I recall waking up and feeling this heaviness lingering over me. I tried to shake it off, but it weighed hard on my mind and spirit. I remember thinking, *I hope that doesn't happen.* But then my arrogant human side thought, *That will never happen, because Eric's in Arkansas. Plus, I don't have long hair like that.* Then I got up from the bed to get ready for work.

Although I fleetingly dismissed the dream in my mind that uncanniness feeling lingered. After the shower, getting dressed and even still when I got in the car, backing out of the driveway, that eerie feeling stayed with me. That's when I finally said a small prayer as I drove away from the house. I hoped that my dream would not be a reality as I went on to work. Then I went on with my everyday life, soon forgetting all about that one distinct dream.

Better Without

CHAPTER EIGHTY-EIGHT

I have always been good at letting things go. Having major indifferences with my mom growing up taught me that it is best to not harp on people's wickedness. And most importantly, to not allow others' hateful ways to darken your spirit. I always respected my mother, even during the moments when she heavily provoked me to do otherwise. Yet, I honored her as the Bible says that we should do. Granted, our relationship was not close by any means, but still I respected and helped her out financially when she asked me to. At one point, I even kept a second job, just so I could have the extra cash on hand for when she called. Yes, it was not an easy task being her eldest child and daughter. However, I withstood those tribulations and forgave my mother of her shortcomings, and I know for that alone, I was blessed considerably.

Even with lowlife Tim, although I saw the creep in passing at work, he got no more energy or time from me. By that, I mean there were no angry desires for vengeance anymore. Nah, I let all that go. I figured; what Tim didn't know about me *did* hurt him. Tim misjudged the high caliber of woman that I was even at that young age. He was oblivious to my spiritual background and unaware of my rich faith and wisdom. Tim didn't know he was messing with a strong and smart black woman with a mighty inner light.

Tim didn't like that he was so easily dismissed, and it hurt his ego. Although within our interactions, I eventually grew fond of Tim, he never had what it took to "break me down" because my heart was already settling for less than what it desired. And although Tim was on the short end vertically, he didn't fall short of being like every other insecure man that a woman comes across. In many cases, men are attracted to the inner light a woman exudes, captivating them. However, that same radiance within a woman is the very thing an insecure man will start to resent. In those cases, they attempt to break us, mentally and/or physically, dulling that light that emits from within. In my case, Tim resented that which first appealed to him, all because he was foolish enough to think he could contain my radiance on his own terms, and that was undoubtedly a mistake on his part.

With as much wrath as Tim had awakened within me at one point, it was certainly a good thing that I disregarded him. I definitely would not have come out unscathed. I know my shine would have been dulled by vengeful anger, physical bruises or incarceration. And it would have been by my own doing, because it would have been my choice to succumb to that venom and alter my actions to be outside of my normal character. If I'd allowed that, I could have gone into beast mode, getting down with the nitty-gritty of guerrilla warfare. No doubt I would have gone there, if that's what it took to beat Tim physically. And if by chance, I did stand victorious from the war with Tim, who around me would have been a casualty or hurt in the process?

I am grateful that I had better sense that enabled me to come out on top and unharmed. Tim was beneath me and if I had stooped to his level, participating in the constant back and forth battles on the strength of hate and retaliation, it would have most definitely depreciated my value, lowered my standards, and dismantled my happiness, which in any case is never good. Ultimately, Tim would have gotten his way after all, by controlling something that he knew he couldn't—my light. His negative actions, triggering negative responses from me, would have flawed my character and dimmed my shine. However, I avoided all of that by simply being wise enough to dismiss that fool completely.

I didn't even bother to discuss the situation with mutual acquaintances of ours. When I would happen to run into one of them, I never even mentioned Tim's name. Although a few of them made efforts to steer conversations in that direction of Tim's discrepancies, I had nothing to share with them. Why would I want to spread my business? For sympathy or validation? That was unimportant and irrelevant. Besides, I was sure his friends were well aware of the situation, so there was nothing further to discuss.

Indeed, through the years, it has been a life struggle to not allow negative behavior to have a looming effect on my temperament. I have experienced firsthand how hatred could change one's psyche. Those negative vibes can alter or transform the person you naturally are, if it is not counteracted. When I dwelled on the actions of my mother, my anger toward her took away from my genuinely happy self, so it was a must that I forgive her.

When that rage and resentment brews to the surface and causes one to react hastily, retaliation may feel justified and temporarily satisfying at that moment. Yet inevitably, it only darkens the spirit and disrupts the peace surrounding you. Therefore, choose the high road.

A Reality

CHAPTER EIGHTY-NINE

If there is one thing I've learned through my life dealings with people, it is that you cannot allow their circumstances or poor behaviors to reflect on you. Despite those tempted urges provoked by the assailant that would cause you to act out negatively. It's easy to give into that anger of being wronged, to be mad and whoop somebody's ass. However, will it make the situation better or worse? Perhaps in some cases it seems better, especially when it comes to training your kids favorably. However, amongst adults, we should be able to discuss the situation at hand without losing our cool or self-discipline. Now to me, that exerts authority and power when we maintain self-control in spite of what we're dealing with.

The fact remains, the enemy does not discriminate whatsoever. Satan will use anyone who will allow it, in an attempt to cause confusion, separation, or a disruption of the positive flow of God's energy in our lives. That is why it is vital to continue to do your part in God's will despite the adversities and hardships, because ultimately it is your relationship with the Lord that truly matters. That is the love that will sustain you through it all; regardless of how deep and low the enemy attacks.

Rising above the evil is never an easy task. However, by doing so and keeping your head to the sky, being faith filled and being grateful for what you do have, is pleasing to God. How is that so? Because by not taking matters into your own hands, we complicate things less, and allow God to be *the* God in our lives; trust in Him and He will cover us on every end.

Treasured peace will not be disturbed when you step aside and simply let God do His thing; His way on His time. By doing so, there are no innocent bystanders. No unwanted bloodshed caused by straying bullets from those being caught in the crossfire undeservingly. Nope, when God is in charge, he'll let only the trespassers get exactly what they deserve. And God is so cold with it, their demise will by their own wicked hands and heart. That's where karma plays its role. Your enemies will hang themselves, with you having lost no sleep.

With the situation involving Tim, a year later, I would hear that he died. I got the news from a friend of mine who knew that he and I had dated. From what I gathered; Tim went out of the country to Mexico for some sort of optometry mission trip. He came back to the U.S. and developed pneumonia. He was sick with it for weeks before deciding to go to the hospital. There at the hospital, things took a turn for the worse, and Tim ended up dying two or three days later. He left behind a wife who was five months pregnant with their first child, who he never got to see.

My friend, who told me the news wasn't being gossipy, but came to me with some genuine concerns. Apparently, it was also rumored that Tim died from complications of having the AIDS virus. The friend, Etienne, at one time wanted to date me, but when he understood that the interest was only on his part, he became a really good friend to me. Etienne thought that I had contracted the virus, since Tim and I were involved at one point. However, whatever or whoever Tim got a hold of was way after me and during his marriage. Thankfully, I was just fine, and I appreciated Etienne's honesty and regard of me.

See how life works? Although Tim hit a nerve in me that transmitted pure rage, for my benefit, I harnessed that negativity and let it go. Taking the high road, I let God be the God in my life as He should be always in all of our lives. And at the end of the day, it proved worth it. The Bible reads that vengeance is His, says the Lord, and in this situation, it certainly was. Who knows what Tim was doing behind closed doors here in the U.S. or down in Mexico? Whatever the case, his demise came from his own doing.

.

Under the Radar

CHAPTER NINETY

Although I did not allow Tim to hinder my shine after that whole ordeal, I defensively camouflaged it myself. I had gotten orthodontic braces, which were a dental necessity. I got eyeglasses prior to the fallout with Tim. I could see just fine without them. However, I wore them all the time as a shield to conceal my beauty. In addition to the braces, I looked like a real nerd, and I liked that.

See, after Tim, I was tired of men just seeking me for my looks. It seemed that I would catch the attention of many, but it was mostly due to lust. The ones I did give my number to always wanted to see me. Hardly did they want to sit on the phone, converse and get to know me as person. They admired my beauty as an attainable object and that would be as far as their little minds would go.

Fed up with that, along with my ortho braces and eyewear, I began to dress in a homely fashion. I wore roomy t-shirts and joggers that hid my bodily figure, protecting myself from unwanted attention.

Rekindle

CHAPTER NINETY-ONE

As I was in my Clark Kent phase of life at age 23, flying below the radar, my path crossed with Rendell Schwann again. Our eyes met, and that was all it took. Rendell was able to see through the disguise of the baggy clothes and glasses. He knew of all that I was trying to conceal underneath those loose-fitting clothes. Rendell took to me like a magnet, and we became active in each other lives once more.

Honestly, I can't recall distinctively how or where our reintroduction occurred, but it didn't take long for us to get familiarized with one another again. Being with Rendell felt so natural, it was like, "Honey, I'm home." Touching and loving on him once again felt like a continuation of what was meant to be, but our love connection now had some major kinks.

Although Rendell and I were intimate with each other, I could feel that I didn't have all of him. We never spoke of it, but Draco's involvement had an immense negative impact on the both of us. Neither of us knew how to get beyond the hurt and shame from that past we both knew of.

Yet, there was this pulsating interconnection, a strong binding love between Rendell and me that neither of us could deny. The feeling felt tragic. This was who my heart yearned for, yet he was emotionally distant, and I understood why. Therefore, I loved what parts of Rendell I could at his own pace.

Eric Returns

CHAPTER NINETY-TWO

Months later, I had gotten a call from Eric's mom, who told me he had come back to town. Surprised by the news, I asked what brought that on. Mrs. E. said, "Julia." She went on to explain that Julia had been calling Eric, crying and talking about how her kids needed him. He felt bad and decided to come back to Tulsa.

A week or so later, I got a visit from Eric. I happened to be at home when he called and said he'd like to talk to me. I was at the duplex alone, doing some cleaning. DeLon may have been over to a relative's house. However, shortly after I hung up the phone, Eric pulled up. Hearing him turn toward the house, I quickly slipped on a pair of shoes and met Eric outside next to his white Dynasty.

Eric still made me a little anxious when I got around him, and rightfully so. Although the most physical he ever got with me was a failed face-slap, his threats toward me, however, were dangerous and somewhat traumatizing apparently.

Eric stood there, looking sweaty. It seemed like he had lost weight, because his clothes were baggy, and he appeared uneasy about something. I asked why he looked so slim.

"I lost my muscle," he responded. Since he had been out

the pen, he hadn't been lifting weights, so all his bulkiness had diminished. I didn't even know muscles could go away like that, but apparently so.

Eric was looking around, nervous. I got concerned, so I asked him what was wrong. By his body language, I could tell he did not want to answer. He leaned back on the Dynasty, crossed his legs and looked toward the ground. After a short pause, Eric opened up.

He said, "Man... Momma gave Julia my number where I was, and she called and called and called. She was crying and hollering about how the kids need me, she need me; so I come down to see about her and the kids. I go over to her apartment, and she had another dude over there."

Hearing that I felt for him, but I wasn't surprised. Julia was a stripper and apparently a whore too. Nevertheless, his mom though. She wouldn't even give me the number to where Eric was, but she gave it to Julia. Go figure.

Eric saw a dark brown, ole skool car that looked just like the one he got shortly after we met. He pointed to the car and said, "Remember that, Olivia?" I recognized the car right off, but acted like I didn't. He looked at me with his head leaning to the side and lips turned sideways, like, *you know you lying.* And I was, but I didn't want him think there was a chance of going back down memory lane with me, so I belittled that déjà vu moment.

It was warm outside that day, and Eric and I were just standing there, so I cut the visit short. I told him I had to finish cleaning and started to walk to the front door. Eric followed me, and in a glimpse, I noticed he had a sawed-off shotgun hidden under his shirt. Frightened and shocked, I did a double-take, but Eric's reflexes were a lot swifter than mine because he concealed that firearm so quickly. He was so fast, I wondered if my eyes were playing tricks on me, so I asked him.

"Do you have a gun?"

Eric, avoiding the question, looked away from me, toward the street. Then he turned back to me, spread his arms far apart as wide as they could possibly go, and asked if he could have a hug. I looked at him and without saying a word, I shut the door right in his face.

A week went by, and I hadn't heard from Eric, but I knew he was still in town. I figured he was doing his own thing, like I was doing mine. He had his own set of friends he hung out with outside of the gang bangers. Eric still was a very attractive guy, and I doubt he had any problems finding new female friends.

It was early Thursday morning when I got a call. Rendell and I were just getting up, about to get dressed for the day when the phone rang. It was a relative of mine who called to let me know that my Aunt Mary had a bad stroke and had been rushed to the hospital. I was startled by the news. I knew she was having issues with getting her blood pressure under control, but never thought it would get to that point. My Auntie had been stressing over getting a divorce and losing her possessions. Sadly enough, a stroke had to put things in perspective for her. That car, house, and money didn't mean anything without the health to be able to enjoy it all.

Forty minutes later, my home phone rang again. This was a first; I rarely if ever did I get calls in the morning, and on this day, it happened twice. It was about 6:30 a.m. when I looked over to the clock before answering. I said, "Hello?"

On the other end of the receiver was Mrs. E. She said, "Olivia."

I responded, "Yes?"

Mrs. E said, "Eric is dead. He got shot in the back of Gibbs quarter store."

Stunned, I didn't have anything else to say, but "What!?" She repeated it again, then broke down crying.

It was an early Thursday morning on August 24, 2000. My son's father had lost his life ten days after he turned twenty-four. My aunt had a debilitating stroke that would change her life forever. Both ordeals were very heavy situations to encounter on a morning before going to work.

I got off the phone, still taken aback, and told Rendell what had happened. He was shocked too, but of course the news didn't have a huge impact on him like it eventually would me. I am unsure if my outer shell was just too hardcore or what; but I took in the news, yet still went on to work. I was saddened and stunned, but not a tear fell from my eyes.

Hit by It

CHAPTER NINETY-THREE

It wasn't until two days later when the death of Eric really sunk in. I was over to Eric's mom's house, and Julia was there too. She was on the front porch sobbing when I pulled up. I got out of the car, walked up to the front door, but instead of walking past Julia and going right in, I stopped and sat down next to her.

It was strange; I had no words of solace for her. I mean, although she was grieving hard, I was Eric's baby's mother and I had not yet wept. She was his friend, but her short-wave involvement was nothing in comparison with my history with Eric. However, I sat there quietly beside Julia on the porch, gazing out at the neighborhood street. Then through her tears, she started to speak.

Julia's face was soiled with tears, and she was rocking back and forth. Then out of nowhere, she said, "I rode over there to the place where Eric got shot. I dropped to my knees and laid right on the blood-stained concrete where his body fell." Then Julia went on to tell me all the good things Eric had done for her and her kids.

Listening to Julia and envisioning Eric's good deeds as she spoke, it finally hit me, the grief. Eric was just trying to find his way like the majority of us, and it's especially difficult to do so when your behavior imitates others just to fit in. Eric was a good guy, and I was saddened that his life was cut short, before he could see the man inside of him develop on the outside. That moment right there cracked the shell and from then on, my heart was in complete sorrow from the death of my son's father.

As I sat there, I could hear voices inside the house. Amongst other conversations going on, I could hear someone ask, "Is that Olivia out there?" Still with no words said on my part, I turned my attention away from Julia, got up and went in the house, leaving her outside. I walked in, gave hugs to Eric's mom and sister, Tammy, then sat on the living room sofa.

Tammy was in the midst of telling us what she had heard happened to Eric. She had talked to the friend whom Eric had dropped off right before he got killed, some eyewitnesses, and the cops. Eric's friend told Tammy that she and Eric had just come from playing pool and drinking beers. Eric took her home, but decided to stay and visit a little longer, so he cut off his car. When he got ready to leave, the car would not start. The girl said she had to get up early that next morning, so she left him tending to his car. After some time of not hearing from him, she thought Eric had gotten the car started and left already. But then she heard some arguing outside. When she realized it was Eric out there, she got up to see what was happening and then heard the gunshots.

Tammy said witnesses divulged information too. They told her that night they saw three boys in the age range of seventeen to eighteen, wearing blue and orange colored clothing, walking in the neighborhood. Eric was outside with his car when the group of boys walked up to him and attempted to rob him for his chrome Dayton wheels. Eric was cussing the young boys out, talking noise of some sort until they took out their guns.

The cops told Tammy what the evidence showed. A policewoman disclosed that from the looks of the crime scene, Eric tried to run, because one shoe was off of his foot at a distance from where his body lay, and as he turned to do so, the young boys shot at him, hitting him eleven times, but it was one shot that caused the fatality. The cop told Tammy it was a bullet in the back that went through his chest that caused Eric's death. Learning that Eric got shot eleven times made me gasp, and the tears began to flow even more as I listened to Tammy tell us what the police reported.

Eric's funeral was two days later. His relatives on his mother's side owned a funeral parlor in Okmulgee and had recently opened up one in North Tulsa. Mrs. E. contacted them to prepare Eric's body for the going away services. I had heard of Bigelow's funeral parlor doing exceptional work already, but since this was a family member, no corners were cut. And knowing Mrs. E., no expenses were spared either when it came to burying her only son and youngest child.

Funeral Day

CHAPTER NINETY-FOUR

The funeral was on a Tuesday morning at eleven o'clock. The service was being held at the Wesley United Methodist Church. It was a red bricked church located on the hill off North Cincinnati. Eric and his parents were not Methodist, but more than likely due to the size, this was the place his funeral services had to be held. I walked in holding my child's hand, and we sat in the first pew.

As I sat there, I looked up at Eric's casket. It was granite grey with chrome handles. The conducting pastor began to speak, but I only heard bits and pieces of what he was saying. Looking at the casket, all I could think of was how my connection to that one person through my son was now gone, and the last time I saw him was when I slammed the door in his face.

I began to cry uncontrollably. Seeing me distressed, caused my child to cry. I tried to console him, but I was blinded by my own tears and weak with grief. DeLon understood that his father was deceased even at age six. Although their relationship was not close, the experience in tragically losing a close family member did affect our son. After a while with DeLon and I both sitting there crying our hearts out, my Aunt Armostean came from behind and grabbed him. I remember being handed tissues to wipe my eyes, but there were too many tears flowing to keep a dry face.

After the funeral services, Eric's casket was rolled out to the entryway, so that whoever wanted to see his body, could. As family members and friends made their exit from the church nave, they each viewed Eric's body in passing. I walked out now, more composed than before, and observed Eric's shell laying in his casket. He looked like himself, but with silver undertones. He had a nice grey suit on, and the body just looked like it was resting; I stood there and looked on for a short while, then walked out the church and escorted into the limousine.

As I was riding up to Okmulgee for Eric's body to be buried at their family plot, gazing out the window and up at the sky, I realized something significant. It was only Julia and me in the very back of that limousine. Then I remembered that dream I'd had a while ago about attending Eric's funeral. The dream matched up exactly with everything that had taken place. My hairstyle was in a medium bob, because I had gotten it styled in a ponytail that hung to my jawline. The church was red-bricked and full of people. Then in the limousine, there was a space between me and Julia. I knew right then without a doubt that Eric's spirit was with us too, unseen, but sitting right in-between us.

Recollecting the scenes of the dream that was now a reality, my mouth dropped in amazement. Although I could not see Eric, I kept looking at that space between me and Julia. I could not believe this was actually happening. I cried some more in astonishment.

When we arrived at the burial site, I got out of the vehicle and knew Eric was close by. During the burial ceremony, I looked around and smiled, knowing that Eric's spirit was there too with us. After Eric's body was buried, we were walking back to the limousines, and remembering that dream, I looked back and waved goodbye to him because I knew, he was there too watching us leave.

The Reckoning

CHAPTER NINETY-FIVE

For weeks after Eric's funeral, strange occurrences were happening. I had dreams and through those dreams, I got closure for Eric's death. In one dream, I was at my duplex in bed, but got up because I heard some water dripping. I went to the kitchen to find a black man sitting on top of my stove that was next to the fridge with its door open. I walked past the man as he looked at me with a smile. I stopped right in front of the refrigerator and saw water dripping from underneath it. I bent down to get a closer look when I noticed a phone receiver with a coiled cord attached to it.

I picked it up and said, "Hello?"

Then I heard a hello on the other end. It was Eric's voice.

Surprised, I said, "Eric, is this really you?" He said yeah. I remember asking him all sorts of questions. One question I distinctively remember asking was, what did God's voice sound like? Eric said that His voice sounded like large bodies of water in motion.

He went on to ask if I remembered this Andy Griffith movie. Eric said the movie title, which I remembered clearly then, but irritably I do not recall now; but it was a one-word title of about seven letters and it began with the letter G. It was not a movie that I remembered seeing. However, in that movie, Eric said there was a sound in it that came close to the sound of God's voice.

Excited to be actually talking to Eric after his death, I stupidly said, "Ok, enough about Him. I want to know about you." And shortly after that comment, the connection faded away and I woke up.

Gob-smacked, I sat up on the bed in disbelief. Then I thought to myself, how foolish was I to not want to know more about God! He was the one who allowed that conversation to even take place, granting me closure. And there I was talking about, "enough about Him." As if that was something I could come back to later. I felt amazed and ashamed all at the same time, yet still very fortunate to have had that opportunity.

After Eric's death, the days seemed to go by so slowly. At my house, grieving, I realized I had not heard from Rendell since the morning I got the call from Mrs. E regarding Eric's death. I tried to call Rendell to see why I hadn't heard from him, but there was no answer. I was in this all alone, and I mourned deeper.

It took about a year for me to get out of that slump. I was depressed, but got through with no medical interventions. I just continuously cried at every quiet moment I got. At times, I even screamed at the top of my lungs, releasing the hurt and sadness that I felt within. During that healing year, in an attempt to press forward, I even enrolled myself in a community college. However, I ended up dropping a whole semester of classes, because I could not focus like I needed to. I had not yet fully overcome the glumness.

Since Rendell was not there for me during that critical

time in my life, I made the decision that I did not need him in it. He never called or came by to check on me for weeks after that. When he finally did call, I didn't even bother to answer.

It was sad too, because I loved Rendell so much. However, because he wasn't there for me at that very low point in my life, especially when he was right there when I got the news, I felt he wasn't worthy anymore to be in my life like that. I made up my mind then, that we would be strictly friends and so we were.

Looking Ahead

CHAPTER NINETY-SIX

Years went by, and I would see Rendell sparingly after we became distant. I buried my feelings for him and just went on about my life without him in it, and I was comfortable with that. Looking ahead and not back at Rendell, I wasn't reminded of my past mistakes with Draco. There was no shame to face or worries about Ren treating me unfairly or not taking our relationship seriously. And that was achieved by having little to no interactions with Rendell, which meant no relating between us. He and I would just be cool, making him another friendly face in the crowd.

Yet, when our paths did cross and we would see each other, although the conversation was always casual and light, Rendell had that internal effect on me still. I would see him out in public, and he would be like a breath of fresh air to me. My heart would flutter and I would think to myself every time, *I still love him.*

Inevitably, life goes on. Rendell and I were living our lives separately. After being abstinent for five straight years and wishfully hoping that Rendell would return to me in the process, I got tired of being alone and decided to seek out a relationship. I entered into one that lasted four-and a-half years; after that relationship, I had a few other short-lived ones, years later.

The majority of my adulthood though, I mostly spent

being a single woman. I wasn't coupled with anyone which was by choice. A lot of the time, if I wasn't feeling them, I didn't waste their time nor mines either for that fact. I believe in true connection and having genuine feelings shared amongst one another. Therefore, I was content with being single, even if what I sought, was never found. I had my son and was satisfied with him being the only child until I got maritally united with that special one.

Rendell, however, took another approach. He was in his thirties by then, and ready to have kids. He found himself a couple of females to have his babies with, out of wedlock. And dealt with everything that came with that, excessive hair-greying stress included.

Meanwhile, I devoted my time and energy to work, school and worship services. By this time Delon and I regularly attended church when I wasn't at work. I also participated in singing with the church choir from time to time when I wasn't occupied with taking college courses. Rendell, however, veered into the streets to make money along with doing whatever he wanted to do, a benefit he would always say came along with being an adult.

After I decided on no looking back and no regrets, I was a happily single woman. I was going to work and school, sometimes holding down a second job on top of being a single parent. I knew I had good things going for me, so it never interested me to have one-night stands or spontaneous relationships. No, I wanted my time to be spent efficiently and held to a high regard, because I realized I was—and still am—a prize to have. I have always been a one-man woman who gives the love I want to receive from my significant other. So, within my intimate relationships, there has to be other mutual connections outside of just having a physical one.

One could say that I was selective. Some of my closest friends would even say I was too picky, but I knew what I liked, and having just anybody would not do. That's why in addition to the five-year period that I went without sex, there would be other long segments in life where I went without as well; and was still just as content. It gave me peace that empowered my inner being, and I loved that more than having casual sex. Therefore, I was very particular about who I chose to get involved with. If it were to happen, there would have to be some sort of endearing moment that occurred between he and I. A special kind of interest for that spark of attraction to be embodied, and cause me to accept his advances. It was difficult to come across a man who carried certain attributes or qualities that attracted me to him which made my dating life seldom and far in between.

For years, I would say to myself that I was very selective, whenever the question arose, "Why aren't you married?" I believed it too, wholeheartedly. However, the real truth finally dawned on me eighteen years later.

I just happened to be at the casino with my cousin Kim, who invited me out, when I saw Rendell. Seeing him, I went over to say hello. He was slapping on that button playing the slot machine when he noticed me. Seeing me, Rendell did a double-take. He then looked at that slot machine, then back at me and cashed out as he offered to buy me a drink. We went over to the bar, had a drink and talked about all sorts of stuff. The conversation was very pleasant.

Rendell made me laugh as he always did, but just being with him made me feel warm inside. I realized then that I wasn't married, not because I was too picky, but because none of those other men were him. He was the only true man that I could undeniably dedicate my heart to for an infinite lifetime, and want to, for that matter, loving unconditionally.

After a while of sitting at the bar, it got late and I was ready to go. Rendell offered to drive me to my car. I rode in his vehicle as he drove me to mine. When we got to my car, I stepped out of his SUV and was about to shut the door when he caught my attention for the last time of the night.

"Olivia!" Rendell called my name abruptly, causing me to turn to him where I stood. And out of his mouth, he spoke the words that had resonated in my heart for all these years. Whenever our paths would cross, every time our eyes met, my heart would flutter, and those exact words, would always come to mind. Those exact words, at that moment, Rendell finally spoke out loud.

He said, "I still love you."

Hearing those words ring through my ears sparked something within me. It was a feeling that I had not felt in many years, a yearning for a love that I was no longer familiar with. Rendell had reignited that flame of passion within me that had been dispirited throughout the years. Instantly, I felt an enormous sense of aspiration. A newfound hope for a renewed love, joy and fulfillment that I thought no longer existed between he and I. Those exact four words that Rendell spoke rekindled my ambition for us. I was immediately empowered, because of the love that I carried for him still after all these years, he too, actually shared for me.

Radiating from within, I looked up at him with this huge grin on my face and blew him a kiss goodbye. Then I shut his vehicle door closed, got in my car and drove off. Parting ways with Rendell once again.

With that sudden sense of inspiration also came fear. Any attempt to pursue that internal flame between us would also mean facing the daunting facts of the past. I was aware that Rendell thought there was some dishonesty on my part with my initial involvement with Draco. Also, there were some major key components of our past relationship that Rendell had also forgotten, his part. And I had gone all this time with being silent concerning his "best friend," thinking it was better that way. However, now the air had to be cleared. I could no longer run away from my past, but face it head on with this new found sense of revelation.

Although we had managed to be just friends all this time, eighteen years had to pass before we could finally see each other in that way again simultaneously. My son was now an adult and remained my only child, and that angelic voice that I heard was not a figment of my imagination—DeLon never had a father. And due to the negative influences around my son, it would cause our relationship to be strained and distant, as well as trigger him on a downward spiral.

Rendall had three kids of his own in middle school at that time. We both were either at the end of a relationship or recently out of one. However, eighteen years is a lot of crucial time to be absent from each other's lives, and time had made changes within us both individually. Although the love was still present between us, we were not as innocent-minded as we were before. Within those eighteen years, life had taken its toll and we both were exposed to some things and negatively impacted in one way or another.

For me, despite the mental and physical scars of life, my spirituality remained strong. However, for Rendell, it was a different story. With his mental and physical scars from life, his spirit darkened.

The lapse of time missed, along with a shameful past, made for a tall hurdle to cross and a major obstacle to overcome. For this relationship to succeed, Rendell and I, both as consensual partners would have to be mature enough and completely willing to look over each other's faults. That involves genuinely and wholeheartedly forgiving one another; allowing the hurtful past to pass by, never affecting us again. Which in turn; permits those wounds, even the ancients ones, to mend and heal entirely, once and for all.

However, that is more easily said than done, as you will further read about in detail in Volume 2.

The Hand Lesson

CHAPTER NINETY-SEVEN

Despite whatever I felt or thought, there is no excuse for disobeying the Lord. Leaving the park that day with that piece of paper in hand, I was fully aware of what I should have done. By doing the opposite, I regretfully was showing God that I, a mere nineteen-year-old mortal, knew better than He. Disobeying that angel was the most profound decision I had ever made. And at that moment when I left that park with Draco's number in hand, I was unknowingly removing myself from under God's protection to an extent and giving the devil permission to toy with my life in an attempt to destroy it.

My rebellious nature kicked in, and I challenged God. And just like a good parent who only wants the absolute best for his or her child, when one gets out of line, they correct them. During my trials and tribulations, my eyes were opened as to what and whom God wanted to shield me against. In God's true nature, He wants the absolute best for us. However, if we are wayward, we have to endure the punishment to be able to realize our faults.

Contrarily, if we are obedient to His will and pleasing unto His eye, we are rewarded abundantly. The Lord will pour blessings on top of blessings that go as far as the human eye can see. But understand, when we give into malice or mischief, it brings forth or unveils an evil presence in spiritual places that intervenes and attempts to block all the goodness of what God has in store for us. This is why it is critical that we be obedient to His will and maintain self-discipline. I have learned, to go against the Lord God, is to go against yourself.

The Angel at that park was only trying to protect me from myself and the unforeseen peril that lurked ahead. Reaching out to Draco caused many things to unfold for years to come. Of course, I did not understand then what my disobedience would expose me to, but the Angel did. The Angel knew about the levels of deception, hate and jealousy that would surround me on this journey, despite my good nature.

If only I had just taken heed to that warning. If only I had simply stayed still no matter I how I felt. My life would not have been subjected to such turmoil and this unintended grief, if only I had simply obeyed.

My dare-devilish ways caused me to endure a great deal of pain throughout this life. However, unlike the effects of the iron incident or the daring plot to escape Big Mama's wrath, those were superficial repercussions. When I became defiant to God's instruction, I suffered way beyond physical discomfort. The depth of hurt that I endured then, and still to this day, was something that I could never fathom at the softhearted age of nineteen.

I leaned to my own understanding instead of taking heed to the God-sent warning. And because of that, I became susceptible to the enemy's fiery darts. Through my anguish, I have learned that satan will use whoever or whatever he can to cause malice in one's life. The enemy's whole purpose is to destroy whatever godliness you have in you and around you. Therefore, beware.

I did not know I would endure such hardship and be ambushed on every level. Attacks: on my well-being, on my child, on my empowering earthly love. God did not intend for me to be on this journey incomplete, battling these demons from every angle. However, because God is all-knowing of the past, present and future of every life that walks on this earth, He already knew the result of all my mistakes before I would ever make them. Therefore, I was already equipped to undergo these life tribulations from birth. And that is, but a portion of the omnipresence and powerful nature of the Almighty God. Although, I have fallen short and caused my life's path to become twisted and coiled, the Lord still made a way.

On this passage of redemption, my eyes were opened to the levels of deception, envy and hate. I saw that no one is exempt from being attacked or used by the enemy. Regardless of how innocent or good-natured one may be, anyone can become a victim at any moment. The offender could be the closest and most entrusted family member or friend to you. I came to the realization that people can resent you for your happiness or simply for being who you naturally are. Oftentimes, they may hate you for something that you innately possess and don't even realize yet, is an asset. Indeed, I have witnessed much jealousy and resentment out of the eyes of many, yet still I press on.

I found out on this journey what the angel was ultimately trying to protect me from. As humans, we don't know the true feelings of those surrounding us. We can't hear those inner thoughts and see the jealousy brewing in the hearts of others. I was left to fend for myself. I didn't have the mental support required to press on without some hindrance, so my personal progress was delayed.

As for the two most important men in my life. My dear son, due to the fact that there was no other person around to uplift his mother in his eyes, his mind was easily influenced to go against me. And being heavily swayed to think so highly of material things by those he felt cared for him, DeLon would eventually succumb to a wayward lifestyle with no esteem for God or me. And in regards to the only man who could eternally capture my true love. Rendell having lacked that nurturing, firm guidance of a genuinely-loving and God-fearing partner by his side; a true helpmate that aids the other in staying on the right track, withstanding worldly temptations; he too had begun to get lost in this world and succumb to its ungodly ways. What biblical teachings he strongly believed in when we first met, eighteen-plus years ago, Rendell now doubted and even questioned God's existence altogether.

Nevertheless, that is how the enemy works— it causes doubt then division with lies. And that is what the Angel attempted to shield me from having to endure with its warning. However, when I leaned to my own understanding, and not that of the Lord's, I became vulnerable to such afflictions and separation. Despite what I understood to be true in my heart at that moment, I was incapable of foreknowing the trail of hardships that lurked ahead that not only affected me, but those that I closely loved and cherished as well.

Due to my decision to keep that piece of paper in hand.

Therefore, trust and please believe that God is God for a reason—and Angels Don't Warn for Nothin'!

To: Nicole

thank you friend
for your support.

Stay Blessed.

Truly
Regretta

Made in the USA
Columbia, SC
19 June 2022

61913782R10254